Supercharge Power BI
Power BI Is Better When You Learn to Write DAX
3rd Edition

by
Matt Allington

Holy Macro! Books
PO Box 541731
Merritt Island, FL 32954

Supercharge Power BI - 3rd Edition

© 2021 Tickling Keys, Inc.

All rights reserved. No part of this book may be reproduced or transmitted in any form or by any means, electronic or mechanical, including photocopying, recording, or by any information or storage retrieval system without permission from the publisher. Every effort has been made to make this book as complete and accurate as possible, but no warranty or fitness is implied. The information is provided on an "as is" basis. The authors and the publisher shall have neither liability nor responsibility to any person or entity with respect to any loss or damages arising from the information contained in this book.

Author: Matt Allington

Layout: Jill Bee

Copyediting: Kitty Wilson

Cover Design: Emrul Hasan, Shannon Travise & Maddie Allington

Cover Illustration: Freepik

Indexing: Nellie Jay

Published by: Holy Macro! Books, PO Box 541731, Merritt Island FL 32954, USA

Distributed by: Independent Publishers Group, Chicago, IL

First Printing: January, 2021.

ISBN: 978-1-61547-069-3 Print, 978-1-61547-155-3 e-Book

Library of Congress Control Number: 20211931632

Table of Contents

Introduction

In my view, Power BI is the best thing that has happened to business intelligence (BI) software since the introduction of Microsoft Excel. You might find this a strange comment as you may be thinking that Microsoft Excel is not a BI product. But I beg to differ. Prior to the introduction of the personal computer, there was only one type of BI solution possible: "enterprise BI" using enterprise BI software. Since the introduction of business-focused personal computers (e.g., early Apple devices and IBM-compatible PCs), there have been two types of BI solutions: enterprise BI and self-service BI. I would argue that Excel was one of the first self-service business intelligence software products broadly available to businesses. (There were several others, including VisiCalc and Lotus 123, before Excel, but Excel has been the most successful.)

A self-service BI solution is a solution that an end user builds. Enterprise BI solutions are important and have their place; they are enterprise-wide, scalable, robust, certified, reliable, etc. They are also expensive, and they take time to build, deploy, and maintain. Not every business-reporting problem can—or should—be solved by using an enterprise solution. For example, say that you have a short-term need to report on some measurable activity in your business. You want to measure the progress toward a short-term target (say 1 month), and then the reporting need goes away. It would not be practicable to build an enterprise-grade BI solution to report on such an activity. Both the cost and time horizon would make enterprise BI impracticable for such a need. There will always be more demands for reporting in an organisation than can be met by enterprise BI—and that's where self-service BI comes in. Self-service BI has existed since the late 1970s/early 1980s, when business personal computers became popular and software tools—including Microsoft Excel—began to enable business users to solve problems.

Microsoft launched Power BI in July 2015 with little fanfare. There were plenty of competitive critics out there, saying that the product was immature and not a real competitor to their own products—and they were right. In fact, I didn't love Power BI until it was almost 2 years old. At that point, I felt that Power BI had achieved the minimum level of maturity needed to be considered a serious BI product. When I look back now and compare the latest versions of Power BI with the 2-year-old version, I'm amazed at how far it has progressed.

Power BI is still evolving, and there are so many great things about it that it is hard to know what to mention first. Perhaps one of the most important things to note about Power BI is that it is designed with business analysts and Excel users in mind. You do not need to be an IT professional to be able to use this software well. But it is not only a self-service BI tool; it is also a fully featured enterprise-grade BI software tool. Brilliant strategy, don't you think?

Power BI has everything needed to complete an enterprise or self-service BI project across four important phases:

- **Data acquisition:** Power BI has a powerful data acquisition engine that helps a user fetch and load the data needed. The underlying technology that supports data acquisition is called Power Query (accessed via the Transform Data menu inside Power BI Desktop). The programming language inside Power Query is called M.

- **Data modelling:** Power BI's powerful data modelling engine allows a user to model loaded data to make it more useful than it is in the raw state. The underlying technology that facilitates data modelling has various names across different software products, including VertiPaq, SQL Server Analysis Services (SSAS) Tabular, and Power Pivot for Excel. (I refer to the modelling engine as SSAS Tabular in this book.) The programming language is called DAX (short for Data Analysis Expressions).

- **Data visualisation:** Power BI's modern visualisation engine has been built using the latest web technologies so you can build interactive, engaging reports. The Power BI visualisation engine has been open sourced so that anyone with the necessary skills can build new custom visuals to use and share within Power BI.

- **Report distribution:** Finally, Power BI has a framework that supports multiple ways to share data and reports with others, including a cloud-based web environment and native mobile apps. The sharing framework makes it easy to share reports and dashboards with other people who need to see and interact with the data. The tool to share Power BI reports is called the Power BI service, or PowerBI.com.

This book, Supercharge Power BI: Power BI Is Better When You Learn to Write DAX, teaches you the skills you need to use SSAS Tabular, the modelling engine at the core of Power BI, and the DAX language. SSAS Tabular brings everything that is good about enterprise-strength BI tools directly to you right inside Power BI Desktop without the time and cost impacts normally associated with large-scale BI projects. In addition, it is not just the time and money that matter. The fact that you can do everything yourself directly inside Power BI is very empowering. Analyses that you would never have considered viable in the past are now tasks that can be achieved within the current business cycle.

It is worth pointing out that you can use Power BI without learning DAX and data modelling. However, Power BI is definitely better when you learn to write DAX. If you don't invest time in learning DAX and data modelling, you will be able to take advantage of only the basic capabilities of Power BI. Imagine knowing how to use Excel basics like clicking on buttons and menus but not knowing how to write any formulas. Your limited knowledge would cause you to miss out on a lot of what Excel has to offer. You would be able to produce only very basic and simplistic spreadsheets. In much the same way, if you learn Power BI basics but don't learn the DAX language and how SSAS Tabular works, you will be limited to simplistic capabilities that restrict the value you can get from the tool.

There is another significant benefit to learning data modelling and DAX for Power BI. These skills are fully transferable to Power Pivot for Excel and also to Microsoft enterprise BI projects (using both Power BI and SSAS Tabular enterprise software). Although in this book you will be learning the DAX language using the Power BI user interface, you will be able to easily migrate your new skills into Power Pivot for Excel should you want to do that. And who wouldn't?

Why You Need This Book

I am a full-time Power BI consultant, trainer, and BI practitioner. I have taught many Excel users how to use Power Pivot for Excel and Power BI at live training classes (see http://xbi.com.au/live-training), and I have helped countless others online at various Power BI forums. This teaching experience has given me great insight into how Excel users learn Power BI and what resources they need to succeed. Power BI is very learnable, but it is very different from Excel; you definitely need some structured learning if you want to be good at using this tool. I have learnt that Excel users need practice, practice, practice. This book is designed to give you practice and to teach you how to write DAX. If you can't write DAX, you will never be good at Power BI or Power Pivot for Excel.

I refer above to Excel users, and that wording is quite deliberate. I have observed that Excel professionals learn DAX differently than do IT/SQL Server professionals. IT/SQL Server professionals are simply not the same as Excel business users. SQL Server professionals have solid knowledge of database design and principles, table relationships, how to efficiently aggregate data, etc. And of course there are some Excel users who also have knowledge about those things. But I believe IT/SQL Server professionals can take a much more technical path to learning DAX than most Excel users because they have the technical grounding to build upon. Excel users need a different approach, and this book is written with them in mind. I am not saying that an IT/SQL Server professional would not get any value from this book/approach; it really depends on your learning style. Further, I am not saying that IT/SQL Server professionals don't need to learn in a structured way; indeed, most do. What I am saying is that if you are an Excel business user who is trying to learn DAX, this book was written with your specific needs in mind.

Incremental Learning

I am an Excel user from way back—a long way back actually. (I first learnt to use Lotus 123 before Microsoft Excel was released.) I'm not the kind of guy who can sit down and read a novel, but I love to buy Excel reference books and read them cover to cover. And I have learnt a lot about Excel over the years by using this approach. When I find some new concept that I love and want to try, most of the time I just remember it. But sometimes I add a sticky note to the page so I can find it again in the future when I need it. In a way, I am incrementally learning a small number of new skills on top of the large base of skills I already have. When you incrementally learn like this, it is relatively easy to remember the detail of the new thing you just learnt.

It's a bit like when a new employee starts work at a company. Existing employees only have to learn the name of that one new person. But the new employee has to learn the name of each person in the entire company. It is relatively easy for the existing employees to remember one new name and a lot harder for the new person to start from scratch and learn all the names. Similarly, when you're an experienced Excel user reading a regular Excel book, you already know a lot and need to learn only a few things that are new—and those new bits are likely to be gold. It is easy to remember those few new things because often they strike a chord with you. Even if you don't remember the details, the next time you face a similar problem, you'll remember that you read something about it once, and you'll be able to go find your book to look it up.

Well, unfortunately for seasoned Excel users, Power BI is a completely different piece of software from Excel. It shares some things in common (such as some common formulas), but many of the really useful concepts are very different and completely new. They are not super-difficult to learn, but indeed you will need to learn from scratch, just as that new employee has to learn the names of many people. Once you get a critical mass of new Power BI knowledge in your head, you will be off and running. At that point, you will be able to incrementally learn all you want, but until then, you need to read, learn, and, most importantly, practice, practice, practice.

Passive vs. Active Learning

I think about learning as being either passive or active. An example of passive learning is lying in bed, reading your Power BI book, nodding your head to indicate that you understand what is being covered. When you learn something completely new, you simply can't take this approach. The DAX language was released in Power Pivot for Excel some 3 years before Power BI was first introduced, and I read a lot of Power Pivot books early in my discovery. Despite all my reading, the first time I sat in front of my computer and wanted to write some DAX, I was totally lost. What I really needed to do was change from a passive learning approach to an active approach, where I was participating in the learning process rather than being a spectator.

Passive learning on its own is more suited to incrementally adding knowledge to a solid base. Passive learning is not a good approach when you are starting something completely new from scratch. I'm not saying that passive learning is bad. It is useful to do some passive learning in addition to active learning, but you shouldn't try to learn a completely new skill from scratch using only passive learning.

Learning to Play Golf

I decided to take up golf when I was 53 years old. I had reached a stage in my career where I was working from home full time and had enormous flexibility as to when I did my work. I needed to find a new hobby to give me some downtime as my previous hobby—helping people on Excel forums in my spare time—was now my full-time job. I simply couldn't relax by helping others on forums anymore (unfortunately). And I needed to get out of the house, as my work and home had become the same place. I decided to take up golf as it was a perfect fit for my needs.

You're probably wondering what my new golf habit has to do with Power BI. Well, I read a really good book about golfing techniques (a Tiger Woods book, so it should be good). I also watched countless YouTube videos of professionals playing the game and countless more videos on various techniques to help improve my golf. But none of these insights from others made as much of a difference in my golf game as getting out there and practicing and playing the game. You can read all the Power BI books you like, but you will not be any good at DAX or data modelling until you actually do it yourself.

How to Get Value from This Book

There are 46 "Here's How" worked-through examples and 73 individual practices exercises in this book. That gives you almost 120 opportunities to learn and practice. (Did you see what I said there? These are opportunities for you to practice.) Make the most of these opportunities to develop your skills; after all, that is why you purchased this book.

If you think you can get value from this book by reading it and not doing the practice exercises, let me tell you: You can't. If you already know how to complete a task and you have done it before, then just reading is fine. However, if you don't know how to do a task or an exercise, then you should practice in front of your computer. First, try to do an exercise without looking at the answers. If you can't work it out, then reread the worked-through examples (labelled "Here's How") and then try to do the exercise again. Practice, practice, practice until you have the knowledge committed to memory and you can do it without looking.

Don't Treat This Like a Library Book

As kids going to school, most of us were taught that we should not write in library books. And I guess that is fair enough. Other people will use a library book after you are finished, and they probably don't want to read your scribbles. Unfortunately, the message that many of us took away was "Don't write in any book ever." I think it is a mistake to think that you can't write in your own books. You bought it, you own it, so why can't you write in it? In fact, I would go so far as to say you should write in the reference books you own. You bought them for a reason: to learn. If you are reading this book and want to make some notes to yourself for future reference, then you should definitely do that.

But I guess I am forgetting the eBook revolution. You can't write in an eBook, but I know you can highlight passages of text in a Kindle, and I assume you can do something similar in other eBooks. You can also type in your own notes and attach them to passages of text in many eBooks. There are lots of advantages of eBooks, and the one that means the most to me is the fact that I can have a new book in front of me just moments after I have decided to buy it.

Personally, I prefer to read a tactile object so I can flip through the pages, add sticky notes, and so on. But that is just me, and we are all different. I am sure there are plenty of people in both camps. On the upside, eBooks are usually in colour, and printed books (like this one) are more often in black and white. Whichever camp you are in—eBook or physical book—I encourage you to write in this book and/or make notes to yourself using the eBook tools at your disposal. Doing so will make this book a more useful, personalised tool well into the future.

Getting Help Along the Way

Hopefully you will be able to complete the practice exercises in this book on your own. But sometimes you might need to ask someone a question before you can move forward. I encourage you to become a member of my community forum at http://xbi.com.au/scpbiforum and participate as someone who asks questions and also as someone who helps others when they get stuck. Answering questions for other people is a great way to cement your learning and build depth of knowledge. You will notice from the URL that this is an Aussie forum; however, it is open to everyone. At this writing, only 15% of all traffic at the forum is from Australia, with the balance coming from more than 130 other countries around the world. I suggest that you sign up and get involved; your DAX will be better for it.

You can find a subforum dedicated to this book at my community forum (linked above). In the unfortunate event that there are errors in this book, you can go to this subforum for details.

How This Book Is Organised

I've organised this book to make sense to a new Power BI user starting from the beginning as well as to be useful as a reference guide. The general structure of the chapters is as follows:

- Each chapter's title begins with either "DAX Topic" or "Concept." A "DAX Topic" chapter covers one or more specific DAX formulas, including the syntax and usage; a "Concept" chapter covers one or more principles that you need to understand in order to be competent with Power BI. I've ordered the chapters so that you can learn incrementally. Each "Concept" chapter starts with a description of the concept, and each "DAX Topic" chapter starts with some information about the DAX language to help you understand the topic.

- Almost every chapter provides at least one worked-through example. When you see "Here's How," you know you're reading one of those, and it's time to sit in front of your computer and follow along with me as I explain the concept. See the "Table of Here's How Sections" on page 278.

- Almost every chapter includes a number of practice exercises that help you practice what you have learnt. You will find guidelines to complete the exercises, and you can also find the answers in Appendix A. I recommend that you complete the exercises first and only then look at the answers to ensure that you got the correct results. This way you can cement your learning as you work through the book.

- As in Excel, there is often more than one way to do something in DAX. If you do an exercise differently than I show how to do it, as long as you get the correct/same answer, all is good.

Here's How: Getting Power BI Desktop

All the instructions in this book use Power BI Desktop as the data modelling tool. To download this free tool, follow these steps:

1. Navigate to http://powerbi.com.
2. Go to the Products menu (see #1 below) and select Power BI Desktop (#2).

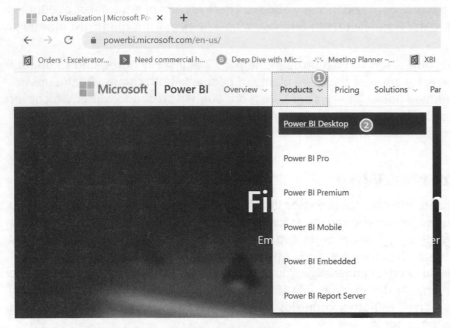

Note: At this writing, there are five other links under Power BI Desktop in the Products menu shown above (though this list changes quite often):

- Power BI Pro and Power BI Premium are licencing models for Power BI.
- Power BI Mobile links to the free Power BI apps for iOS and Android devices.
- Power BI Embedded allows developers to build Power BI reports directly inside their own custom software.
- Power BI Report Server is an on-premises version of Power BI for companies that do not wish to use a cloud-based solution.

3. Once you arrive at the Power BI Desktop page, click the Download Free button.

Go from data to insight to action with Power BI Desktop

Create rich, interactive reports with visual analytics at your fingertips—for free.

Download free >   See download or language options >

Note: You need administrator rights on your PC to be able to install the software. Also, the default download is the 64-bit version of Power BI Desktop that is installed from the Microsoft Store. This is the best option for most people. Here are a few key points for consideration:

- Where possible, you should install Power BI Desktop 64-bit from the Microsoft Store. When you install the software this way, Windows will automatically keep the software up to date. The software changes monthly, and you need to keep up with the updates. Make sure you install the software with the name Power BI Desktop.

- The 64-bit version of Power BI will work even if you have 32-bit Microsoft Office on your PC. If for some reason you need the 32-bit version of Power BI, you can click See Download or Language Options and download it from there.

- If you can't install from the Microsoft Store (some companies disable this feature), you can click See Download or Language Options and download a standalone installation package from there.

Updates to Power BI Desktop

Power BI Desktop is constantly being updated, and new software updates are released every month. This is great because each month you will be able to access new and exciting features developed by the team at Microsoft. If you install Power BI Desktop from the Microsoft Store as outlined above, you will always have the latest version; there is nothing else you need to do. If, however, you use one of the standalone installation packages, you will need to keep the software up to date yourself.

When there is a new version of Power BI Desktop available for you to install, you see a notification in the bottom-right corner of the application, as shown below.

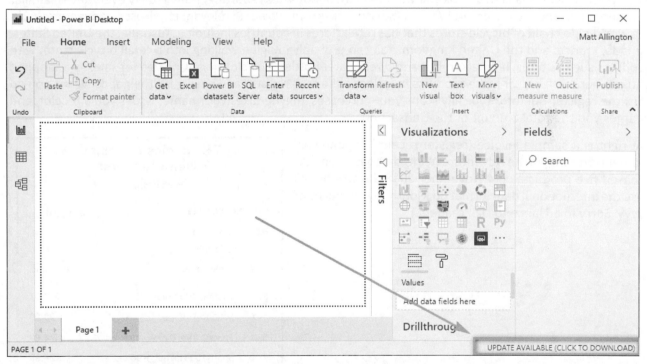

You can simply click on this notification to download the latest version. To complete the installation, you need to have admin rights, and you also need to close Power BI Desktop.

Note: One downside of Microsoft releasing new versions of Power BI Desktop every month is that it is inevitable that some of the screenshots in this book will look different from what you see on your screen, given that you will surely have a newer version of the software than I used while writing this book. Please keep this in mind as you read.

Power BI Pro vs. Power BI Free Accounts

Power BI Desktop is a free data model authoring tool that is used to build data models and reports. After you build a report, you can share it as a file with other Power BI Desktop users (just as you can an .xlsx file). With Power BI Desktop, you can also publish your reports to PowerBI.com, where the reports can be easily shared with other Power BI users; this is how reports are typically shared.

You need a Power BI account in order to use PowerBI.com. There are two types of Power BI accounts: free and Pro. A free account allows you to use most of the functionality of PowerBI.com, but there are some significant exceptions. You cannot share your work with others other than through public (unsecure) sharing, and you can't use some features, including Analyze in Excel, unless you have a Pro (or Premium) account. If you want to share reports and dashboards with other users, you need to either ensure that each of those users has a Power BI Pro account or post the reports on a Power BI Premium workspace. You can read more about Power BI licencing at https://powerbi.microsoft.com/en-us/pricing.

The AdventureWorks Database

It is surprisingly difficult to create your own database of meaningful data to use for data analysis practice. Think about the data that exists in a commercial retail business, for example: data on customers, finances, sales, products, territories, etc. And it is not a simple task to create a meaningful quantity of realistic data from scratch; it is a lot of work. Microsoft has created a number of sample databases that anyone can download and use for free. I use a modified version of the Microsoft AdventureWorks database throughout this book. You will need to download a copy of this modified version, in Microsoft Excel format, by going to http://xbi.com.au/sample-db. (Note that you do not need to have Microsoft Excel installed to load this data into Power BI Desktop, although most people will have Excel anyway.) This is the same sample database I use in all my training classes.

Not everyone who reads this book will want to learn about sales reporting, but virtually everyone is familiar with shopping, and the AdventureWorks database makes using Power BI relevant for all users. AdventureWorks is a worldwide chain of bicycle stores that has retail stores in countries including Australia, the United States, Canada, France, and the United Kingdom. You can probably imagine walking into a retail bicycle store, with products such as bikes, helmets, tubes and tyres, water bottles, and clothing displayed for sale. As a shopper, you can purchase one or more products by going to the cash register and paying for the goods. When you do this, the register operator typically scans your purchases, maybe takes your name, issues you a receipt, and charges you the total amount of the transaction.

At right is a sample invoice (register receipt) for one customer (Jon Yang) in the AdventureWorks database. Jon purchased five products on 4 November 2018. (In this book I use the international date format dd Month yyyy or dd/mm/yyyy. Sorry in advance to U.S. readers.)

Tax Invoice / Receipt
Adventure Works
Australia

OrderNo: **SO57418**		4/11/2018

Bill To: Jon Yang
Cust No.: 11000

Item	Description	Amount
573	Touring-1000 Blue, 46	$ 2,384.07
541	Touring Tire	$ 28.99
530	Touring Tire Tube	$ 4.99
214	Sport-100 Helmet, Red	$ 34.99
488	Short-Sleeve Classic Jersey, S	$ 53.99

Subtotal:	$ 2,507.03
Total ex tax:	$ 2,507.03
Tax (8%):	$ 200.56
Total Inc tax:	$ 2,707.59

The data that is produced during this transaction gets stored in the AdventureWorks database as shown below.

ProductKey ▼	OrderDate ▼	CustomerKey ▼	SalesOrderNumber ↑	OrderQuantity ▼	UnitPrice ▼	ExtendedAmount ▼
604	Sunday, 4 November 2018	28308	SO57416	1	539.99	539.99
477	Sunday, 4 November 2018	28308	SO57416	1	4.99	4.99
479	Sunday, 4 November 2018	28308	SO57416	1	8.99	8.99
214	Sunday, 4 November 2018	28308	SO57416	1	34.99	34.99
605	Sunday, 4 November 2018	22170	SO57417	1	539.99	539.99
538	Sunday, 4 November 2018	22170	SO57417	1	21.49	21.49
480	Sunday, 4 November 2018	22170	SO57417	1	2.29	2.29
573	Sunday, 4 November 2018	11000	SO57418	1	2384.07	2384.07
541	Sunday, 4 November 2018	11000	SO57418	1	28.99	28.99
530	Sunday, 4 November 2018	11000	SO57418	1	4.99	4.99
214	Sunday, 4 November 2018	11000	SO57418	1	34.99	34.99
488	Sunday, 4 November 2018	11000	SO57418	1	53.99	53.99
599	Sunday, 4 November 2018	15833	SO57419	1	539.99	539.99
363	Sunday, 4 November 2018	12689	SO57420	1	2294.99	2294.99
485	Sunday, 4 November 2018	12689	SO57420	1	21.98	21.98
478	Sunday, 4 November 2018	12689	SO57420	1	9.99	9.99
477	Sunday, 4 November 2018	12689	SO57420	1	4.99	4.99
563	Sunday, 4 November 2018	25064	SO57421	1	2384.07	2384.07
489	Sunday, 4 November 2018	25064	SO57421	1	53.99	53.99

The data shown in the image above comes from the `Sales` table, but a lot more data related to the transaction is stored in other tables, such as the `Customers` table and the `Products` table.

Naming Conventions

This book uses best-practice naming conventions for DAX in Power BI:

- There are no spaces in table names, like this:

    `TableName`

- Columns in tables always include the table name followed by the column name in square brackets, like this:

    `TableName[ColumnName]`

- Measures never include a table name, they often include spaces, and they are wrapped in square brackets, like this:

    `[MeasureName]`

- Measure and column formulas are written with the formula name (without the square brackets) followed by the formula, like this:

    `Total Sales = SUM(Sales[ExtendedAmount])`

1: Concept: Introduction to Data Modelling

In the past, the term data modelling was often unfamiliar to business users as data modelling tended to be the domain of IT BI professionals. But this is no longer the case, thanks to the introduction of self-service BI tools such as Power BI and Power Pivot for Excel.

What Is Data Modelling?

Data modelling is the process of taking data from various sources; loading, structuring, and relating data logically to other data; and enhancing, embellishing, and generally preparing the data for use. The objective is to allow the data to be used without having to write a custom query every time you want to look at a different subset of data.

The data modelling process includes:

- Determining the optimal structure and shape of the source data to analyse, including whether to bring in all the data, a subset of the data, or summary data.

- Loading the data from the source into the data model (Power BI in this case).

- Defining the logical relationships between the various tables (which is similar to what you do with VLOOKUP() in Excel, except the data stays in the source table in Power BI).

- Defining data types (e.g., specifying whether a column of data is a column of decimal values or a column of currency values, a column of text, etc.).

- Creating new insights from the source data so that you can analyse concepts that don't exist natively in the source data but that can be calculated or created inside the data model. For example, if you have a table of transactional data with cost price and selling price, you can extend the data model to include calculations for margin, margin percentage, etc., even though these concepts are not explicitly in the source data. Once you have modelled these new facts in the data model, they can be reused over and over by people using your workbook.

- Giving meaningful names to your new business insights (i.e., to your measures).

Power BI, Power Pivot, and SSAS Tabular

The data modelling engine that is used inside Power BI is the same one used in Power Pivot for Excel and SQL Server Analysis Services (SSAS) Tabular. The engine has quite a few names, including xVelocity, VertiPaq, SSAS Tabular, and Power Pivot. Despite the different names, the engine is essentially the same across all of these software products (with the exception of any version differences related to version release timing). It therefore follows that virtually everything you learn in this book about data modelling and DAX can be applied to Power Pivot for Excel and SSAS Tabular. In this book I most commonly refer to Power BI, but you should keep in mind that most of the content also applies to these other products.

Remember: Power BI Is a Database Tool, and Excel Is a Spreadsheet Tool

One very important concept you simply must understand is that Power BI is a database tool, and Excel is a spreadsheet tool. A database and a spreadsheet are not the same. A database has structure; it consists of one or more tables of data. Each table has zero, one, or more rows of data and one or more columns. Each column has a defined data format, and the data in each column must conform to that format. A database does not have a column-and-row reference system. A spreadsheet (e.g., an Excel worksheet) lacks the structure of a database. A spreadsheet, like a database, has columns and rows, but these columns and rows lack structure. You can put any data you want into any cell in a spreadsheet, and you can refer to a cell by using a cell reference. You have to follow a lot of rules with a database that don't apply to a spreadsheet.

Remember that Power BI is not Excel. You need to think differently if you are to master Power BI than you need to think to master Excel.

Power BI Is a Data Model–Based Tool

Power BI is a data model–based BI reporting tool. Not all BI tools are data model based. One example of a non-data model–based BI tool is SQL Server Reporting Services (SSRS). Non-data model–based BI reporting tools require the report writer to first generate a query to fetch the data from a database (typically SQL Server) and return the results of that query to SSRS so the results can be rendered in a report. With a non-data model–based reporting tool, you can typically use a user interface that helps with the generation of the query, or you can use a scripting language such as T-SQL to fetch the data that you need for each report.

Traditional Excel—that is, the spreadsheet tool without the modern BI add-ins of Power Query and Power Pivot—is also a non-data model–based BI tool. In the case of traditional Excel, the user loads data into the spreadsheet and then logically relates and aggregates the data using Excel formulas and builds a report (often on a new sheet) to summarise and present the results (the report).

Now don't confuse "a tool" here with "a data model–based tool." Excel is definitely a tool; it is a very flexible tool that lets you build virtually any report without being a programmer. In fact, I think Excel is probably the best and most popular BI tool ever invented. But it is not a data model–based tool because traditional Excel doesn't have a data model.

There is nothing wrong with using a non-data model–based BI tool; it is just a different approach from using a data model–based tool. The biggest issue with non-data model–based reporting tools is that every time you need a new report, you have to start again, often from scratch. Each report has a single purpose, and there is very little reusability or extensibility.

A data model–based tool like Power BI has many benefits, including the following:

- The author of the data model builds a reusable model that can be used to solve the current reporting requirements as well as (often) future requirements without the need to write further queries to retrieve a new subset of data.

- The author can often be a business user (normally with good Excel skills) and doesn't have to be a professionally trained database administrator or SQL professional.

- The data model is conceptual in nature, supported by a user-friendly interface that lets you build the data model logically, with minimal coding. Keep in mind that you do need to do some coding (formula writing) for a good data model, but it is fairly easy—no harder than building a typical spreadsheet in Excel—when you have the skills, as you will see later in this book.

The term data modelling can be a little bit scary, but there is no reason to be concerned. When you learn the DAX language and join your tables of data in Power BI, you are actually learning data modelling. By the time you have finished this book, you will be well on your way to being an accomplished data modeller using Power BI. Just use the techniques covered in this book and keep in mind that what you are actually doing is learning to be a data modeller.

With all this in mind, it's time to build your first simple data model.

2: Concept: Loading Data

The first step in data modelling is to load data into Power BI Desktop. The image below shows the data connector that appears when you connect to a SQL Server database from Power BI Desktop. (There is a different data connector for each data source. You'll see how to get to the various data connector screens later in this chapter.) There are two modes that you can use in Power BI Desktop when loading data from a database tool such as SQL Server: Import and DirectQuery.

Most data sources do not provide these two options and instead only allow you to use Import mode. This book focuses on Import mode. When you use Import mode, Power BI Desktop loads a complete copy of the source data into the data model as the first step in the process. Once it is loaded, you can share your .pbix workbook with others, and there is no need for anyone else to have direct access to the source data. Alternatively, you can publish your reports to PowerBI.com and share the contents with others from there. When you publish a report to PowerBI.com, a complete copy of the data is loaded into the cloud also, without the need for it to access the source data. The data that is loaded into your data model retains a connection to the original source. It is a simple task to refresh the data when the data at the source changes. Such a refresh can either be triggered manually or set to automatically occur on a schedule.

When you load data into Power BI Desktop, you have to decide which data to load, including which tables, which columns in each table, etc. I call this the shape of the data. The following "Here's How" shows how to load data that has been prepared for you. But you need to be aware that the process of deciding which data to load is an important part of the data modelling process, as discussed later in this chapter.

Here's How: Loading Data from a New Source

If you don't already have a copy of the custom version of the AdventureWorks database used in this book, you should download the sample Excel file now (from http://xbi.com.au/sample-db), unzip it, and place it in a location that is easy for you to find. In the following steps, you will load the following tables from the AdventureWorks database:

```
Sales
Products
Territory
Calendar
Customers
```

For convenience and ease of access, I have extracted all the relevant data from the AdventureWorks database into individual sheets inside an Excel workbook; that is what you will find inside the .zip file. The following steps show you how to load these database tables from the Excel workbook and prepare them for use in Power BI:

1. Open Power BI Desktop. You should see a blank Power BI Desktop file with a ribbon along the top, as shown below.

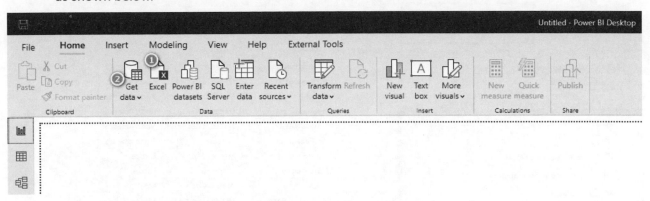

2. From the Home tab in Power BI Desktop, select Excel (see #1 above). Alternatively, select Get Data (#2 above), All, Excel (#1 below) and then click Connect (#2 below).

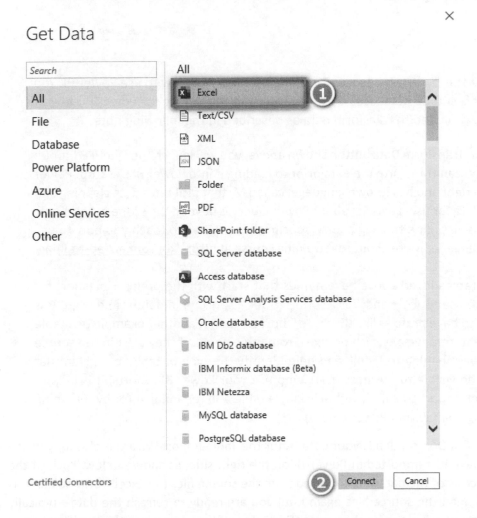

3. Browse to the location of the sample Excel file you downloaded earlier and click Open.

4. When Power Query connects to the file, you see a list of all objects that can be imported into Power BI. In this instance, you see a list of sheets inside Excel that contain data that can be loaded. You need to select the five sheets that contain the tables of data needed for this book, as shown below. At this point, you should not load the other sheets of data.

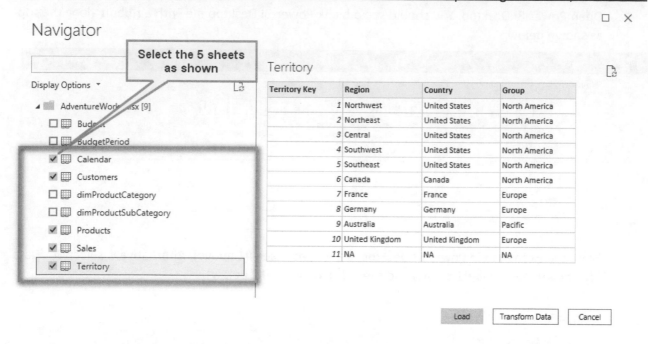

Tip: The sample data for this book has been well prepared for learning how to use Power BI. You should not assume that a source database has the correct table structure for Power BI; few of them do. In most cases, you need to transform data as described in the following note.

Note: If you now click the Transform Data button shown above, you will launch the Query Editor (in Power Query), where you can transform the data prior to loading it into Power BI Desktop. Power Query is a tool in its own right and has its own language, called M, that facilitates data cleaning and shaping to prepare the data for use. Learning about Power Query is beyond the scope of this book, but I have a comprehensive online training course specifically designed to teach you how to use this powerful tool. You can learn more about that training course at http://xbi.com.au/pq-training.

Notice that two of the tables listed above have names that start with the prefix `dim` (short for dimension): `dimProductCategory` and `dimProductSubCategory`. In database design, it is very common for tables to have prefixes like this. `fct` (short for fact) is another example of a table prefix. It is best practice to remove any such prefixes from table names if they exist in the source data. These prefixes have meaning to IT folk and help identify the type of table, but given that these table names will be visible to business users who use your Power BI reports, it is best to remove the prefixes after import by simply right-clicking a table and renaming it (or by renaming the tables during loading from within Power Query).

5. Click Load, and Power BI Desktop loads your data. After the Table Import Wizard is closed, you see the five tables you have just imported in Power BI on the right side, as shown below. Each of the tables is a complete copy of the data you imported from the source files (an Excel workbook, in this example). You don't need the source files again until you are ready to refresh the data—typically when the data changes at some time in the future. This is one of the many great things about Power BI: You can simply refresh the data when the data changes, and your workbooks are updated with the new data.

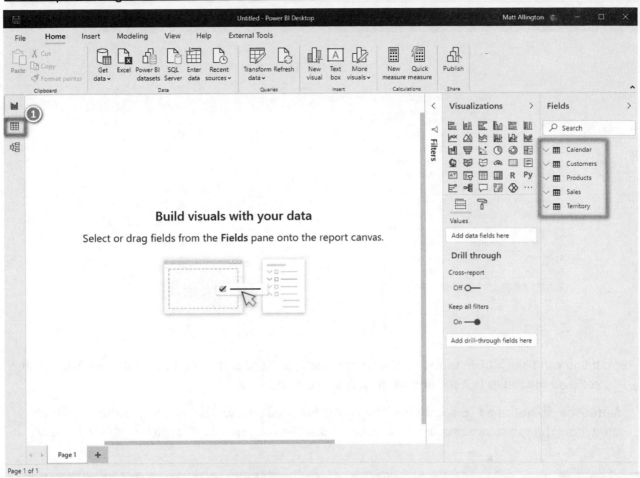

6. Switch to the Data view by clicking the Data icon (see #1 above). You can now see the data in the tables, as shown in the image below.

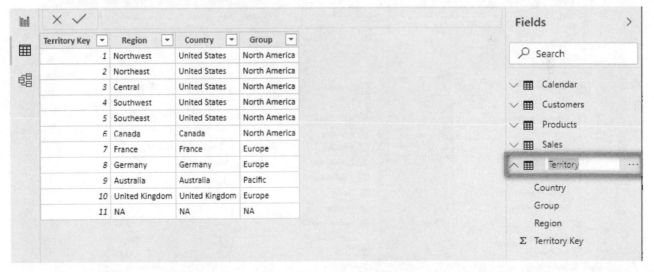

7. In the Data view, double-click the `Territory` table name on the right, as shown below, and rename it `Territories` for consistency (e.g., naming all tables with plurals—except `Calendar`, of course).

8. For the next stage of the data modelling process, which involves creating the logical relationships between the tables, switch to the Model view by clicking the Model icon (see #1 below).

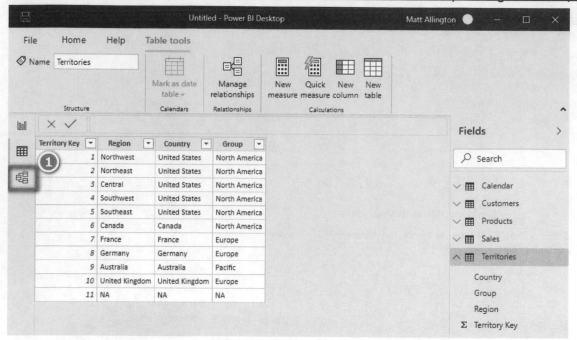

9. If you can't see all five tables on the screen, click the Fit to Screen button (#1 below). You can also collapse the tables (#2, #3, and #4) to save space in this view.

> **Note:** You do not need to see all the columns in the Model view. The purpose of this view is to show how the tables are related. If you want to see the column names, switch to the Data view. Trust me.

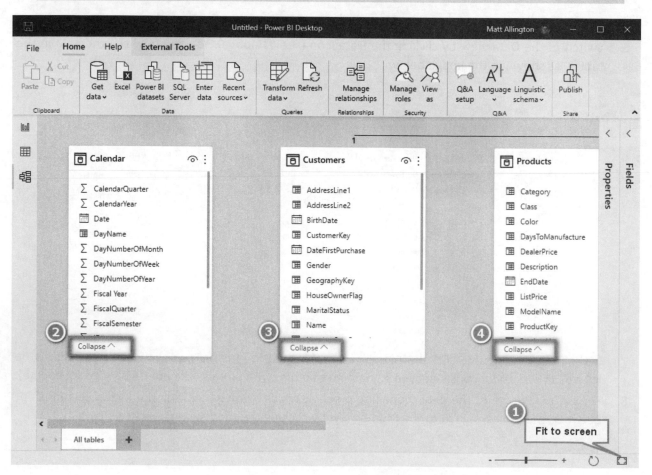

In the image shown below, two of the tables have automatically been joined. Power BI, by default, automatically attempts to logically join the tables of data together. These automatically created relationships may or may not be correct; in this case, they are indeed correct.

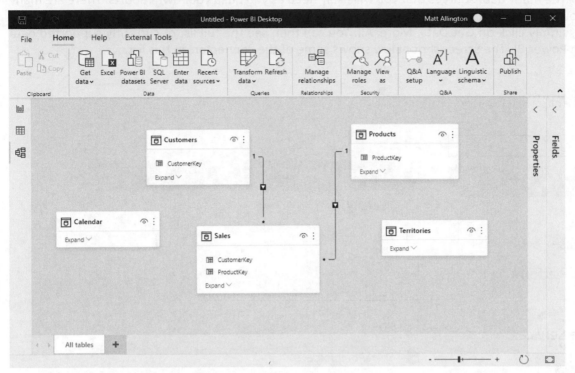

10. If desired, change the layout of these tables by dragging and dropping. As you will learn later in this chapter, I recommend positioning the tables so that any transactional tables (there is only one, `Sales`, in this case) are at the bottom of the screen and the lookup tables are at the top.

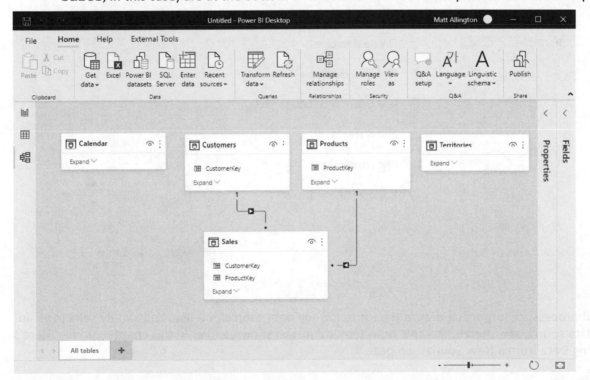

When you've completed these steps, you need to create relationships between the `Sales` table and the other four tables. You'll learn how to do so in the next "Here's How" section.

Other Data Sources

In this book, I teach you how to import data from the AdventureWorks Excel sample file, but this file is only an example of the many data sources that you will likely need as you build your own reports. There are many other data source connectors available in Power BI (though technically they are part of Power Query). To see a full list, simply click on Get Data, More, All. You can then see the full list of currently supported data connectors in Power BI. The screenshot below shows some of the connectors in this list.

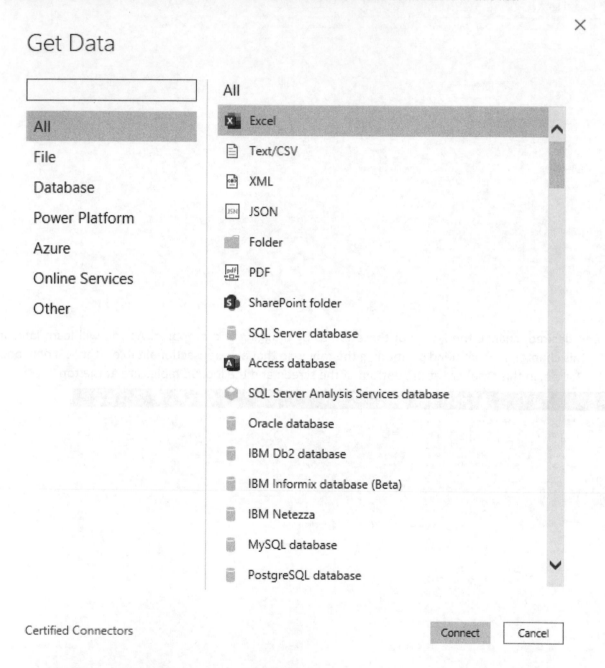

The general process for importing data is the same for any data source you use: You simply select the appropriate data source and then follow the import wizard just as shown earlier in this chapter, under "Here's How: Loading Data from a New Source" on page 8.

Here's How: Creating Relationships in Power BI Desktop

The Introduction provides a high-level overview of the AdventureWorks database. Here we look more closely at some of the tables in that database. The `Sales` table holds records of sales transactions. It has the following features:

- One row of data is generated for each item scanned at the cash register and stored in the `Sales` table.
- There can be many rows of data in the `Sales` table that together make up a single customer invoice.
- Each customer can shop many times, so there may be more than one invoice for each customer in the `Sales` table.
- The date, the customer number, the product codes, the quantity, the cost price, and the selling price of each item sold (among other data) are stored in the `Sales` table.
- Only the absolute minimum amount of data needed to identify the customer, the product, the time period, and the store are recorded in the `Sales` table. This data is presented in "key" columns, such as `Customer Key` (e.g., customer number) and `Product Key` (e.g., product number).

Note: As described later in this chapter, I call the transaction tables data tables and the other tables lookup tables.

Each transaction in the `Sales` table contains a customer key that uniquely identifies which customer purchased each item. All the other information about that customer (e.g., name, address) is stored in the `Customers` table. When using traditional Excel, it is common to write a `VLOOKUP()` formula to fetch the name of the customer who purchased each item and bring it back to the `Sales` table. This is not required in Power BI. Instead, the two tables of data (the `Sales` table and the `Customers` table) can be logically related using the common customer key that exists in both tables. When these tables are joined using the customer key, there is a one-to-many (`Customers` to `Sales`) relationship between these two tables. Exactly the same principle applies to the `Products`, `Calendar`, and `Territories` tables.

To join a lookup table to a data table in Power BI Desktop, follow these steps:

Note: It is important to follow these steps now as doing so will create a foundation for all the practice in the rest of this book.

1. Expand the `Sales` and `Calendar` tables to view all the columns (if needed).
2. Select a column from the data table (the table at the bottom of the Power BI Desktop screen, as shown below). To do this, click the `OrderDate` column in the `Sales` table and hold down the left mouse button (see #1 below).
3. Drag the column up and hover over the matching key in the lookup table (in this case, the `Date` column in the `Calendar` table) until you can see that you are hovering over the correct column in the `Calendar` table (see #2 below).
4. Release the mouse button to complete the relationship.

   The `Sales` and `Calendar` tables are now joined with a one-to-many relationship on the `Date` column.

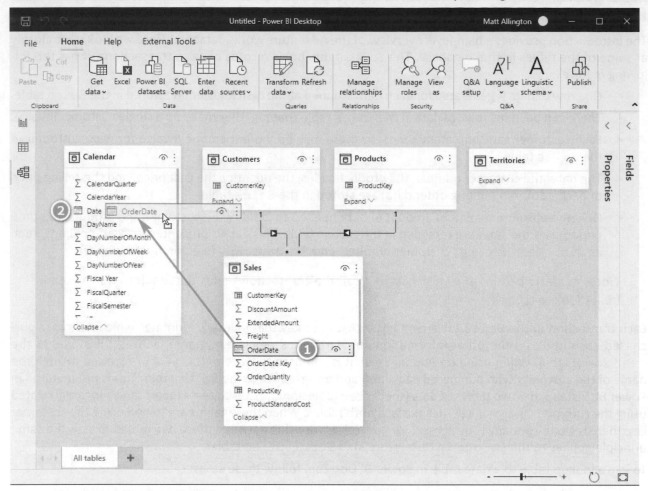

5. Complete the same process for the remaining tables. See if you can work out on your own which are the correct columns to join before you look at the answers below. Note that it is not mandatory for the key columns to have the same name, although it is good practice to name them the same.

Data Table	Column		Lookup Table	Column
Sales	ProductKey	=>	Products	ProductKey
Sales	CustomerKey	=>	Customers	CustomerKey
Sales	SalesTerritoryKey	=>	Territories	TerritoryKey

Because these are one-to-many relationships, the joins are specifically single-directional (and you see an arrow pointing downward toward the `Sales` table). Always drag from the data table up to the lookup table rather than the other way around (as you would if you were writing a `VLOOKUP()` in Excel). It will work the other way, but this is the correct way to do it.

As you can see in the image below, an asterisk appears at the end of the relationship that points to the data table (`Sales`), and a 1 appears at the end that points to a lookup table. In each case, an arrow points toward the `Sales` table. (You'll learn more about these arrows later in this chapter.)

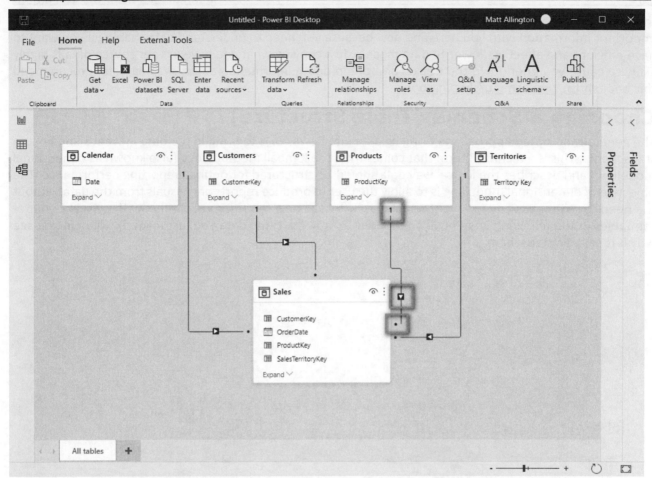

By putting the data table at the bottom, you create a visual clue that the tables at the top of the screen are lookup tables. (Get it? You have to "look up" to see the lookup tables.)

6. Save the Power BI Desktop file by clicking the Save icon, as shown below, and give your file a suitable name and location so you can find it again later.

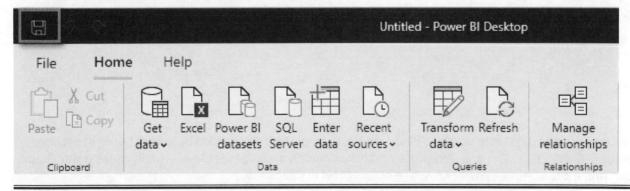

Shaping Data

It's time to pause for a minute to discuss the optimal shape of data for Power BI. When I say "shape" of data, I am talking about things like how many tables you import, how many columns are in each table, how many rows are in each table, which columns are in each of the tables, etc.

Shaping data is a huge topic, and I don't have room here to discuss it fully. But I do want to give some foundational advice in this section and the sections that follow to get you started. One reason this advice is important is because the shape of data in transactional systems (and relational databases) is seldom the ideal shape for Power BI. When an IT department executes an enterprise BI project, one of the important first steps is to shape the data so it is optimal for reporting. This step is normally completely hidden from the end user (i.e., you), and hence the end user is shielded from the need for shaping. But I am sharing this important information with you here and now because you need to understand data shaping if you want to have efficient and effective Power BI data models. Just copying what you have in your source data is highly likely to cause you grief down the track. For more in-depth information about shaping data, I recommend this book: http://xbi.com.au/shaping-book.

Choosing a Schema (Table Structure)

The generally accepted approach to bringing data into Power BI is to bring in the data in what's known as a star schema. This is a technical term that comes from the Kimball methodology (also known as dimensional modelling) and describes the logical way data should be structured for optimal reporting performance. The objective of dimensional modelling is to allow the user to produce reports and visuals from the data without the need to write a new query over the database for each new reporting requirement. The visual layout of the tables in the following image (which includes exactly the same data you just loaded) will help you see why it is called a star schema.

In a star schema, the data table or tables (Sales in this example) are surrounded by lookup tables (Customers, Products, Territories, and Calendar in this example), and together they visually make a star shape. You can find more comprehensive coverage of this topic in Chapter 6.

> **Note:** Dimensional modelling is a huge topic. I have a comprehensive online training course on dimensional modelling that I produced with Ken Puls and Miguel Escobar that you can find at http://xbi.com.au/dm-training.

The Visual Layout of Tables in the Model View

When it comes to visually positioning tables in the Model view, I teach business users to position the tables such that the lookup tables are located at the top of the window and the data tables are at the bottom of the window, as shown below.

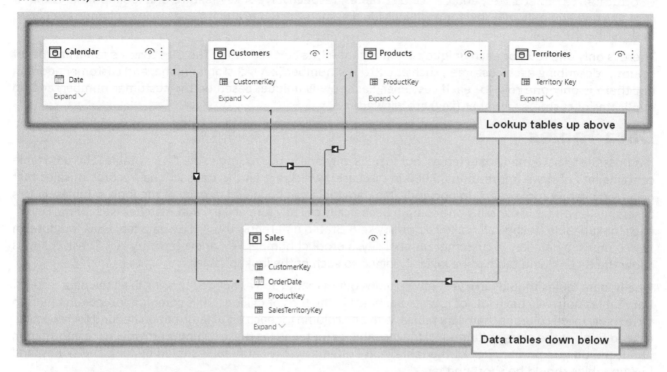

Note: While the optimum data model shape is a star schema, other shapes work, too. For example, you can use a snowflake schema, with secondary lookup tables joined to the primary lookup tables; however, the extra relationships can come at the cost of degraded performance and possibly also confusion to users, particularly if they are building their own reports.

If you compare the image above with the one just before it, you will see that they both have exactly the same logical relationships (links) between the tables: They are both star schemas, even though they have different visual layouts.

The visual layout in the image just above is the one conceived and recommended by Rob Collie, and I call it the "Collie layout methodology." The Collie layout methodology involves placing the lookup tables at the top of the window and the data tables at the bottom. The importance of this for business users learning Power BI will become evident later in the book. For now, just trust me and follow the Collie layout methodology.

Understanding the Two Types of Tables: Lookup Tables and Data Tables

In the IT world, lookup tables are referred to as dimension tables, and data tables are called fact tables. For business users, though, I suggest using the terminology lookup tables and data tables.

A data table contains transactional information. The data table we use in this book, the Sales table, contains sales transactions. Lookup tables contain information about logical groups of objects, such as customers (Customers table), products (Products table), and time (Calendar table).

Before Power BI, an Excel user needed to create one big flat table in Excel before creating a pivot table. Often that meant writing VLOOKUP() formulas to bring data from other tables into the one allowed big flat table. It is no longer necessary to bring data from the lookup tables into the data tables by using VLOOKUP() in Power BI. Instead, you can simply load the lookup tables and join them to the data table(s) with a relationship.

Lookup Tables

You should have one lookup table for each "object" that you need for reporting purposes. For example, in the data being used here, these objects are customers, products, territories, and time (in the `Customers`, `Products`, `Territories`, and `Calendar` tables, respectively). A key feature of a lookup table is that it contains one and only one row for each individual item in the table, and it has as many columns as needed to describe the object.

There is only one row for each unique customer in the `Customers` table. The `Customers` table has lots of columns describing each customer, such as customer number (key), customer name, and customer address, but there is only one row for each customer. Each row is unique, based on the customer number, and no duplicates of customer number (key) are allowed.

Data Tables

It is possible to have many data tables, but there is only one in this example: the `Sales` table. This data table contains lots of rows (more than 60,000 in this case), which are all the transactional records of sales that occurred over multiple years. Importantly, the data table can be joined to each of the lookup tables. In this case, the `Sales` table contains one column (technically called a foreign key) that matches each of the keys in each lookup table (technically called a primary key). Stated differently, the `Sales` data table has four foreign key columns: a date key, a customer number key, a product number key, and a territory key. These columns allow the `Sales` data table to be logically joined to each of the lookup tables.

Ideally, data tables should have very few columns but as many rows as needed to bring in all the data records. Data tables normally have lots of rows (sometimes in the tens of millions). It is common for lookup tables to have many more columns than data tables, with one column for each bit of information needed for reporting. I like to think of the extra columns in a lookup table as metadata as these columns provide more information about the unique primary key of the table. And I often say that data tables should be long and skinny, and lookup tables should be short and fat.

The Shaping Bottom Line

When it comes to shaping data, you need to remember the following:

- There are two types of tables: data tables, which contain the data you want to analyse, and lookup tables, which contain metadata about the objects you are going to analyse, such as the name, address, and city of each customer.
- The rule of thumb is to load one table for each object. This is both efficient for the database to process and easy for users to understand.
- The optimal way to shape your data is to use a star schema, but other schemas, such as a snowflake schema, can work, too, though they may be less efficient.
- For business users, I recommend positioning tables in the Power BI Model view, using the Collie layout methodology. (You'll learn more about why you should do this in Chapter 5.)

Here's How: Making Changes to a Table That Is Already Loaded

Sometimes you will want to make changes to the data that is loaded after the initial load is complete. This is a technical Power Query topic, but I cover it here so you will know what to do.

Say that you want to make changes to the `Calendar` table so that you only bring in dates for the years 2017 and 2018, and you also want to remove the fiscal date columns from the table. You can do this by using the Query Editor. The following steps walk you through how to make changes like these to a table that is already loaded:

1. In the Fields pane on the right (in the Report view or the Data view), right-click on the `Calendar` table and select Edit Query.
2. In the Power Query Editor that appears, navigate to the `CalendarYear` column and click the drop-down arrow (see #1 below).

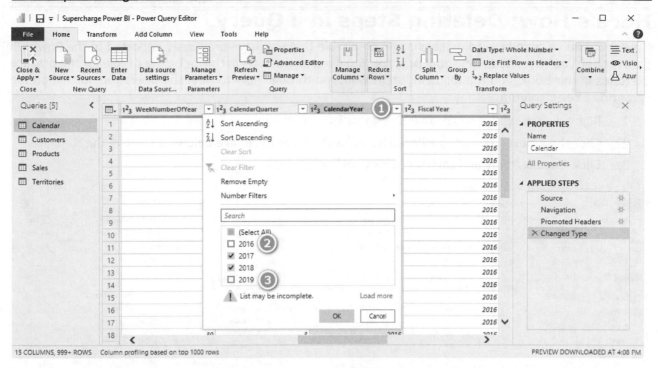

3.   Deselect the years 2016 and 2019 from the drop-down list (see #2 and #3 above) and then click OK.

4.   Remove the three fiscal columns by first selecting them all using either the Shift or Ctrl keys (see #1 below) and then right-clicking on one of the selected columns and selecting Remove Columns (#2).

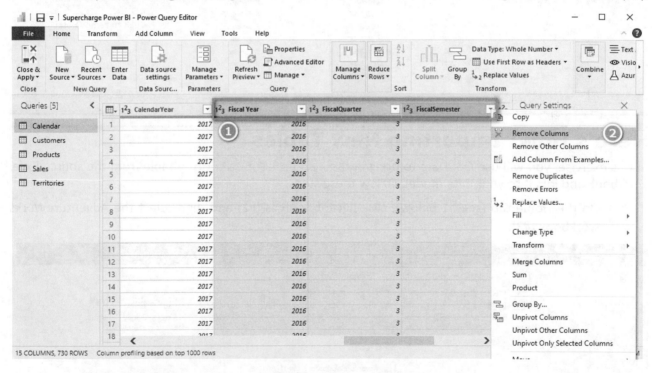

5.   Click Close & Apply and then save the .pbix workbook.

Note: When you are using the Power Query Editor as shown above, you are actually using the Power Query technology (the Data, Get Data menu options in Excel and the Home, Get Data menu options in Power BI). As mentioned earlier, using Power Query is a big topic that is not covered in detail in this book. I recommend that you refer to my online training course, at http://xbi.com. au/pq-training, to learn more about this important topic.

Here's How: Deleting Steps in a Query

Now that you've seen how to make changes to a table that you have previously imported to the Power BI data model, you're ready to get some practice. You need all the rows in the `Calendar` table for the practice exercises in this book, and the following steps walk you through how to clear the filters you applied on the `CalendarYear` column:

1. Right-click the `Calendar` table and select Edit Query.

2. Click the X next to the step Filtered Rows, as shown in the image below, to remove the step.

3. Click Close & Apply and save the .pbix workbook.

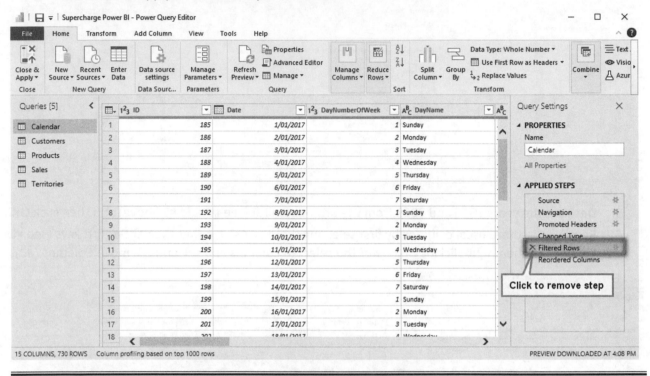

Here's How: Importing New Tables

In this exercise, you will use Get Data to bring in the `ProductSubCategory` table from the source Excel workbook and join it to your data model. Follow these steps:

1. On the Home tab (see #1 below), click Recent Sources (#2) and then select the AdventureWorks workbook (#3).

2. Select the `dimProductSubCategory` table (see #1 below) and click Transform Data (#2).

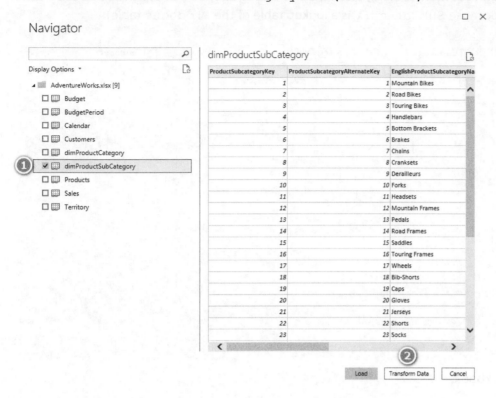

3. Remove the `dimProduct` prefix from the Name box on the right, as shown below, so you are left with `SubCategory` as the query name, and then click Close & Apply. Power BI automatically connects the new `SubCategory` table to the existing `Products` table. As mentioned earlier, Power BI attempts to do this by default where possible. Sometimes it gets it right, and sometimes it gets it wrong. It is best practice to always check the Model view for relationships after you load a table of data.

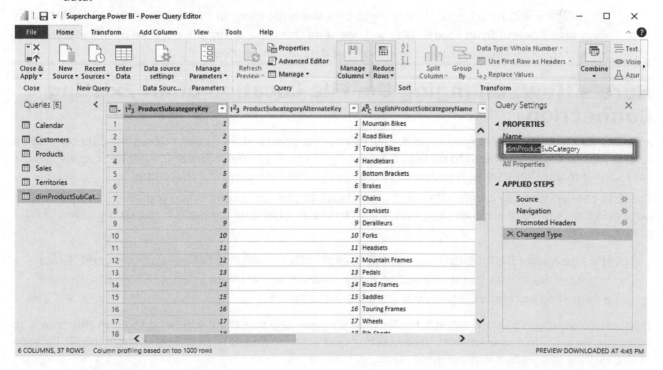

4. To apply the Collie layout methodology, place the `SubCategory` table above the `Products` table, as shown below (because `SubCategory` is a lookup table of the `Products` table).

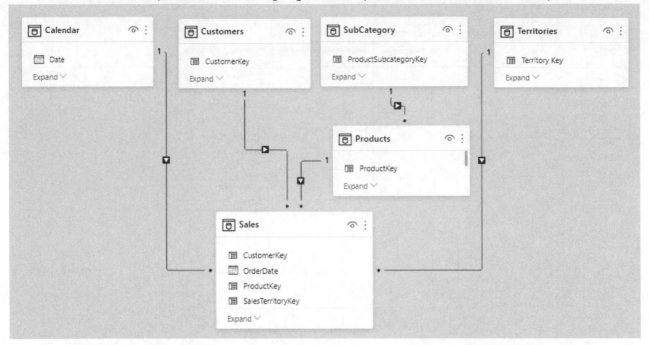

5. Save the .pbix workbook.

Note: Now that there is a second lookup table (`SubCategory`) connected to another lookup table (`Products`), this is technically a snowflake schema. This shape will work, but it may be less efficient than a star schema. In addition, this shape may be confusing to users of the report because it does not follow the "one object, one table" rule; there are two tables that contain information about products. It is not wrong to do it this way. It is just a guideline to try to build models that follow the "one object, one table" rule where possible to keep the model easy to understand.

6. To delete this `SubCategory` table, right-click the table name in the Report view or the Data view and select Delete from Model. (You will not need this table again; the purpose of this exercise was simply to show you how to add new tables of data, when needed.)

Here's How: Changing the File Location of an Existing Connection

It's important to know how to move a source file to a new location and then point the existing data connection to that new location. You need to do this, for example, if you ever send a Power BI workbook as well as the data source to another user or if you need to change file locations on your own computer.

The data connections you create in Power BI are relative to your computer. When you send a Power BI workbook and data source to another user, that person has to edit the data connection so that it will work on his or her own PC.

Note: You need to follow the steps in this section only if you send both a workbook and a data source to another user. But that is not normally what you do. Normally you don't need to distribute the data at all because it is loaded in Power BI already.

To simulate what can happen when a file location changes, the first thing you need to do in this case is to move the Excel file to a new location so the existing query cannot find it. Then you can change the file location of the existing connection. Follow these steps:

1. In Windows Explorer, create a new folder.

2. Navigate to your Excel file and move it into the new folder.

3. Try to refresh your queries (by clicking Refresh on the Home tab) and note that it doesn't work, as shown below.

Refresh

✕

⚠ Calendar

Could not find file 'D:\Matt\Supercharge Power BI\AdventureWorks.xlsx'.

⚠ Customers

Could not find file 'D:\Matt\Supercharge Power BI\AdventureWorks.xlsx'.

⚠ Products

Could not find file 'D:\Matt\Supercharge Power BI\AdventureWorks.xlsx'.

⚠ Sales

Could not find file 'D:\Matt\Supercharge Power BI\AdventureWorks.xlsx'.

⚠ Territory

Could not find file 'D:\Matt\Supercharge Power BI\AdventureWorks.xlsx'.

[Close]

4. Click Close.

5. On the Home tab, select Transform Data (see #1 below) and then Data Source Settings (#2).

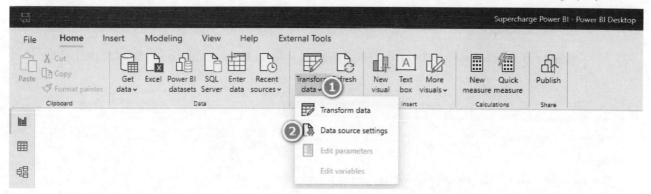

Tip: Be careful here. When a menu item (like the Transform Data menu above) has a small down arrow next to the description, it means that there is a drop-down menu just below the icon, and you will get different results if you click the icon than if you click on the down arrow below the icon.

6. Select the data source that relates to the Excel source file (see #1 below) and then click Change Source (#2).

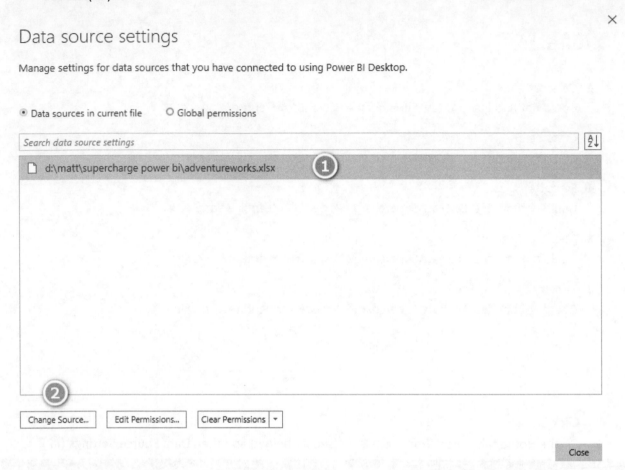

7. Browse to the new location by using File Explorer (see #1 below) and then click OK (#2).

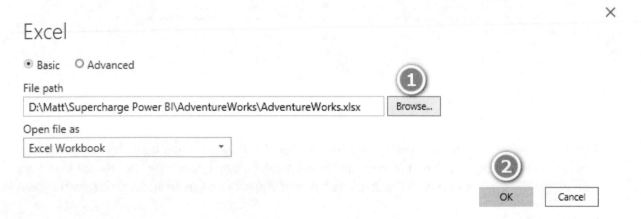

8. Click Close in the Data Source Settings dialog and click Apply Changes to make the changes.

There Are No Pivot Tables in Power BI

The Power BI report canvas is very different from what you are used to using in Excel. This can be quite confronting to Excel users who are getting started with Power BI. But the good news is that you will be comfortable with it in no time. In October 2020, Microsoft updated the blank report canvas experience. Now, instead of seeing a blank page (as in PowerPoint), you see some watermark instructions that provide hints on how to load some data. This is a big step forward in helping beginners know what to do next.

In Microsoft Excel, the most common way to aggregate data for BI-style reporting is to use a pivot table. But there are no pivot tables in Power BI. What's worse (and confronting) is that you can't even edit data inside the Data view in Power BI Desktop after the data is loaded; it is read only. Although Power BI has no pivot tables, it does allow you to use a matrix. A Power BI matrix is very similar to a pivot table and is (in my view) the best visual to use when you are learning to write DAX. Throughout this book, you will in many cases set up a matrix and then place your new measures inside that matrix so that you can visualise the results of your work. Once you have seen that the results of your measures are working as you expect, it is very easy to change the matrix into another type of visual to better display the data.

At this writing, there is no pivot table object in Power BI, but there is a matrix that does pretty much the same thing. The matrix visual object is a very close substitute for a pivot table, and it is the best visualisation to use when you are beginning to build models. It allows you to "see" the results of your calculations in the form of numbers and text. There is also a table visual that you can use. The table is similar to a matrix, but it doesn't have an option to cross-tabulate your data into rows and columns, as you can in a matrix and a pivot table. You can explore the difference by switching between the two visualisation types in a report.

Here's How: Inserting a Matrix

There are several ways to insert a matrix into a report. I suggest that you do it like this:

1. Ensure that you are in the Report view by clicking the Report icon (see #1 below).
2. Click the Matrix icon (#2).

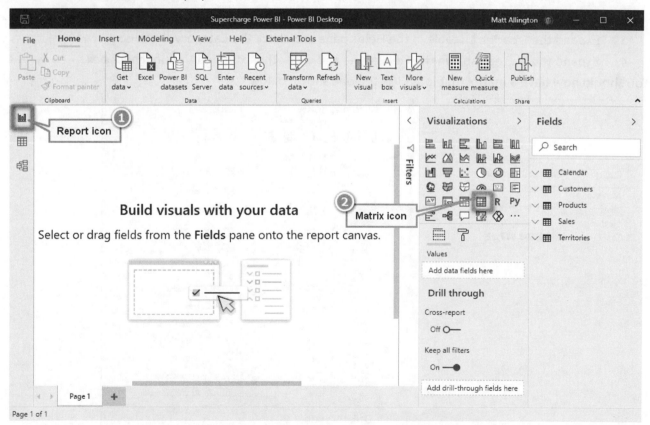

A new matrix placeholder appears on the canvas (see #1 below). Note the Fields pane (#2) and the Rows (#3), Columns (#4), and Values (#5) drop zones on the right-hand side. If you have experience using pivot tables in Excel, you will recognise this as being very similar to the Excel pivot table experience.

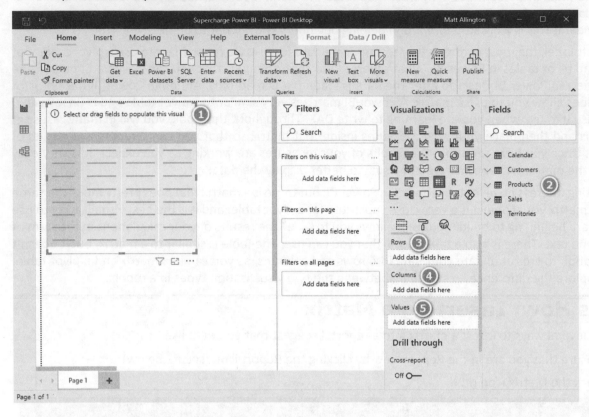

3.   Expand the `Products` table in the Fields pane and check the Category check box.

4.   Expand the `Sales` table in the Fields pane and check the ExtendedAmount check box.

You should now have a matrix that looks like the one shown below.

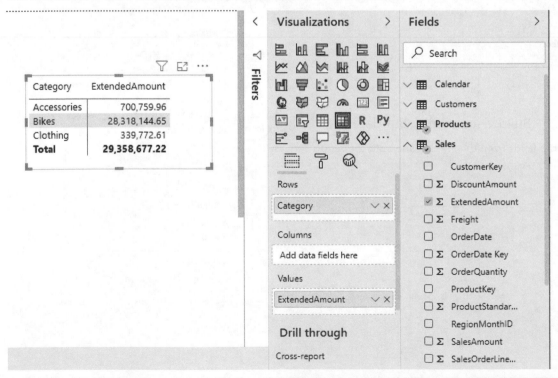

3: Concept: Measures

Measures have been around for many years in the enterprise versions of Microsoft BI tools, such as SQL Server Analysis Services. Measures have now made it into the world of business users who want to create Power BI reports. There is nothing confusing or hard to learn about measures. A measure is simply a DAX formula that instructs Power BI to do a calculation on data. In a sense, a measure is a lot like a formula in a cell in Excel. The main difference between a formula in a cell in Excel and a measure is that a measure always operates over the entire data model, not over just a few cells in a spreadsheet. You'll learn more about this later, but for now you can think of a measure as a formula that calculates a result from the loaded data.

Techniques for Writing DAX Measures

With Power BI, you write measures in the formula bar, as shown below.

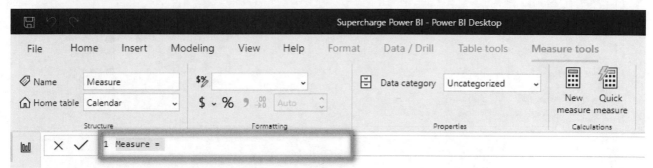

The formula bar is not visible unless you have a measure selected in the Fields pane on the right-hand side of Power BI. When you select a measure in the Fields pane, the formula bar appears just below the ribbon, as shown above.

> **Note:** There is another way to write measures in Power BI: by using a third-party tool called Tabular Editor. Using Tabular Editor is a more advanced technique that has a lot of productivity benefits over using the formula bar. You can read more about Tabular Editor at http://xbi.com. au/tabular-editor.

There are two ways you can start the process of writing a new measure in Power BI. One way is to select the Modeling tab (see #1 below) and then click the New Measure button (#2).

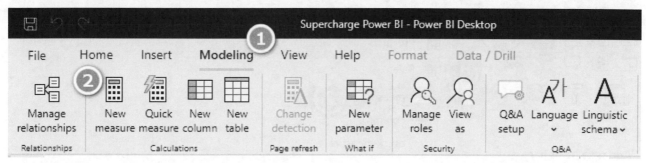

I don't recommend using this approach to create a new measure as it has one major problem: Any time you create a new measure by clicking the New Measure button (see #1 below), the measure is automatically added to the table that is in the Fields pane on the right (#2). It is far too easy to place the measure in the wrong table when you use this approach. I therefore recommend that you use the second approach, described next.

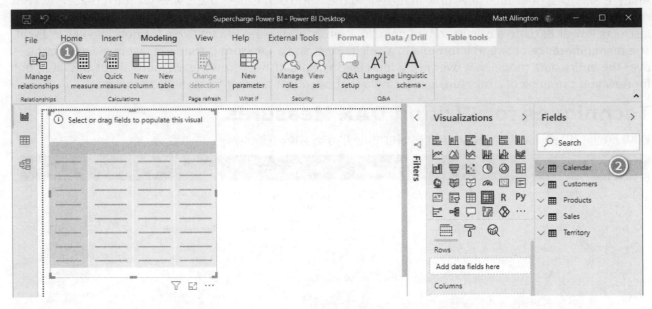

The second way to write a new measure in Power BI is to go to the Fields pane and right-click the table where you want to store the measure (see #1 below). (Best practice is to store the measure in the table the data comes from. You'll learn more about this later.) Then select New Measure from the menu (#2) and write the measure from there.

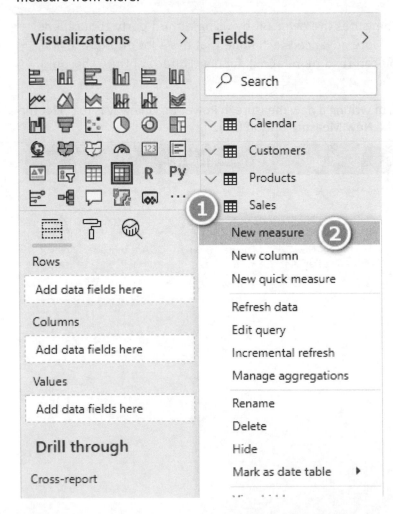

Here's How: Writing Measures

The approach to writing new measures described here is the best approach I have found to ensure that you get the best possible outcome with the least amount of rework. Follow these steps:

1. Create a new blank matrix on you report page (or use an existing one if you already have one set up from earlier). Make sure that you have the matrix selected on the report canvas. You can see the drag handles (see #1 below) when the matrix is selected.

2. Add some relevant data to the rows in your matrix. For the sample database used in this book, I suggest that you go to the Products table and place Products[Category] on Rows in the matrix. To do this, in the Fields pane, select the Products[Category] column (see #2 below) and then drag and drop the column into the Rows drop zone for the matrix (#3). Keep an eye out for the dotted line around the drop zone. When you see the dotted line, you can release the column, and it will be correctly placed in the matrix.

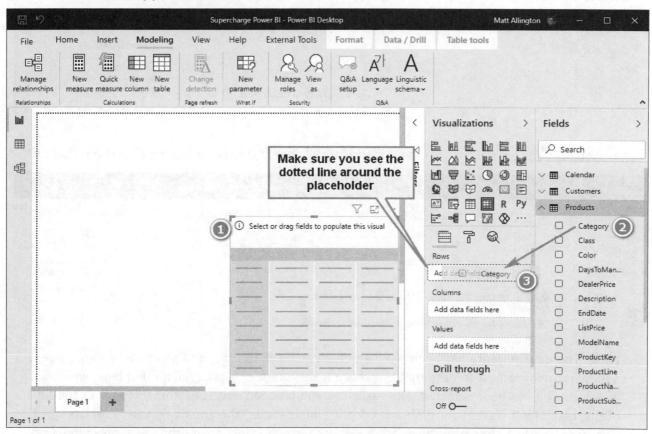

Note: You should always place a measure in the table the data comes from. In this case, you will write the measure [Total Sales], and the "data" you are using is in the Sales[ExtendedAmount] column, which is in the Sales table.

3. Right-click the `Sales` table in the Fields pane (see #1 below) and select New Measure (#2).

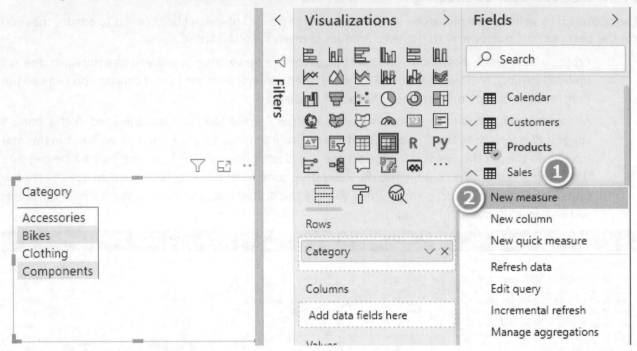

You now see `Measure` `=` appear in the formula bar at the top of the page, as shown below.

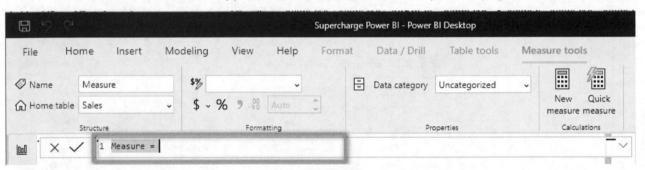

Note: The new measure has been given a default name, `Measure`, and an equals sign has been added automatically. Also note that the entire text `Measure  =` is highlighted in blue, which indicates that it has been selected. The easiest way to proceed now is to simply type over the top of this text. Don't waste your time and effort trying to "save" the equals sign and edit the word `Measure`. It is just not worth the effort. It is much faster and less error prone to simply type over the top.

4. In the formula bar, type the following DAX formula directly over the highlighted text `Measure  =` (see #1 below):

```
Total Sales = SUM(Sales[ExtendedAmount])
```

Press Enter.

Note: If you are used to using IntelliSense in Excel, the editing experience here should be familiar to you. You can use the up and down arrows on the keyboard to select from an IntelliSense list and then press Tab to select an item from the list. You will read more about this later.

5. Apply the formatting you need before doing anything else. You will already be positioned on the Measure Tools tab on the ribbon (see #2 below). Apply the formatting shown below (#3 and #4) and then press Enter again.

Tip: Get used to applying formatting to a measure immediately so you don't forget to do it.

Note: It is possible to set your own number formatting directly (see #5 below). You can learn more about this at http://xbi.com.au/format-strings.

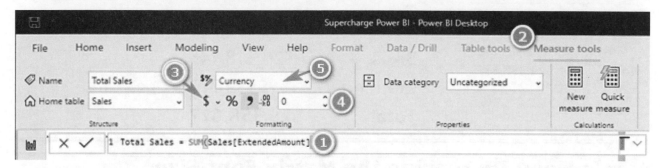

6. Check to make sure you still have the matrix selected by ensuring that you can see the drag handles (see #1 below), navigate to the `Sales` table in the Fields pane (#2), locate the new measure `[Total Sales]` (#3), and drag and drop the measure into the Values drop zone for the matrix (#4). (You could also simply click in the check box next to Total Sales in the Fields pane.)

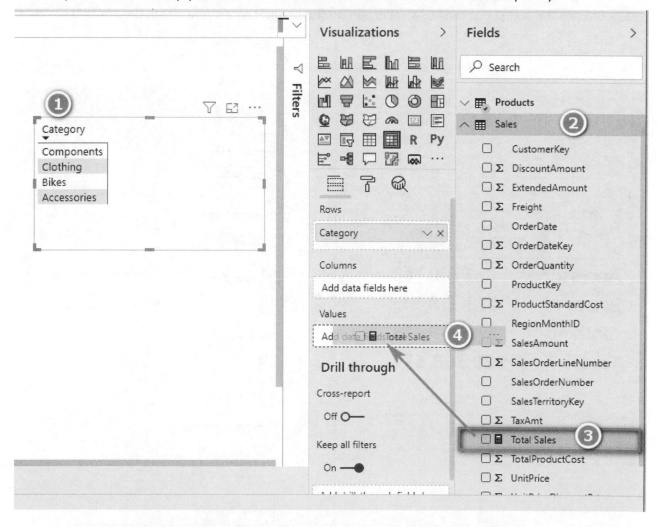

Tip: Following this procedure will save you time because you will not have to go back and fix things you missed. Practice writing measures this way right from the start, and you will develop a good habit that will serve you well in the future.

Your matrix should now look similar to the one shown on the left below. You may want to increase the font size of your matrix to make it easier to read, as shown on the right below.

Category ▲	Total Sales
Accessories	$700,760
Bikes	$28,318,145
Clothing	$339,773
Total	**$29,358,677**

Category ▲	Total Sales
Accessories	$700,760
Bikes	$28,318,145
Clothing	$339,773
Total	**$29,358,677**

Here's How: Increasing the Matrix Font Size

To increase the font size in a matrix, follow these steps:

1. Ensure that the matrix is selected (see #1 below).

2. Navigate to the Format pane (#2) and select Grid (#3).

3. Change the Text Size setting to an appropriate size or enter a new font size in the box (#4).

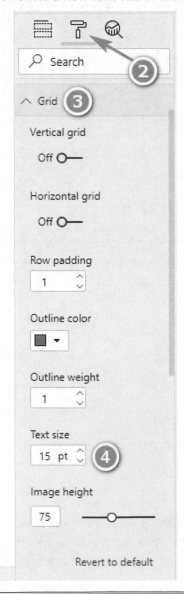

Avoiding Implicit Measures

There are several ways to add up the values in a column. You can do it by simply dragging the name of a column of numbers from the Fields pane (see #1 below) and dropping it in the Values drop zone for the matrix (#2). That column now appears in the matrix (#3). When you use this method, you get the same answer you get by using the measure [Total Sales].

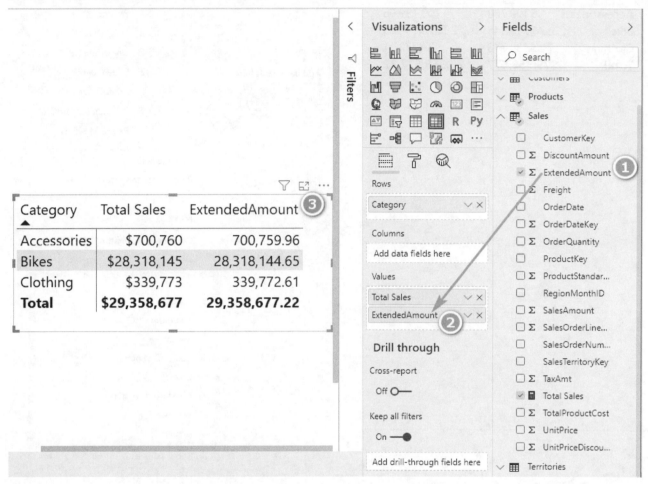

If you then click the drop-down arrow next to the column `[ExtendedAmount]` (see #1 below), you can see a few different options for aggregating the data, including the default aggregation Sum (#2).

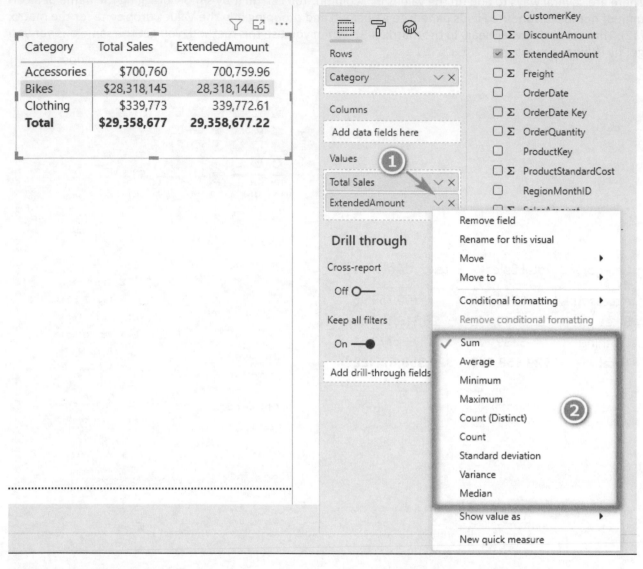

When you drag a column in this way, you create what I call an "implicit measure" (although Kasper de Jonge tells me this is not the official name). Doing it this way is not wrong, but personally I am not a fan of using implicit measures, and I recommend that you avoid using them—for a number of reasons:

- The name of an implicit measure is not very helpful. Compare the name of this implicit measure, `[ExtendedAmount]`, with the name `[Total Sales]` that you provided when you explicitly wrote the measure yourself. You can change the name of an implicit measure after you add the column to the visual, but the name changes only for the current visual (a matrix in this case). If you later add the same column again in a different visual, you need to change the name again if you want consistency.

- No formatting is applied when you drag to create an implicit measure. Again, you can use the formatting from the source column, but you cannot have different formatting for different visuals.

- You can't reference implicit measures inside other measures, so implicit measures have limited use. Implicit measures work on single columns, but they cannot work if you need data from more than one column.

- You won't learn how to write DAX if you always use implicit measures.

So do yourself a favour and don't drag and drop your table columns. Of course, if you just want a quick look at a column of data for some testing, then doing this is fine. But you should undo the change immediately after you have taken a look. If you want to keep a measure, you should write it from scratch, using your DAX skills. It will be your skill in writing DAX that will set you apart from other users of Power BI.

Here's How: Using IntelliSense

When you type a DAX formula in the formula bar, I recommend that you learn to leverage the IntelliSense tooltips that appear. Follow these steps to see how it works:

1. Begin typing a function name into the formula bar, as shown below, and you see the IntelliSense pop up to show you the syntax of the function (on the first line) and also what the function does (on the second line).

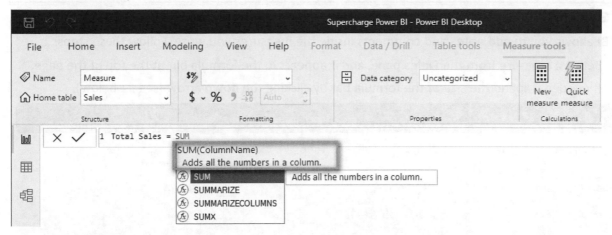

> **Tip:** IntelliSense is your friend. Reading the information it provides will help you build your DAX knowledge and skills.

2. Follow the DAX best practice of typing the table name before the column name. Power BI has a very good user interface that helps you do this. If you start typing the name of any column in your data model, as shown in the example below, where I've typed `ex`, IntelliSense prompts you with the full name in the format `TableName[ColumnName]`, as you can see below, highlighted in blue.

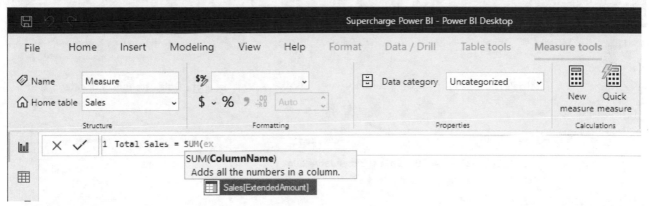

> **Tip**: Always, always, always include the table name before the name of a column in your formulas. Doing so is best practice because it fully qualifies the column name in its home table, which makes it easier to differentiate columns from measures.

3. Simply use the up and down arrow keys to highlight the column you want from the list presented by IntelliSense and then press Tab to select the column highlighted in blue. The table name is then included automatically.

4. Type) (a closing parenthesis) and press Enter.

> **Tip:** Try to use the keyboard and not the mouse to select from the tooltips, particularly if the list is short. This method may be slower for you to start with, but it will be faster in the long run if you learn to do it this way.

Here's How: Editing Measures

It is easy to go back and edit (or simply review) measures after you have written them. Follow these steps:

1. Find the measure you want to edit in the Fields pane and click the measure once to select it. The formula bar reappears at the top of the page.

2. Click in the formula bar and edit the measure as required.

Here's How: Adding Comments to Measures

Power BI allows you to add notes and comments inside the measures you write. Follow these steps:

1. Select a measure from the Fields pane, and it appears in the formula bar at the top of the page.

2. If needed, expand the size of the formula bar by clicking the down arrow (see #1 below).

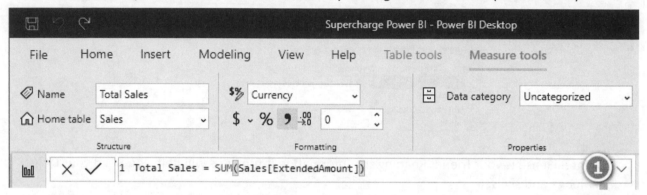

3. Start a new line in the measure by pressing Shift+Enter.

4. Add comments as shown below. Use a double slash (//) at the start of a single-line comment and use the /* */ pattern to create a multi-line comment, as shown below.

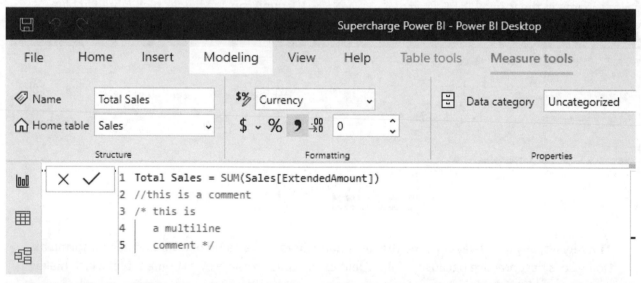

When Something Goes Wrong as You Write DAX

At some point, you will start the process of creating a new measure, and something will go wrong. For one reason or another, you will need to stop what you are doing and go and do something else. In cases where you are partway through writing a formula but you need to stop, you can use the comments feature so that you don't have to scrap your work in progress.

The following figure shows a complex partially written measure (which is not from AdventureWorks).

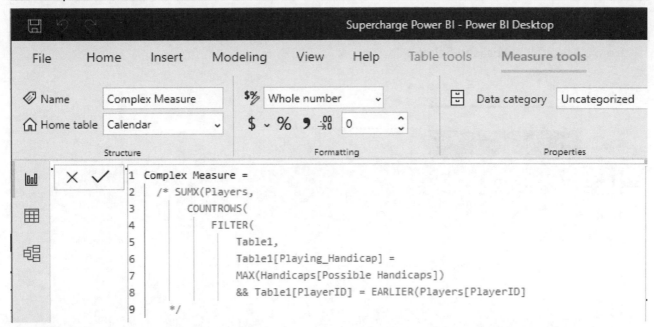

The particular formula shown in this example is not important; the point is to show you an example of a partial formula that you would not want to lose. You can wrap the measure inside the multi-line comment indicators /* */ in order to make the entire measure a comment that can be stored in your table without throwing an error.

Here's How: Creating New Pages in Power BI

Power BI has a tabbed page navigator at the bottom of the Report view where you can see the various pages created. It is easy to create a new page by clicking the plus symbol. You can also duplicate an existing page by right-clicking any existing page and selecting Duplicate Page.

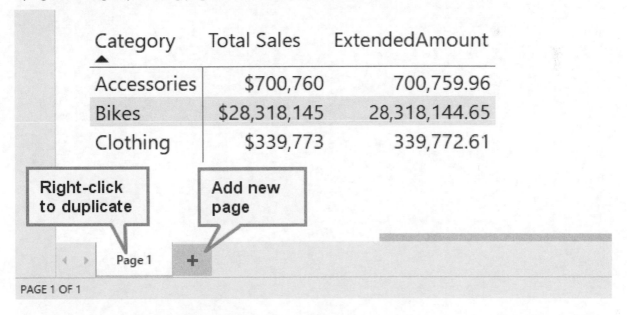

Duplicating is a great approach, especially when you are writing DAX, because it means you get a new page that already has one or more visuals (e.g., a matrix) that you can use for the next measure. While learning from this book, I recommend that you rename the duplicated pages to something more descriptive so you can more easily find the exercises again later. You can duplicate instead of add new pages if you want to add similar visuals to a new page.

Note: When you have many pages in a report, you can see only some of them on the screen. Just as in Excel, if you right-click on the page navigator arrows, you can see a list of all pages and select from a list of all pages (see below).

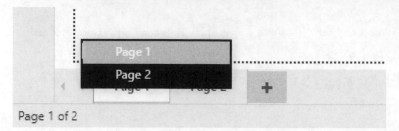

Page 1 of 2

4: DAX Topic: SUM(), COUNT(), COUNTROWS(), MIN(), MAX(), COUNTBLANK(), and DIVIDE()

This chapter introduces some basic DAX functions to get you started with writing measures. Most of the DAX functions in this chapter accept a column as the only parameter, like this: =FORMULA(*ColumnName*). The exceptions are =COUNTROWS(*Table*), which takes a table (not a column) as the parameter, and DIVIDE(), covered later in this chapter.

With the exception of DIVIDE(), all the functions in this chapter are aggregation functions, or aggregators. That is, they take inputs from a column or table and somehow aggregate the contents; these functions handle the aggregation differently for each formula.

Think about the column Sales[ExtendedAmount], which has more than 60,000 rows of data. You can't simply put the entire column into a single cell in a matrix because Power BI can't place a column of 60,000+ numbers into a single cell in the matrix.

The following example shows a DAX formula that uses a "naked" column, without any aggregation function. This does not work when you're writing a measure, as indicated by the error message.

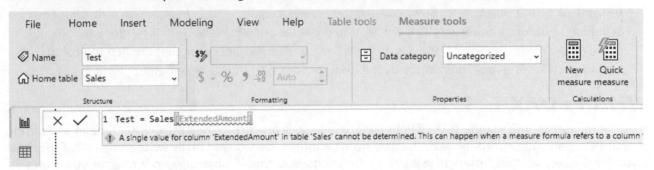

You have to tell Power BI how to aggregate the data from this column so that it returns just a single value to each cell in the matrix. Each of the aggregators in this chapter effectively converts a column of values into a single value.

The correct way to write this measure is shown below.

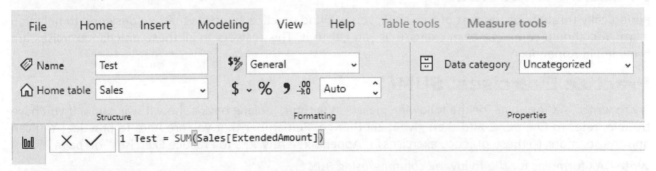

> **Note:** Did you notice that this example uses the table name and the column name in the formula? Remember that it is best practice to refer to the table name and the column name when referring to a column in DAX. Never refer to a column without specifying the table name first. Power BI does this for you automatically, but it is still possible to delete the table name manually (accidentally or deliberately)—and you should not do so! In just a bit, you will understand why I say this.

IntelliSense Problems

Sometimes IntelliSense can be confusing. IntelliSense prompts you with a list of the available functions, tables, columns, and measures only if you are writing a formula correctly. This can be very useful because you get a list of the valid syntax. But the downside is that it can be confusing if you can't see the list of possible functions, tables, columns, and measures that you are looking for and you don't know why. If at any time when you are writing a formula you can't see the functions, measures, columns, or tables you are looking for, you should stop and check your syntax. If the syntax is incorrect, IntelliSense stops prompting you with suggestions. Over time, you will learn to trust IntelliSense, and you will learn to stop and check your syntax when it is not working as you expect it to.

Reusing Measures

One important shortcut in DAX is that you can reuse measures in order to write other measures. Say that you create a new measure called [Total Sales]. When this measure exists in the Power BI data model, it can be referenced and reused inside other measures. For example, after creating the measure [Total Sales], you could use the following formula to create a new measure for 10% tax on the sale of goods:

```
Total Tax = [Total Sales] * 0.1
```

Note that the new measure [Total Tax] is a calculation based on the original measure [Total Sales] multiplied by 0.1.

It is good practice to reuse measures inside other measures.

> **Note:** There is no table name in front of the measure name above: It is [Total Sales] and not Sales[Total Sales]. Remember that although you should always include the table name in front of a column (for example, Sales[ExtendedAmount]), it is best practice to omit the table name before a measure. This convention provides an important clue: A reader can look at Sales[ExtendedAmount] and [Total Sales] and immediately tell that the first is a column and the second is a measure simply by the existence (or not) of the table name.

Writing DAX

It's time to start to write some DAX of your own to get some practice. When I say write, I mean sit in front of your PC, open your workbook with the data from Chapter 1 loaded, and really write some DAX. Especially if you have never written formulas using these functions, you should physically do it now, as you read this section. Imagining yourself doing it in your mind is not enough.

If you haven't already done so, go ahead and load the test data by following the steps in Chapter 2. Once it is loaded and prepared, you are ready to create the new measures in the following practice exercises.

Practice Exercises

Periodically throughout the rest of this book, you will find practice exercises that are designed to help you learn. You should complete each exercise as you get to it. The answers to all these practice exercises are provided in Appendix A.

Practice Exercises: SUM()

Try to write DAX formulas for the following measures without looking back at how it was done. If you have trouble, refer to Chapter 3 and then give it another go. Remember that you are here to practice! You can find the solutions to these practice exercises in "Appendix A: Answers to Practice Exercises" on page 252.

Write DAX formulas for the following columns, using SUM().

1. [Total Sales]

You should have already written this measure earlier in this book (see "Here's How: Using IntelliSense" on page 37). If you didn't, write a new measure that is the total of the sales in the ExtendedAmount column from the Sales table.

2. [Total Cost]

Create a measure that is the sum of one of the cost columns in the Sales table. This measure uses exactly the same structure as the [Total Sales] measure, but it adds the cost of the product instead of the sales amount. You can use any of the product cost columns in the Sales table; all the cost columns are the same in this sample database.

3. [Total Margin $]

Create a new measure for the total margin—that is, the amount of profit AdventureWorks makes on the sale of each item, which is total sales minus total cost. Make sure you reuse the two measures you just created in this new measure.

4. [Total Margin %]

Create a new measure that expresses the total margin from Practice Exercise 3 as a percentage of total sales. Once again, reuse the measures you created above. I don't cover the `DIVIDE()` function until later in this chapter, but you can try to work out how to use it by using the IntelliSense if you like. Rely on your Excel experience to write the formula.

5. [Total Sales Tax Paid]

Create a measure for total sales tax paid. Look for a tax column in the `Sales` table and add up the total for that column.

6. [Total Sales Including Tax]

The `[Total Sales]` measure above excludes tax, and you need to add two measures together to create the `[Total Sales Including Tax]` measure.

7. [Total Order Quantity]

This is similar to the other measures you've just created, but this time you add up the quantities purchased. Look for the correct column in the `Sales` table.

How Did It Go?

As you worked through the practice exercises, did you do the following?

- Did you create a matrix first and put `Products[Category]` on Rows in your matrix? (Or did you put something else on Rows, as appropriate for these measures?) Creating a matrix is a best practice because it enables you to you get feedback immediately after you write a measure; it allows you to see the results right away.

- Did you right-click the `Sales` table in the Fields pane and select New Measure to start the process? Doing so guarantees that the measure gets placed in the correct table, so you don't lose it. Remember that you should always put a measure in the table where the data is stored. Therefore, the measures in these practice exercises belong in the `Sales` table.

- Did you reference all columns in your measures in the format *TableName[ColumnName]* (i.e., did you always reference the table name)? Remember that you should never reference a column in DAX without first specifying the table name; always use the table name and the column name. Power BI makes this easy for you most of the time.

- Did you apply formatting to your measure immediately after you wrote it?

- Did you use the keyboard and look at the IntelliSense when you typed the measures? Remember that you should try not to use the mouse. Doing so might be faster for you now, but relying on the mouse will prevent you from getting faster with the keyboard in the future. Learn to use the keyboard and follow the process covered in "Here's How: Using IntelliSense" on page 37.

Remember that the answers to all the practice exercises in this book are provided in Appendix A. Try to avoid peeking at the appendix when you should be thinking and typing. If you do the thinking now, you will learn how to do it, and that will give you the skills and the solid foundation you need to master Power BI.

Okay, it's time to move on and learn about a new DAX function.

The COUNT() Function

As you write the formula shown below using COUNT(), take the time to consider again at how IntelliSense can help you write DAX.

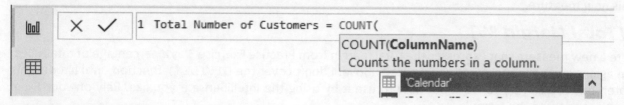

Remember that whenever you type a new formula, you can pause, and IntelliSense shows the syntax and a description of the function. The description includes some very useful information. For example, in the figure above, the tooltip says that this function "counts the numbers in a column." This gives you three very useful pieces of information. You've already worked out the first one: It counts. In addition, this tooltip tells you that the function counts numbers and also that the numbers need to be in a column. This should be enough information about the COUNT() function for you to use it to write some measures.

Practice Exercises: COUNT()

Now it is time to write some DAX formulas using the COUNT() function. Find the solutions to these practice exercises in "Appendix A: Answers to Practice Exercises" on page 252.

> **Note:** Don't forget to set up a matrix before you work the following exercises. A good approach is to assign a name to the page in your last exercise, such as SUM(), and then duplicate the page for the next exercise, giving it a different name, such as COUNT(). This way, you can easily look back at your work later for a refresher. Whenever you set up a new matrix for a new exercise, make sure you have something meaningful on Rows, such as Products[Category]. Look at the image in "How Did It Go?" after these practice exercises if you are not sure how to set up the matrix.

8. [Total Number of Products]

Use the Products lookup table when writing this measure and count how many product numbers there are. Product numbers and product keys are the same thing in this example.

9. [Total Number of Customers]

Use the Customers lookup table and just count the customer numbers. Customer numbers and customer keys are the same thing in this example.

How Did It Go?

Did you end up with the following matrix?

Category	Total Number of Customers	Total Number of Products
Accessories	18,484	35
Bikes	18,484	125
Clothing	18,484	48
Components	18,484	189
Total	**18,484**	**397**

If not, check your answers against those in "Appendix A: Answers to Practice Exercises" on page 252.

Note: The matrix above is a bit confusing because [Total Number of Customers] doesn't seem to be correct. It is returning the same value for every row in the matrix, and this is not something you are probably used to seeing. But if you think about it, it actually does make sense. You are not counting how many customers purchased these product categories; you are counting the number of customers in the master customer table, and the number of customers doesn't change based on the product categories; the customers are either in the master table or not. (You'll learn more about this in Chapter 5.)

The COUNTROWS() Function

Let's move on to another counting function, COUNTROWS(). I prefer to use COUNTROWS() instead of COUNT() as it just seems more natural to me. These functions are not exactly the same, even though they can be used interchangeably at times. If you use COUNT() with *TableName[ColumnName]* and the column is missing a value in one of the rows (for some reason), then that row won't get counted. COUNTROWS() counts every row in the table, regardless of whether every column has a value in every row. So be careful to select the best formula for the task at hand.

Practice Exercises: COUNTROWS()

For these exercises, rewrite the two measures from Practice Exercises 8 and 9 using COUNTROWS() instead of COUNT(). Find the solutions to these practice exercises in "Appendix A: Answers to Practice Exercises" on page 252.

10. [Total Number of Products COUNTROWS Version]

Use the COUNTROWS() function to count the number of products in the Products table.

11. [Total Number of Customers COUNTROWS Version]

Use the COUNTROWS() function to count the number of customers in the Customers table.

How Did It Go?

Not surprisingly, for Practice Exercises 10 and 11, you should get the same answer you got with COUNT(), as shown below.

Category	Total Number of Customers COUNTROWS Version	Total Number of Products COUNTROWS Version
Accessories	18,484	35
Bikes	18,484	125
Clothing	18,484	48
Components	18,484	189
Total	**18,484**	**397**

A Word on Naming Measures

You may have noticed that I sometimes use very long and descriptive names for measures. I encourage you to make measure names as long as they need to be to make it clear what the measures actually are. You will be grateful you did down the track, when you are trying to work out the fine difference between two similar-sounding measures.

Here's How: Changing Display Names in Visuals

It is possible to change the display name of a measure or column once it is in a visual. Doing so will only change this single use of the measure inside this single visual; the change has no impact on the actual name of the measure. Here are the steps for changing a display name:

1. Select the visual.
2. Find the measure or column in the Values section of the Fields card on the Visualizations pane and click its down arrow (see #1 below).

3. Click Rename for This Visual (#2). As the name suggests, this renaming applies only to this single visual and does not change the actual name of the measure or column in the model.

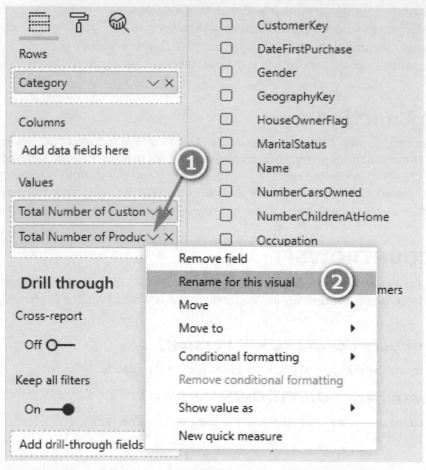

Here's How: Word Wrapping in a Visual

Changing a measure's name is useful when you want a shorter name to appear in a visual. Sometimes the name of a measure makes sense only in certain situations (i.e., in some visuals and not in other visuals). For such situations, if you want to keep using a longer descriptive name but want to make it fit in a matrix, you can resize the columns in the matrix. Here's how:

1. Hover your mouse to the right side of the column header in the matrix.

2. Click and drag the mouse to the left, as shown below.

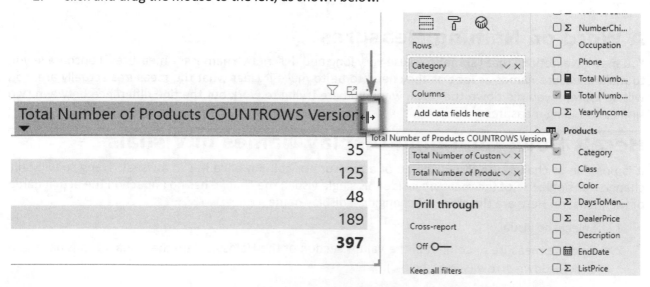

The following image shows the result of applying word wrap to the matrix shown earlier in this chapter.

Category	Total Number of Customers COUNTROWS Version	Total Number of Products COUNTROWS Version
Accessories	18,484	35
Bikes	18,484	125
Clothing	18,484	48
Components	18,484	189
Total	**18,484**	**397**

The DISTINCTCOUNT() Function

DISTINCTCOUNT() counts each value in a column once and only once. If a value appears more than once in a column, it is still counted only once. Consider the Customers table. In this case, the customer key is unique, and by definition, each customer key appears only once in the table. (Keep in mind that customer key = customer number.) So in this case, using DISTINCTCOUNT() with the customer key in the Customers table gives you the same answer as using COUNTROWS() with the Customers table. But if you were to use DISTINCTCOUNT() with the customer key in the Sales table, you would actually be counting the total number of customers that had ever purchased something. This is not the same thing as the number of customers in the Customers table. The answer may or may not be the same, but the business logic and hence the DAX logic are different.

Practice Exercises: DISTINCTCOUNT()

To practice using DISTINCTCOUNT(), create a new matrix and put Customers[Occupation] on Rows in the matrix and [Total Sales] on Values. Then use DISTINCTCOUNT() to write the following measures. Find the solutions to these practice exercises in "Appendix A: Answers to Practice Exercises" on page 252.

12. [Total Customers in Database DISTINCTCOUNT Version]

You need to count a column of unique values in the Customers table. Which column will you use? How will you know which column or columns are distinct? Is the customer name distinct? How can you be sure?

Earlier you saw one possible way to count a column of unique values in the Customers table. Now you need to write a measure using the DISTINCTCOUNT() function to find out how many distinct customers there are in the Customers table. When you are done, add the [Total Number of Customers] measure you created earlier to the matrix as well. You should end up with a matrix like the one below.

Occupation	Total Sales	Total Customers in Database DISTINCTCOUNT Version	Total Number of Customers
Clerical	$4,684,787	2,928	2,928
Management	$5,467,862	3,075	3,075
Manual	$2,857,971	2,384	2,384
Professional	$9,907,977	5,520	5,520
Skilled Manual	$6,440,081	4,577	4,577
Total	**$29,358,677**	**18,484**	**18,484**

How Did It Go?

Did you get the same answer as above in the new measure? Did you remember to format the measure to something practical (e.g., a whole number with thousands separators)?

> **Note:** You now know two ways to find how many distinct records there are in a lookup table: Use `COUNTROWS()` for the table and use `DISTINCTCOUNT()` for the primary key. These are not the only ways to solve this problem. In the case of the `Customers` table, you could also use `COUNT()` for `Customers[CustomerKey]` to get the same result. This works because, by definition, the primary key column of a lookup/dimension table must be unique, so counting a primary key column must give the same result as using `DISTINCTCOUNT()`.

13. [Count of Occupation]

Create a new matrix and put `Customers[YearlyIncome]` on Rows. Then create the measure `[Count of Occupation]`.

Even though the description of the measure is "Count of Occupation," you need to use `DISTINCTCOUNT()` to count the values in the `Occupation` column in the `Customers` table. Don't get confused with the business language "count of occupation" and the DAX formula. You want to end up with a matrix like the one shown below. The way to read this matrix is that there are customers in three different occupations that have incomes of $10,000, there are customers across four occupations that have incomes of $30,000, etc.

YearlyIncome	Count of Occupation		YearlyIncome	Count of Occupation
$10,000	3		$10,000	3
$20,000	3		$20,000	3
$30,000	4		$30,000	4
$40,000	4		$40,000	4
$50,000	3		$50,000	3
$60,000	3		$60,000	3
$70,000	3		$70,000	3
$80,000	3		$80,000	3
$90,000	3		$90,000	3
$100,000	2		$100,000	2
$110,000	2		$110,000	2
$120,000	2		$120,000	2
$130,000	2		$130,000	2
$150,000	2		$150,000	2
$160,000	2		$160,000	2
$170,000	2		$170,000	2
Total	**5**		**Total**	**5**

> **Note:** The table on the right has some conditional formatting applied. The next "Here's How" describes how to add conditional formatting.

Here's How: Applying Conditional Formatting

It is much easier to read a matrix if you apply some of the formatting features that come with Power BI. For example, compare the matrix above left with the conditionally formatted version above right. I am sure you agree that it is much easier to gather insights from the version on the right. Follow these steps to apply this type of conditional formatting:

1. Make sure you have the matrix selected (see #1 below).

2. Go to the Format pane (see #2 below), select Conditional Formatting (#3), and turn on the formatting effect you want to use, such as Data Bars (#4).

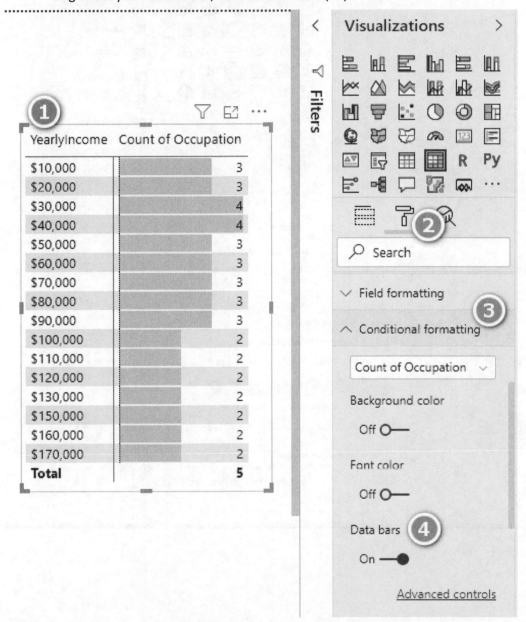

As you can see in the matrix above (#1), using well-placed conditional formatting is a great way to make your matrixes easier to read and helps the important information jump out.

Note: This is not the only way to add conditional formatting. You can also go to the Fields card on the Visualizations pane (see #1 below), click the drop-down arrow next to the measure you want to format (#2), select Conditional Formatting (#3), and then choose the type of formatting you want (#4).

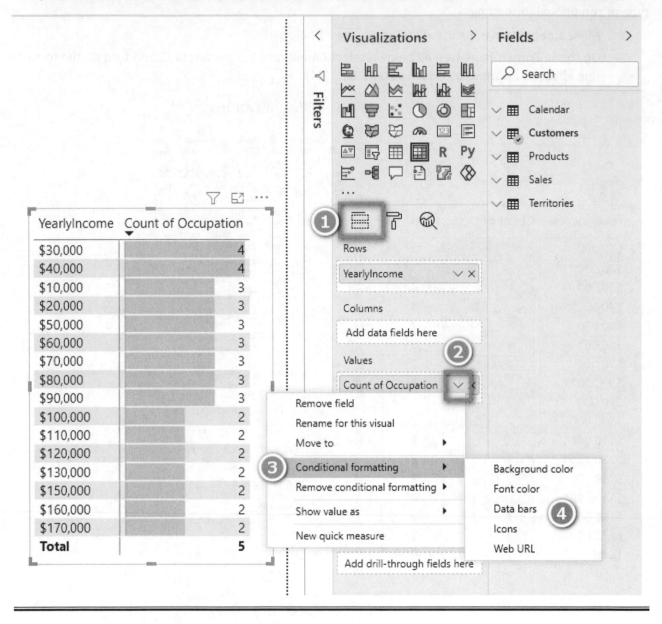

Practice Exercises: DISTINCTCOUNT(), Continued

The following exercises give you more practice using `DISTINCTCOUNT()`. Find the solutions to these practice exercises in "Appendix A: Answers to Practice Exercises" on page 252.

14. *[Count of Country]*

Create a new matrix and put `Territories[Group]` on Rows. Write a new measure called `[Count of Country]`, using `DISTINCTCOUNT()` over the `Country` column in the `Territories` table. This matrix, as you can see below, shows you how many countries exist in each sales group.

Group	Count of Country
Europe	3
NA	1
North America	2
Pacific	1
Total	**7**

15. *[Total Customers That Have Purchased]*

Create a new matrix and put `Products[SubCategory]` on Rows. Then, using `DISTINCTCOUNT()` on data from the `Sales` table, create the new measure `[Total Customers That Have Purchased]`. Apply some conditional formatting to the matrix and then sort the column from largest to smallest (by clicking on the column heading to be sorted). You can see below that Tires and Tubes has the largest number of customers who have purchased at least once.

SubCategory	Total Customers That Have Purchased ▼
Tires and Tubes	8,490
Road Bikes	6,397
Helmets	5,960
Bottles and Cages	4,548
Mountain Bikes	4,089
Jerseys	3,192
Touring Bikes	2,143
Caps	2,132
Fenders	2,110
Gloves	1,376
Shorts	1,019
Cleaners	875
Hydration Packs	719
Socks	559
Vests	557
Bike Racks	325
Bike Stands	243
Total	**18,484**

Note: The measure `[Total Customers That Have Purchased]` does not tell you how many times each customer has purchased. It simply tells you how many unique customers have purchased at least once, over all the sales data in the `Sales` table.

Here's How: Drilling Through Rows in a Matrix

One of the features I really love about Power BI is the ability to nest columns and then drill through. Let's look at how it works, using the matrix shown above:

1. Make sure you have the matrix selected and then locate the `Products[Category]` column in the Fields pane (see #1 below).

2. Drag the column to the Rows drop zone (#2). Take care to check for the yellow line, as indicated below. This line tells you where the column will be dropped (above or below the existing column).

3. Drop the `Products[Category]` column above the `Products[SubCategory]` column, as indicated by the arrow below.

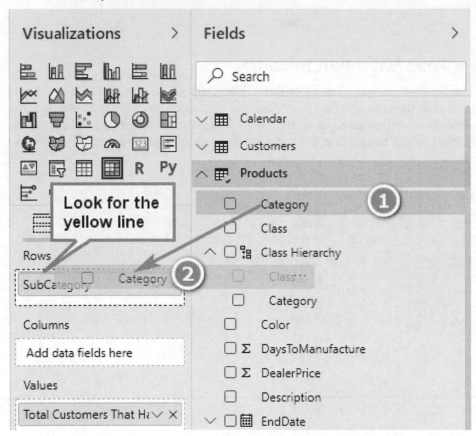

The matrix changes in a few subtle ways, as shown below.

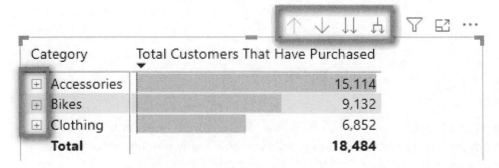

Category	Total Customers That Have Purchased
⊞ Accessories	15,114
⊞ Bikes	9,132
⊞ Clothing	6,852
Total	**18,484**

Note there are four new icons at the top right of the matrix as well as some + (plus) icons to the left of the product categories. In addition, if you right-click on a product category row (see #1 below), the submenu now has some new menu items that were previously not visible.

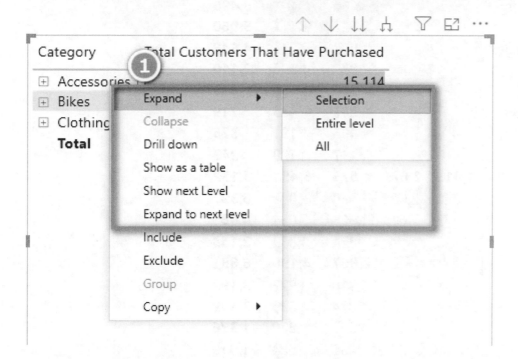

All these new icons and menu items provide new drill-through capabilities for the columns you have added to Rows. Don't get confused here; you add the columns from the tables to Rows in your matrix (by stacking one on top of another), and then you can drill through.

4. Spend a few minutes trying out the various drill-through behaviours for each of these menus. You can drill down and drill up through the matrix.

5. Put `'Calendar'[CalendarYear]` on Columns in your matrix and notice how the matrix changes again.

Note: `Calendar` is a reserved word in DAX; it is also a name of a function, `CALENDAR()`, which returns a calendar table. Personally, I never use the `CALENDAR()` function as I think there are better ways to create calendar tables. It is okay to call a calendar table `Calendar`, but you must always add single quotes when referencing the table inside your DAX formulas, as shown above.

6. Go back to the conditional formatting settings for the matrix, turn off the data bars, and turn on colour scales. You should end up with a matrix like the one shown below.

Note: I have used the Expand to Next Level drill-through feature in this matrix to get the nested layout shown below. This is very similar to how a pivot table looks.

Category	2016	2017	2018	2019	Total
⊟ **Accessories**			6,792	9,435	**15,114**
Tires and Tubes			3,766	5,147	**8,490**
Helmets			2,541	3,617	**5,960**
Bottles and Cages			1,903	2,744	**4,548**
Fenders			879	1,236	**2,110**
Cleaners			376	509	**875**
Hydration Packs			300	425	**719**
Bike Racks			136	191	**325**
Bike Stands			117	129	**243**
⊟ **Bikes**	1,013	2,677	4,875	5,451	**9,132**
Road Bikes	840	2,062	2,558	2,369	**6,397**
Mountain Bikes	173	615	1,961	2,094	**4,089**
Touring Bikes			824	1,332	**2,143**
⊟ **Clothing**			2,867	4,196	**6,852**
Jerseys			1,316	1,922	**3,192**
Caps			874	1,280	**2,132**
Gloves			567	829	**1,376**
Shorts			435	584	**1,019**
Socks			246	317	**559**
Vests			205	354	**557**
Total	**1,013**	**2,677**	**9,309**	**11,377**	**18,484**

Practice Exercises: MAX(), MIN(), and AVERAGE()

MAX(), MIN(), and AVERAGE() are types of aggregating functions (aggregators). They take multiple values in a column as input and return a single value as the result. In the following few practice exercises, you will create new measures using these aggregators.

You should use columns from the Sales table for these exercises. There are some additional pricing columns in the Products table, but those prices are only theoretical prices, or "list prices." In this sample data, the actual price information related to a transaction is stored in the Sales table.

Find the solutions to these practice exercises in "Appendix A: Answers to Practice Exercises" on page 252.

16. [Maximum Tax Paid on a Product]

Use a suitable column from the Sales table along with the MAX() function.

17. [Minimum Price Paid for a Product]

Use a suitable column from the Sales table along with the MIN() function.

18. [Average Price Paid for a Product]

Use a suitable column from the Sales table along with the AVERAGE() function.

How Did It Go?

Did you end up with a matrix like the one shown below?

Category	Maximum Tax Paid on a Product	Minimum Price Paid for a Product	Average Price Paid for a Product
Accessories	$12.72	$2.29	$19.42
Bikes	$286.26	$539.99	$1,862.42
Clothing	$5.60	$8.99	$37.33
Total	**$286.26**	**$2.29**	**$486.09**

Note: Notice that when you add these measures directly to a matrix, you get immediate feedback about whether your measures look correct. This is only a "sense" check, and you should, of course, confirm that your formulas are correct as part of the process.

Here's How: Moving an Existing Measure to a Different Home Table

If you have been following my advice, to create a new measure, you first go to the Fields pane and right-click on the table where you want the measure to be placed, and then you select the New Measure option. However, even if you do it this way, it is possible that at some stage, you will end up with a measure being in the wrong table. This problem is fairly easy to fix. Follow these steps to move a measure to a different table:

1. Locate the measure in the Fields pane and select it. You can use the Search box at the top of the Fields pane, if necessary, to find the measure.

2. Make sure you are on the Measure Tools tab (see #1 below) and select the correct table from the Home Table drop-down list (#2).

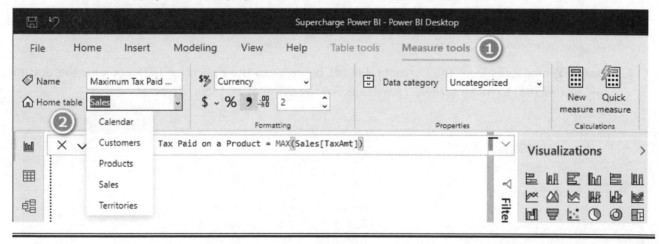

Here's How: Moving All Measures to a New Table

It is possible to move all measures from one table to another table at once. To do this, follow these steps:

1. Switch to the Model view.

2. In the Fields pane, expand the table that contains the measures you want to move (see #1 below).

3. Select one or more measures (see #2 below) that you wish to move from this table. You can use the Ctrl key or Shift key to multi-select measures.

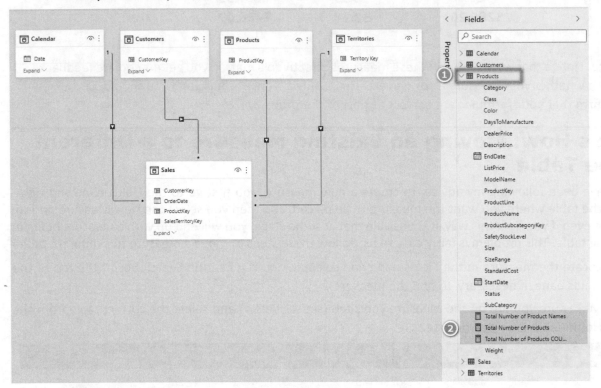

4. Drag the measures from the current table (#1 below) into the new table (#2). Look for the dotted yellow line (#3) to make sure you have selected the destination table correctly.

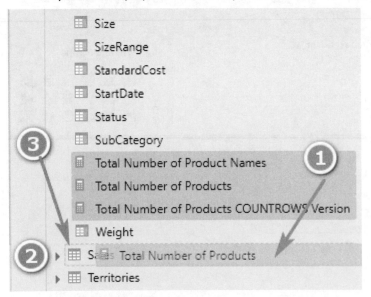

Note: After moving the measures as shown here, make sure to move them back to the correct table before proceeding.

Practice Exercises: COUNTBLANK()

In the following exercises, you use the COUNTBLANK() function to create a measure to check the completeness of the master data.

Create a new matrix and put Customers[Occupation] on Rows. Then start to write the new measure. In these exercises, you need to create measures to find out two things:

- How many customers are missing Address Line 2 from the master data?
- For how many products in the Products table is there no weight value stored in the master data?

Find the solutions to these practice exercises in "Appendix A: Answers to Practice Exercises" on page 252.

19. [Customers Without Address Line 2]

The AddressLine2 column is in the Customers table. As you write the measure [Customers Without Address Line 2], be sure you do the following:

1. Select the table where you want to store the measure and be sure to add it there.

2. Give the measure a suitable name.

3. Start typing the measure. Pause after you have started to type the formula and read the IntelliSense to see what the function does (if you don't already know). As shown below, this measure does exactly what you want it to do: It counts how many blanks are in this column.

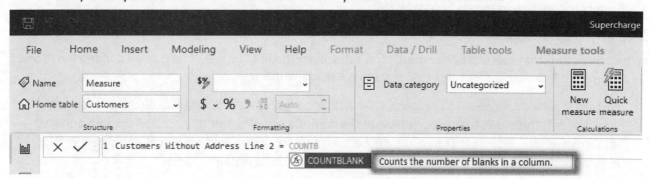

4. Complete the formula, apply the formatting, check the formula, and then click Enter.

20. [Products Without Weight Values]

The column you need to use is in the Products table. You should end up with a matrix like the one shown below.

Occupation	Customers Without Address Line 2	Products Without Weight Values
Clerical	2,878	122
Management	3,007	122
Manual	2,350	122
Professional	5,440	122
Skilled Manual	4,497	122
Total	**18,172**	**122**

Note that the first measure, [Customers Without Address Line 2], is being filtered by the matrix (i.e., Customers[Occupation] on Rows), and the values in the matrix change with each row. However, the second measure, [Products Without Weight Values], is not filtered; the values don't change for each row in the matrix. You have seen this earlier in this book. The technical term for filtering behaviour in Power BI is filter context. Chapter 5 provides a detailed explanation of this filtering behaviour and will help you understand what is happening here and why.

The DIVIDE() Function

`DIVIDE()` is a simple yet powerful function that is also known as "safe divide." `DIVIDE()` protects you against divide-by-zero errors in your visuals. A matrix, by design, hides any rows or columns that have no data (i.e., the formula returns `BLANK()`). If you get an error in a measure inside a matrix, it is possible that you will see lots of rows that you would otherwise not see, and you will possibly also see some error messages that you would rather not see. Power BI error messages include NaN, which means "not a number" and also infinity.

The `DIVIDE()` function is specifically designed to prevent these error messages from appearing. If you use `DIVIDE()` instead of the slash operator (`/`) for division, DAX returns a `BLANK()` method where you would otherwise get a divide-by-zero error, such as NaN (not a number). Given that a matrix filters out blank rows by default, a blank result is preferable to an error.

The syntax for this function is `DIVIDE(numerator, denominator, optional-alternate-result)`. If you don't specify the alternate result, a blank value is returned when a divide-by-zero error occurs.

Practice Exercises: DIVIDE()

Before you can write the following measures, you need to create a new matrix and put `Products[Category]` on Rows. Then add `[Total Sales]` and `[Total Margin $]` to the matrix so you have some data to look at. This helps set the context for the new measures you will write next.

Write the following measures using `DIVIDE()`. Find the solutions to these practice exercises in "Appendix A: Answers to Practice Exercises" on page 252.

21. [Margin %]

Write a measure that calculates the margin on sales percentage (`[Total Margin $]` divided by `[Total Sales]`). To do so, reuse measures that you have already written.

> **Note:** This is a duplicate of a measure, called `[Total Margin %]`, that you wrote at the start of this chapter. This time, however, you write the formula by using the `DIVIDE()` function and give it the name `[Margin %]`. The result will be the same, of course, but technically this new version is safer because it will protect against the errors mentioned above.

22. [Markup %]

Find `[Total Margin $]` divided by `[Total Cost]`.

23. [Tax %]

Find `[Total Tax]` divided by `[Total Sales]`.

How Did It Go?

Did you format the last three measures as percentages, as shown below?

Category	Total Sales	Total Margin $	Margin %	Markup %	Tax %
Accessories	$700,760	$438,675	62.6%	167.4%	8.0%
Bikes	$28,318,145	$11,505,797	40.6%	68.4%	8.0%
Clothing	$339,773	$136,413	40.1%	67.1%	8.0%
Total	**$29,358,677**	**$12,080,884**	**41.1%**	**69.9%**	**8.0%**

5: Concept: Filter Propagation

In Chapter 4 we looked at the COUNT() function and saw some strange behaviour with the [Total Number of Customers] measure. You need to understand the process of filter propagation before you can truly understand what is happening there.

Consider the following matrix.

Category	Total Number of Customers	Total Number of Products
Accessories	18,484	35
Bikes	18,484	125
Clothing	18,484	48
Components	18,484	189
Total	**18,484**	**397**

The result [Total Number of Products] in this matrix is displaying a different value for each product category (i.e., each row in the matrix is showing a different number of products that exist in that category), but the value for [Total Number of Customers] is the same for each product category in the matrix. This happens because the row labels in the matrix (highlighted above) are "filtering" the products in the Products table in the data model before this measure is evaluated. But these same rows (product categories) are not filtering the Customers table at all.

The matrix above first "filters" the data model (in this case, it is the Products[Category] column), and then Power BI evaluates the measures for each row in the matrix with the filters applied; that's what it's designed to do. I call the filters coming from a matrix (or from any other visual or from the Filters pane) the initial filters—initial because it is possible to change the initial filtering behaviour later by using the CALCULATE() function. So the initial filter is the standard filtering coming from a matrix (and/or from any other visual and/or from the Filters pane) before any possible modifications are applied using DAX formulas that include CALCULATE().

> **Note:** CALCULATE() is a massive and complex topic that is covered in depth in Chapter 9.

Cross-Filtering Visuals

So far in this book, we have used only a single visual on a report page. Now is a good time to add a second visual to the report canvas. Do you remember the process? It is important that you click on a blank section of the canvas before adding a new visual. For example, to add a slicer, after clicking on a blank area of your page, you can click on the slicer visual (shown below) to add a new slicer to your report.

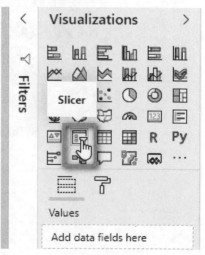

Category	Total Number of Customers	Total Number of Products
Accessories	18,484	35
Bikes	18,484	125
Clothing	18,484	48
Components	18,484	189
Total	**18,484**	**397**

Note: Before you try to add another visual to the report canvas, you should first click on a blank area of the canvas to ensure that you don't accidently have an existing visual selected. If you try to add a new visual while you have an existing visual selected, you will replace the existing visual with the new one instead of adding another new visual to the canvas. If you make a mistake, you can always click Undo, but it's best to get into the habit of clicking on a blank area of the canvas before adding a new visual.

After adding the slicer, locate and drag the `Products[Size]` column onto the slicer, as shown below.

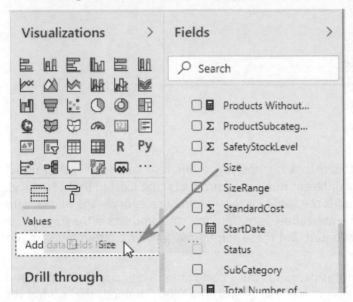

An initial filter in Power BI comes from different areas of the matrix, but it can also come from other areas in the report. Here are a few examples of where initial filters come from:

- Rows (see #1 below)
- Columns (#2)
- Slicers (#3)
- Filters (#4)

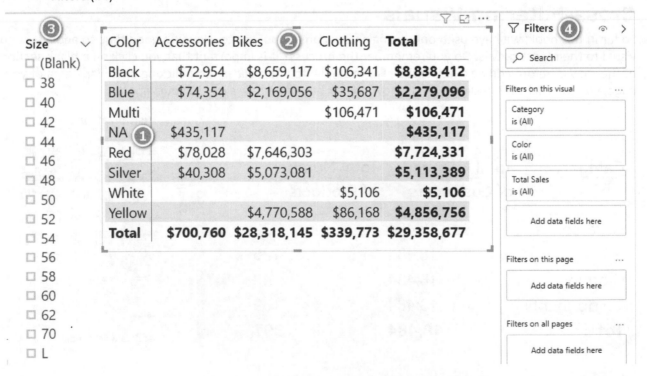

In fact, with Power BI, instead of using a slicer (#3 above), you can use any visual on the canvas to filter any of the other visuals on the canvas. In addition, from the Filters pane (#4), you can choose a visual-level filter (which filters on this visual), a page-level filter (which filters on this page), or even a report-wide filter (which filters on all pages). There is a lot to look for when checking to see what initial filters are impacting the visuals in a Power BI report. Over time, you will learn to find all filtering behaviour quickly and easily.

Reading the Initial Filter

The following matrix, which first appeared in Chapter 4, shows [Total Number of Customers] and [Total Number of Products].

Category	Total Number of Customers	Total Number of Products
Accessories	18,484	35
Bikes	18,484	125
Clothing	18,484	48
Components	18,484	189
Total	**18,484**	**397**

In Chapter 4, this matrix was a bit confusing because it had the same value for [Total Number of Customers] on every row in the matrix. When you learn to read the initial filters in a visual, you will be able to make more sense of what is going on here.

Let's step through the process of reading the initial filter from this matrix. Before we do that, though, you should add the [Total Sales] measure to the matrix so it looks as shown below.

Category	Total Number of Customers	Total Number of Products	Total Sales
Accessories	18,484	35	$700,760
Bikes	18,484	125	$28,318,145
Clothing	18,484	48	$339,773
Components	18,484	189	
Total	**18,484**	**397**	**$29,358,677**

Then point to the cell that's highlighted above and say this out loud (really): "The initial filter for this cell is Products[Category] = Accessories." Then point to the cell underneath the highlighted cell; this cell has an initial filter of Products[Category] = Bikes. You can figure out the rest based on this pattern. It is important that you learn to "read" the initial filter from your visuals because it will help you understand how each value in a visual is calculated. And it is important to refer to the full table name and column name because that forces you to look, check, and confirm exactly which tables and columns you are using in your visuals.

Understanding the Flow of the Initial Filters

Once you know what the initial filters are—there may be more than one—you can mentally apply the following steps to your data model and track how the filters flow through relationships. Technically, the filters propagate from one table to another using the relationships:

1. The initial filters coming from the visual are applied to the underlying tables in the data model. In this example, there is just one table involved, the `Products` table (see #1 below), where `Products[Category]` = "Accessories". The `Products` table is filtered so that only rows in the table that are equal to `Accessories` remain; all other rows are filtered so that they are not in play. (Note that the initial filters can come from more than one table, but in this example, it is just the one table and one initial filter.)

2. The filter applied to the table (`Products` in this case) automatically propagates through the relationship between the joined tables, flowing downhill in the direction of the arrow to the connected table (see #2 below). The filters automatically flow from the "one" side of the relationship to the "many" side of the relationship, in the direction of the arrow; or you can think of the filters as flowing from the lookup table to the data table. Whatever terms you use, it's always downhill. This is one of the reasons it is good for beginners to lay out the tables using the Collie layout methodology (refer to "Shaping Data" on page 17), with the lookup tables above and the data tables below. This mental cue helps you instantly visualise how automatic filter propagation works.

3. The connected table on the "many" side of the relationship, the `Sales` table, is then also filtered (see #3 below). (Remember that there can be more than one connected table.) Only the products that are of the type `Products[Category]` = "Accessories" remain in play in the `Sales` table, and all the other products are filtered away. This is temporary—just for this calculation of this one single cell in the visual.

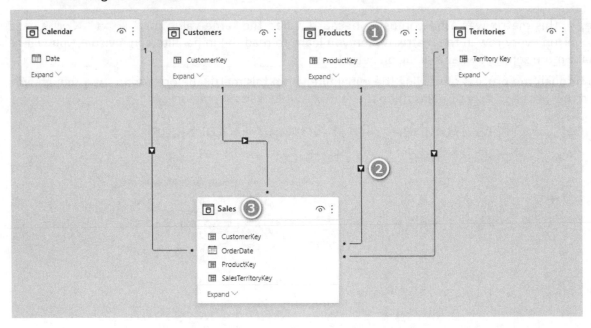

4. After the automatic filter propagation has been completed, then and only then does the measure get evaluated. In this case, the measure is `Total Sales = SUM(Sales[ExtendedAmount])`. It returns the value $700,760 to the single matrix cell we started to look at in this example.

This process is repeated for every single cell in the matrix, including any subtotal and grand total cells.

> **Note:** A subtotal and a grand total do not simply add up the rows above. Rather, every cell goes through the same "filter and then evaluate" process described above, even if it is a subtotal or grand total row.

Understanding Filter Propagation

Keep in mind that you always evaluate each cell on its own, without regard for any other cell in the visual, even if the cell is a subtotal or grand total cell. To see how this works, look at the matrix below and read the initial filter for the highlighted cell out loud: "The initial filter for this cell is `Products[Category]` = "Clothing"."

Category	Total Number of Customers	Total Number of Products
Accessories	18,484	35
Bikes	18,484	125
Clothing	18,484	48
Components	18,484	189
Total	**18,484**	**397**

The initial filter is applied to the tables in the data model using the following process:

1. The initial filter is applied to the table(s). In this example, Products[Category] = "Clothing". The Products table (see #1 below) is then filtered so that only rows in the table that are equal to Clothing remain.

2. This filter automatically propagates through the relationships that exist between the tables, flowing downhill only (in the direction of the arrow), to the connected table(s) (see #2 below).

3. The connected table(s) (Sales in this example) is then also filtered so that the same products in the Products table will remain in the Sales table (i.e., only clothing products will remain in the Sales table after the filter propagates through the relationship) (see #3 below).

4. The filter applied to the Sales table does not automatically flow back uphill to the Customers table (or to the other two tables, for that matter) (see #4 below). Filters only automatically propagate through the relationships downhill from the "one" side of the relationship to the "many" side, in the direction of the arrows. The arrow (see #4 below) indicates that the filters do not flow from the Sales table to the Customers table.

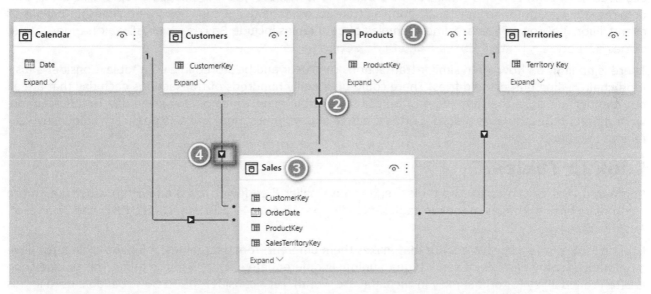

The net result is that the Customers table is completely unfiltered by the initial filter coming from the visual. Because the Customers table is unfiltered, the total 18,484 is returned to the matrix in this cell (and the same is true for every other cell for this measure in the current matrix).

Even if this doesn't seem right to you yet, realise that it is working as designed. Understanding gives you power, so stick with it until you are clear about how it works. Read this section a few times if you need to. You will eventually love the way it is designed and will learn to make it work for you.

> **Tip:** You simply must understand how filter propagation works in Power BI, or you will never be really good at writing DAX. I suggest that you read this chapter multiple times, if necessary, to make sure you are clear about it.

6: Concept: Lookup Tables and Data Tables

All the sample and exercise data in this book has been prepared for you in advance; so far you have been able to simply follow the instructions, using the data provided. But the simplicity of following my instructions shields you from a deep and important topic: how you should structure the tables of your own data that you want to use in your own reports. This chapter covers this topic so that you can understand the various types of tables you can load into Power BI.

Now, be warned: This topic is easy to skim over and dismiss as trivial, but in my experience, proper table structure is one of the things people most commonly get wrong, particularly if they don't know why it is important or don't know how to do it properly. If you get the table structure wrong, everything else becomes orders of magnitude harder.

Tip: Don't brush off this chapter as unimportant. You need to know this stuff if you want to proceed in Power BI with speed and confidence, using your own data.

Data Tables vs. Lookup Tables

As you have already learned, there are two main types of tables that can be loaded into Power BI: data tables (also called fact tables, or transaction tables) and lookup tables (also called dimension tables, reference tables, or master data tables). These two types of tables have some very important differences, as described in the following sections.

Data Tables

Although data tables don't have to be the largest tables loaded into Power BI, they typically are. The Sales table used in this book is a transactional table that contains details of individual cash register transactions that occurred in AdventureWorks retail outlets around the world. Every row in this table represents a line item on a register receipt for an individual shopping transaction. Data tables can consist of millions (or billions or even trillions) of rows of data. Some examples of data tables include Sales, Budget, Exchange Rates, General Ledger, Exam Results, and Stock Count.

There is no limit on how often similar transactions can occur and be stored in a data table. Consider a fast-food chain selling burgers and fries. There could be literally hundreds of transactions each day that are all but identical because the same type of burger can be sold many times on any given day. In this scenario, what differentiates the transactions is often the time of day (time stamp) and also possibly a unique invoice/ receipt number.

Lookup Tables

Compared to data tables, lookup tables tend to be smaller (i.e., fewer rows) and often wider (i.e., more columns). Some examples of lookup tables include Customers, Products, Calendar, and Chart of Accounts.

Lookup tables have a special feature that makes them different from data tables: A lookup table must have a uniquely identifying code of some type to uniquely differentiate each row in the table. This unique code is often called a key (or primary key in the database world). Let's consider the Products table used in this book. AdventureWorks sells lots of different products—397 of them, to be precise. Each of these products has a unique product code (key), a three-digit number that is unique for that product. For example, product key 212 is a Sports 100 Helmet, Red. No other product in the Products table has the same code. If you think about it, this is the way it has to be; there would be chaos if a business used the same product code for different products. The same is true for customers and store ID numbers. In fact, the same is true for the Calendar table, given that the date field is a unique ID (key) for each day in the calendar.

Flattened Tables

To understand the importance of table structure and the different approaches you can take to loading data, it can be helpful to look at a single large flattened table. In the early days of Excel pivot tables (before Power Pivot for Excel), you could only create a pivot table on top of a single table of data. If you wanted to do some analysis over a table full of sales data, you could use a pivot table to aggregate the data.

In the image below, the pivot table (see #2) has been built on the `Sales` table (#1), and the pivot table can easily summarise the total sales for each of the products, as identified in the `ProductKey` column.

Row Labels ⬆	Total Sales		ProductKey ▼	OrderDate ▼	CustomerKey ▼	SalesTerritoryKey ▼	ExtendedAmount ▼
592	$25,425	①	592	3/06/2019	13035	9	564.99
593	$22,035	②	592	3/06/2019	16684	9	564.99
594	$28,250		465	3/06/2019	11965	9	24.49
595	$27,120		479	4/06/2019	16730	9	8.99
596	$25,920		482	4/06/2019	13643	9	8.99
597	$26,460		595	6/06/2019	13036	9	564.99
598	$31,319		489	7/06/2019	18715	9	53.99
599	$30,239		491	8/06/2019	19578	9	53.99
600	$22,140		483	8/06/2019	13634	9	120
604	$194,396		484	9/06/2019	13668	9	7.95
605	$196,016		463	9/06/2019	12351	9	24.49
606	$208,436		541	9/06/2019	19623	9	28.99
Grand Total	$837,755		578	9/06/2019	14262	9	1214.85
			489	10/06/2019	17059	9	53.99

That is all well and good until a report needs some extra data that is not part of the `Sales` table. In the image above, what would happen if you wanted to know the name of the product, or the product category, or the subcategory, or anything else for that matter? Well, in the old days, you would find a `Products` table somewhere, and then you would write a `VLOOKUP()` (or an `INDEX()`/`MATCH()`) to go and fetch the extra columns of data that you needed for your reporting and bring it into the single `Sales` table. From there, it would be possible to use the new columns in your pivot tables. This process of bringing in the missing columns is called denormalising. After you have denormalised, your `Sales` table ends up looking something like the one below (but of course much wider if you need more columns).

ProductKey ▼	OrderDate ▼	Category ▼	ProductName ▼	SubCategory ▼	Color ▼	ExtendedAmount ▼
465	3/06/2019	Clothing	Half-Finger Gloves, M	Gloves	Black	24.49
592	3/06/2019	Bikes	Mountain-500 Silver, 42	Mountain Bikes	Silver	564.99
592	3/06/2019	Bikes	Mountain-500 Silver, 42	Mountain Bikes	Silver	564.99
479	4/06/2019	Accessories	Road Bottle Cage	Bottles and Cages	NA	8.99
482	4/06/2019	Clothing	Racing Socks, L	Socks	White	8.99
489	6/06/2019	Clothing	Short-Sleeve Classic Jersey, M	Jerseys	Yellow	53.99
595	6/06/2019	Bikes	Mountain-500 Silver, 52	Mountain Bikes	Silver	564.99
489	7/06/2019	Clothing	Short-Sleeve Classic Jersey, M	Jerseys	Yellow	53.99
483	8/06/2019	Accessories	Hitch Rack - 4-Bike	Bike Racks	NA	120
491	8/06/2019	Clothing	Short-Sleeve Classic Jersey, XL	Jerseys	Yellow	53.99
541	9/06/2019	Accessories	Touring Tire	Tires and Tubes	NA	28.99
484	9/06/2019	Accessories	Bike Wash - Dissolver	Cleaners	NA	7.95

Technically, you could load the table above into the Power BI data model and use it as is, but doing so is not best practice. If you have very simple requirements—that is, if you use simple functions such as `COUNT()` and `SUM()` —then a single flat table like the one above is fine. If you have a requirement for more complex calculations, such as `[SubCategory % of All Product Sales Variance by Year]` or using the `CALCULATE()` function (which is covered in Chapter 9), then you are well advised not to use a single flat table structure like this. Just because a single flat table is simple does not mean it is the best data model for Power BI. Power BI does not require you to bring all the columns into the one table, as was the case with old Excel pivot tables, and it is not best practice to do this, so you should generally avoid using a single table like this when using Power BI.

> **Note:** The Power BI data modelling engine is a column store database that vertically compresses the data it loads. (Now you see why this engine is also called VertiPaq.) The details behind this are quite technical and beyond the scope of this book. However, there are a couple of key points you should be aware of. The more unique values in a column, the less the data will be compressed. In addition, the number of columns you have in your data tables is much more important than the number of rows; that is, fewer columns and more rows is better than more columns and fewer rows. This is particularly true for large tables.

Joining Tables by Using Relationships

A good approach to solving the problem of repetitive data is to keep the repeating data in separate lookup tables. In the case of products, only one column of information is needed in the `Sales` table to uniquely identify every single product: `ProductKey`, which contains the product code data. If the `Sales` table contains the unique product key, it is possible to fetch any extra information needed from a product master table when it is needed. So rather than requiring you to write a `VLOOKUP()` to go and bring the product information into the `Sales` table, Power BI allows you to load both tables into the data model and create a single relationship between them. Once the relationship has been created, the tables will work together as if they were a single unit, without the need to bring all that data into a single `Sales` table.

As mentioned briefly in Chapter 2, the structure of the tables and any relationships between them in a data model is sometimes referred to as a schema. There are a few different classes of schemas, and the following sections cover the two most common types: star and snowflake schemas.

Star Schema

The image below shows the star schema structure that is used in this book. In this case, the `Sales` table (see #1 below) is a data table and is located at the centre of the star. The other tables (#2, #3, #4, and #5) are lookup tables and are shown as points on the star. This structure is called a star schema due to its shape when laid out like this.

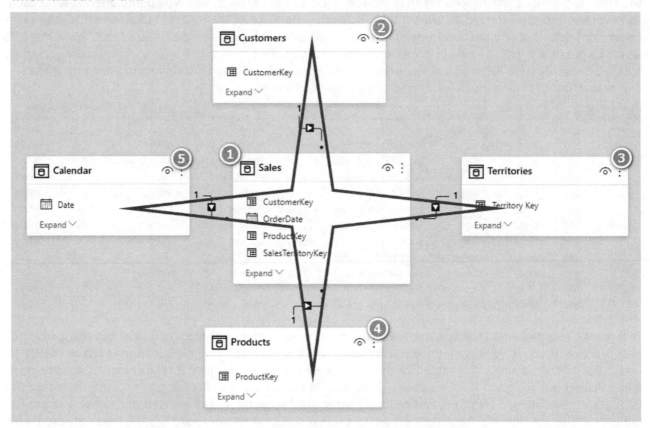

However, as you learnt in Chapter 2, you can reposition tables any way you choose, and I recommend using the Collie layout methodology, as shown below. You can see that the tables here are the same as in the diagram above, but the layout is different. The layout has no impact at all on the way Power BI operates, but it does give you a visual clue as to which tables are the lookup tables and which are the data tables because you have to "look up" to see the lookup tables. (Also, in the old days, you would write a `VLOOKUP()` to go and fetch those extra columns, so there is another link to the past between the words `VLOOKUP()` and lookup table.)

Note: In the database world, a lookup table is called a dimension table.

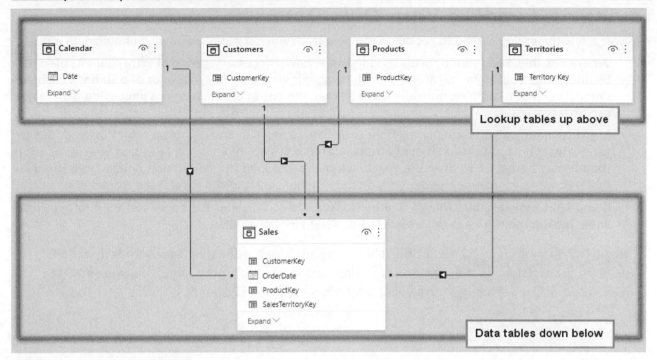

Snowflake Schema

An organisation is likely to have at least one database of some sort to manage some of its data. Such databases are normally built by internal IT staff or possibly by some third-party software company that builds the systems used by the organisation. In traditional relational database systems, the data is often split into many levels of lookup tables. Consider the image below. There is a single data table, Sales (see #1 below), and there are three lookup tables all chained together in a row (#2, #3, and #4). Table #4 is a lookup table of table #3, which is a lookup table of table #2, which is a lookup table of table #1.

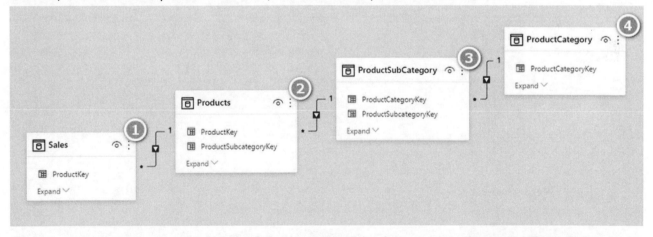

This data structure is common in traditional transactional databases as it is the most efficient way to store the data in those systems. However, this is not the best way to structure data in Power BI because Power BI is not a relational database. There are a few reasons this approach is not the best for Power BI:

- Every relationship comes at a cost. The extra relationships will potentially have negative performance impacts on the database.

- Business users will be building reports using the database design, and they will see all the tables in the data model. The structure above is confusing to and onerous on an end user who is trying to understand where to find information about products.

- Power BI was built from the ground up to be very efficient in the way it stores repetitive data in columns, particularly in the smaller lookup tables, so there is simply no reason to do it as shown in the image above.

Advice on Loading Your Own Data

There are a few things you can do to get off on the right track when it is time to build your own data models:

- Where possible, keep your data tables long and skinny. If necessary, get rid of extra columns of "data" by unpivoting your data, particularly if a data table is very wide (i.e., has a lot of columns). Each additional column of data compresses less well than the last one, which means long, wide data tables can be a real issue.

- Move repeating attribute columns from your data tables and create lookup tables instead. But be careful that you don't overdo it. If a lookup table has only two columns (e.g., Key and Description), then it may be better to drop the Key column and just load the description directly into the data table. How to best handle this depends on the situation, and there is not a single correct way to do it.

- If you have lookup tables joined to other lookup tables, consider flattening them out into a single wider lookup table. This is generally a better design for Power BI.

Note: Definitely do not just accept the table shape and structure coming from your transactional systems. Transactional databases and reporting databases are not the same, and you shouldn't try to use the table structure from your transactional system in Power BI.

7: DAX Topic: Calculated Columns

It's time for a change of pace. I have deliberately left the discussion of calculated columns until now to allow you to get accustomed to the power of measures. I have done this because the mistake I most commonly see Excel users make when learning Power BI is to use too many calculated columns. I'll show you why I think this happens. The image below shows the Data view in Power BI.

As you can see, the Power BI Data view looks a lot like Excel. Most Excel users feel very comfortable when they switch to this view. The table shown above is the `Sales` table. Note that it has the columns `Sales[ExtendedAmount]` and `Sales[TaxAmt]`. But there is no column `Sales[Total Sales Plus Tax]`. What I observe Excel users do, over and over again, is think to themselves "I've got a sales amount, and I've got a tax amount, but I need sales including tax. I'll add a calculated column for that." The problem is that this is the wrong approach. Someone with an Excel background who is new to Power BI may think it's easy to whip up such a formula without learning any new skills; self-taught users often fall into this trap. In order to understand how such a user might proceed, let's create such a calculated column now. Keep in mind, though, that this is not the best way to do this calculation.

Here's How: A Basic (but Wrong!) Calculated Column

To write a calculated column, switch to the Data view and follow these steps:

1. In the Fields pane, right-click on the required table—`Sales` in this case (see #1 below)—and then select New Column (#2).

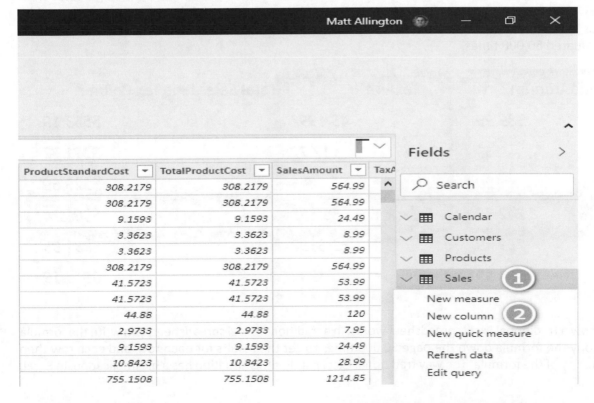

2. In the formula bar at the top of the table, write the following formula:

    ```
    Total Sales Plus Tax Column =
        Sales[ExtendedAmount] + Sales[TaxAmt]
    ```

3. In the Column Tools tab, apply currency formatting with two decimal places.

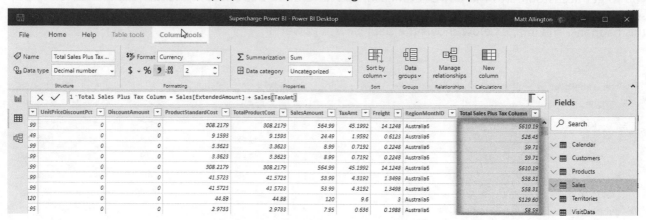

The image above shows the new column. Notice that each row in the new column has a number that is the total of the Sales[ExtendedAmount] column and the Sales[TaxAmt] column for that single row. The first row is $610.19, the second row is $26.45, etc. In fact, the Sales table contains more than 60,000 rows, and so there are now more than 60,000 new numbers stored in this new calculated column in the Sales table.

Important Calculated Columns Concepts

There are a few very important things you must understand before moving on. First, there is only a single formula for the entire calculated column written above. This single formula yields more than 60,000 different results. Keep in mind that with a calculated column, you write a single formula, and that formula is evaluated once for every row in the table.

Take the illustration below as an example. The calculated column formula works through the table, one row at time. When it gets to each row, there is only a single value in each of the two input columns: one value in the Sales[ExtendedAmount] column (i.e., 742.35) and one value in the Sales[TaxAmt] column (i.e., 59.388). For each row, the single value from Sales[ExtendedAmount] is added to the single value from Sales[TaxAmt], resulting in a single result that is stored in the same row of the new column in the table. This process is automatically repeated for every row in the table. If there are 60,000 rows, the formula is logically evaluated 60,000 times.

ExtendedAmount	TaxAmt	Total Sales Plus Tax Column
539.99	43.1992	$583.19
159	12.72	$171.72
120	9.6	$129.60
742.35	59.388	$801.74
769.49	61.5592	$831.05
564.99	45.1992	$610.19

This is not how a traditional Excel spreadsheet works. In a traditional Excel spreadsheet, you write the formula once and copy the formula down the page 60,000 times to get the results for each row, and each row then has its own copy of the formula. The way traditional Excel handles this situation has a big implication. In Excel, if you want to change a row, you can simply change the formula for that row. This is not possible with Power BI calculated columns. You can only have a single formula for an entire calculated column.

> **Note:** Excel has a feature called Excel Tables. It is possible to convert data from a regular Excel spreadsheet into an Excel Table. If you do this, the new Excel Table behaves the same way as a calculated column.

Row-by-Row Evaluation in Calculated Columns

The way Power BI creates a calculated column is by using a trick I call row-by-row evaluation. It is not possible to perform this trick inside a regular measure in Power BI. To see what I mean, follow these steps:

1. Copy the formula you wrote above from the formula bar:

   ```
   Total Sales Plus Tax Column =
         Sales[ExtendedAmount] + Sales[TaxAmt]
   ```

2. In the Fields pane, right-click the `Sales` table and select New Measure.

3. Paste the formula you copied.

4. Change the name of the formula from `Total Sales Plus Tax Column` to `Total Sales Plus Tax Measure`, as shown below:

   ```
   Total Sales Plus Tax Measure =
         Sales[ExtendedAmount] + Sales[TaxAmt]
   ```

   Press Enter.

When you try to write this measure using exactly the same DAX formula that worked as a calculated column, you get the error shown below.

```
1  Total Sales Plus Tax Measure = Sales[ExtendedAmount] + Sales[TaxAmt]
2
```
> ⚠ A single value for column 'ExtendedAmount' in table 'Sales' cannot be determined.

There is a very important reason this DAX formula works in a calculated column and not in a measure: A calculated column has awareness of the presence of rows; it can do row-by-row evaluation. When you write a formula in a calculated column, the single formula is evaluated for every row in the table, one row at a time. A calculated column has the ability to do row-by-row evaluation, but a regular measure does not have this ability, as confirmed by the error message shown above.

Here is a modified version of the invalid measure you just used that does work as a measure:

```
Total Sales Plus Tax Measure Correct =
     SUM(Sales[ExtendedAmount]) + SUM(Sales[TaxAmt])
```

To see why this new version of the measure works, look at what is different: The new version above has every column name wrapped inside a DAX function—in this case, the `SUM()` function. In the original measure that was invalid, repeated below, there are no functions wrapped around the column names:

```
Total Sales Plus Tax Measure =
     Sales[ExtendedAmount] + Sales[TaxAmt]
```

> **Tip:** Compare the two versions of this measure so you are clear on the difference.

No Naked Columns in Measures

You can't write measures in DAX that contain what I call "naked columns." A naked column is a reference to a column name that is not wrapped inside a DAX function; the invalid formula above contains one. Naked columns are allowed inside calculated columns because a calculated column has the ability to do row-by-row evaluation. However, whereas a calculated column understands the concept of row-by-row evaluation, a measure does not. A calculated column is able to work through the table, one row at a time, and find a single value in each of the naked columns (the intersection of the column and the row) in order to do the calculation for each and every row. A naked column is not allowed in a measure because a measure has no ability to do row-by-row evaluation. If you use a naked column in a measure, you are essentially asking DAX to add a column of more than 60,000 numbers to another column of 60,000 numbers. This is a lot like saying, "Take this spreadsheet and add it to this other spreadsheet." You can't add spreadsheets together, and you can't add columns together. What you can do inside a measure, however, is add up all the numbers in a single column, add up all the numbers in a second column, and then add together the totals; this is perfectly fine, as shown with the correct version of the measure above.

> **Note:** It is valid to refer to naked columns in a calculated column as long as the naked columns come from the same table where you are writing the calculated column. You cannot refer to naked columns in a calculated column if the naked columns come from another table.

The Big Problem with Calculated Columns

There is one big problem with calculated columns—and I do mean BIG. The problem is that a calculated column always evaluates every row and permanently stores the answer in the workbook as a value in the new column in the table. This takes up space in the workbook, making your files bigger and hindering their performance. What's more, the compression applied to calculated columns is generally not as good as for imported columns, and so the data may be stored in the workbook less efficiently.

As mentioned at the beginning of this chapter, the mistake I most commonly see Excel users make is to use too many calculated columns. There are two general reasons you should try to avoid them most of the time:

- Calculated columns make your tables and workbooks bigger.
- Mostly (though not always) you can get the same outcome by using a measure, which is a better way.

Consciously avoiding using calculated columns and trying to find a measure-based solution will make you a stronger DAX user. Trust me. Over time, with experience, you will learn when it is best to use calculated columns instead.

Sometimes a Calculated Column Is Your Friend

Calculated columns exist for a reason. In some instances, you simply cannot use a measure—such as when you want to use the results in a slicer. Imagine that you want a slicer in a report so you can filter a chart for either weekdays or weekends. You cannot solve this problem by using a measure. If you want a slicer, you must have a column in a table.

Wait a minute. I just finished telling you not to create calculated columns, and now I am telling you it's okay to do so. Allow me to clarify. In general, you should not use a calculated column if you can:

- Use a measure instead
- Bring the data into a table directly from the source data
- Create the column during data load by using Power Query

If you are missing a column of data that you need (e.g., for a slicer, where a measure will not do the job), I recommend that you prefer the following order to source the missing column:

1. Add it at the source and import it from there.
2. Create it in Power Query on data load.
3. Use a calculated column.

By pushing the column as far back to the source as possible, you increase the possibility of reusability—for yourself and for others—down the track. But the truth is that this is a purist view, and the method you use doesn't really matter that much. If you know how to do something in a calculated column and you don't know how to do it in Power Query, then there is generally no harm in using a calculated column. Indeed, you can and should use calculated columns when you need them. You should definitely use a calculated column when both of the following conditions are satisfied at the same time:

- You need to filter/slice a visual based on the results of a column (i.e., you want to use the column on Filters, Slicer, Rows, or Columns). Measures don't work in this case.
- You can't bring the column of data you need in from your source data or by using Power Query (for whatever reason).

These are the most common reasons for not being able to get a column you need from your source data:

- The column doesn't exist.
- You can't arrange to get the column added (e.g., you don't have access to the source system and/or those who do have access can't or won't do it for you).
- You can get the column added, but not in a timely manner.
- You want to use measures that exist in your data model as part of the formula needed to create the new column (e.g., annual customer sales to determine small, medium, and large customer classifications).

As mentioned earlier, if possible, you should try to get the column you need added to the source data. When you do this, you get the full benefit of compression on data import; in addition, the column is available for reuse in all future workbooks created by you and others. But sometimes this simply isn't possible; other times, it is possible, but you can't wait two weeks (or two years!) to get it done. Calculated columns are useful in such cases. And if a new column becomes available in the future, you can simply delete your calculated column and replace it with the new column coming in from the source.

Here's How: Creating a Day Type Calculated Column

Let's look at an example of where you should use a calculated column instead of a measure. Let's say that you extract the `Calendar` table from your enterprise database, and you want a new column that shows whether each date is a weekend, but you can't arrange to have this column added right now. Of course, you could use Power Query, but this book is about DAX, so this section discusses how to create a calculated column to solve this problem.

Follow these steps to create a calculated column called `Day Type` in the `Calendar` table:

1. In the Power BI Fields pane, right-click on the `Calendar` table and then select New Column.

2. Immediately start typing the following over the top of `Column` = in the formula bar:

```
Day Type =
IF(
'Calendar'[DayNumberOfWeek] = 1 || 'Calendar'[DayNumberOfWeek]=7,
"Weekend","Weekday"
)
```

Note: Note the use of the two pipe symbols (| |) in the formula above. This is the inline text version of a logical OR function. If you are using a U.S. keyboard, the pipe can be found above the backslash (\) key (which is right above the Enter/Return key). If you are using another keyboard, you simply have to go hunting.

You can also write an OR function in DAX as follows:

```
IF(
    OR('Calendar'[DayNumberOfWeek] = 1, 'Calendar'[DayNumberOfWeek] = 7)
    "Weekend","Weekday")
```

Note: You can see here that the OR function in DAX accepts only two parameters—and this is different from the OR function in Excel.

You can also use the IN syntax, like this:

```
IF(
    'Calendar'[DayNumberOfWeek] IN {1,7},
    "Weekend","Weekday"
)
```

Personally, I prefer to use the IN syntax because you only have to mention the column name once, and the list of possible values is very easy to maintain. The OR() function above accepts only two parameters as inputs; if you have more than two logical inputs, you need to use multiple nested OR() functions to make it work.

Note: The inline version of the logical AND is the double ampersand (`&&`), which equates to the `AND()` function.

3. If you are not currently in the Data view, switch to it and check to make sure your column is calculating correctly.

Note: It is very important that you test your measures after you write them. You are a data modeller now! Along with this title comes the responsibility to check that the measures you write are returning the expected results. Switching to the Data view can help you validate this.

4. Note that the formula you just created, as shown below, is a single formula for the entire column. This is not traditional Excel; there can be only one formula in a single calculated column. You therefore have to write the one formula so that it evaluates and handles all the possible scenarios you need.

Date	DayNumberOfWeek	DayName	Day Type
1/07/2016	6	Friday	Weekday
2/07/2016	7	Saturday	Weekend
3/07/2016	1	Sunday	Weekend
4/07/2016	2	Monday	Weekday
5/07/2016	3	Tuesday	Weekday
6/07/2016	4	Wednesday	Weekday
7/07/2016	5	Thursday	Weekday
8/07/2016	6	Friday	Weekday
9/07/2016	7	Saturday	Weekend
10/07/2016	1	Sunday	Weekend

5. Now that you have the new calculated column, go to a new page in your workbook and create a new matrix. Place `Products[Category]` on Rows, place your new column `'Calendar'[Day Type]` on Columns, and then add `[Total Sales]` to the Values section. You end up with the matrix shown below.

Category	Weekday	Weekend	Total
Accessories	$505,721	$195,039	**$700,760**
Bikes	$20,450,873	$7,867,271	**$28,318,145**
Clothing	$244,821	$94,951	**$339,773**
Total	**$21,201,415**	**$8,157,262**	**$29,358,677**

You have successfully extracted some new insights from the data that didn't exist before: You have used data modelling techniques to enhance the data for weekday/weekend analysis. You could also use the new column on a new slicer as an alternate way to filter the data. You cannot use a measure in a slicer, so if you want to use a slicer, you must create a column.

Practice Exercise: Calculated Columns

Write the following calculated column in the `Calendar` table. Find the solution to this practice exercise in "Appendix A: Answers to Practice Exercises" on page 252.

24. Creating a Half-Year Column

In the `Calendar` table, write a calculated column that returns the value H1 for the first half of each year (January through June) and returns H2 for the second half of each year (July through December). Hint: You might want to use an IF statement to do this.

8: DAX Topic: The Basic Iterators SUMX() and AVERAGEX()

The functions covered in Chapter 4—SUM(), COUNT(), COUNTROWS(), MIN(), MAX(), COUNTBLANK(), and DIVIDE()—are what I call "aggregation functions." An aggregation function acts on an entire column or table and uses a specific aggregating technique to return a single value to a cell in a visual on a report.

There is another class of functions that can possibly return the same answers as the aggregation functions— but using a different logical approach. These "X-functions" (so called because each one has an X at the end of its name) are part of the iterator family.

Iterators Use Row-by-Row Evaluation

The main difference between iterators and the other functions we have looked at so far is that iterators are functions that are "aware" of the existence of rows in tables and columns of data. Exactly like a calculated column, an iterating function can do row-by-row evaluation. Iterating functions step through every row in a table, one row at a time, and evaluate the formula for every row.

Iterating Functions vs. Calculated Columns

The big difference between iterating functions like SUMX() and calculated columns is that a calculated column permanently stores the results in the new column. An iterating function generates exactly the same row-by-row results, but it does not permanently store these results anywhere in the workbook.

I have been teaching people DAX for many years. Trust me here: The easiest way to understand how a SUMX() function works is to first build a calculated column so you can "see" what it is doing and then replace the calculated column with the SUMX() version equivalent. To see how this works, let's look at how to write a new version of the [Total Sales Plus Tax Column] equation by using SUMX(). As mentioned earlier, we can start with the calculated column from early in Chapter 7:

```
Total Sales Plus Tax Column =
        Sales[ExtendedAmount] + Sales[TaxAmt]
```

The image below shows (again) the column that is added to the Sales table as a result. You can see the row-by-row results in the new column.

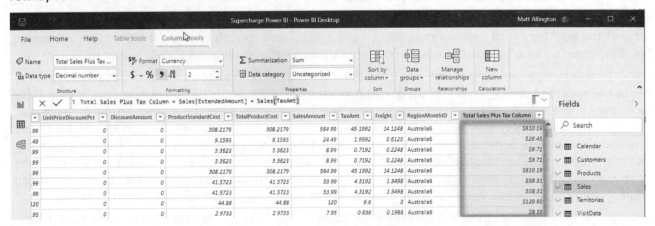

After creating this new calculated column, you could add the new column to the Values section in a matrix (see #1 below). You would then see the total of the column in the matrix (#2) because Power BI automatically sums the total of this column for you (#3).

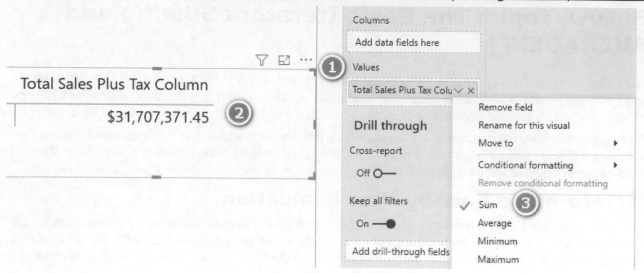

Let me recap the key points of this process before we move on to SUMX():

- The calculated column shown in the first of the two images above has the ability to do row-by-row evaluation.

- Because the calculated column can do row-by-row evaluation, it is perfectly okay to refer to naked columns (from the same table) in the formula expression. It is not valid to write exactly the same formula as in a regular measure because naked columns (i.e., columns not wrapped in functions) are not allowed in measures.

- The Sales table is evaluated one row at a time, and the result from each row is permanently stored in the new column (shown above).

- When you add this new column to a visual, Power BI automatically sums the column of values to show you the total. This is what I call an "implicit measure." If you don't want the sum of the column, you can change the implicit calculation to be something different, such as an average.

Using SUMX(*table, expression*)

Now that you have gotten a fresh reminder of how a calculated column works, let's switch to SUMX(). Remember that the goal here is to look at how SUMX() and a calculated column are almost identical in behaviour. The difference is that a calculated column permanently stores the results, and SUMX() does not.

SUMX() takes two parameters: a table name and the expression to be evaluated. SUMX() steps through every row in the specified table (parameter 1), one row at a time, and evaluates the expression (parameter 2) for each row, generating an interim result for each row. Finally, it adds together the interim results for each row. SUMX() can do row-by-row evaluation, just as a calculated column can, working through the rows one at a time to complete the evaluation. However, the interim results are not permanently stored. This is a good thing because it makes Power BI more efficient, but it can be challenging when learning DAX because you can't see what is going on. This is why I suggest that before you write a formula, you write an equivalent calculated column; doing so helps you visualise what is happening so you can get your head around the concept.

To write the new measure from the preceding section by using SUMX(), you need to create a new matrix, put Products[Category] on Rows, and then write this measure, as shown below, and place it in the Sales table.

```
1   Total Sales Including Tax SUMX Version =
2   SUMX ( Sales, Sales[ExtendedAmount] + Sales[TaxAmt] )
          ①                      ②
```

Note the two parameters inside this measure in the image above. The first parameter (see #1 above) is the table name, Sales. Imagine that you are adding a calculated column to the Sales table. The second parameter (#2) is identical to the calculated column from before. SUMX() does exactly the same calculation as that calculated column: It steps through the Sales table (parameter 1), one row at a time, and for each row, it takes the single value in the Sales[ExtendedAmount] column and adds it to the single value in the Sales[TaxAmt] column. It repeats this process for each of the more than 60,000 rows in the Sales table and keeps the interim results in memory only. It does not permanently store these results, so you can't see them to validate what is happening. When it is done evaluating all rows, it sums the interim results into a total.

Note: The SUMX() function sums the interim results. The AVERAGEX() function averages the interim results.

If you add both the new SUMX() measure and the original calculated column to a matrix, you see that they give exactly the same results, as shown below.

Category	Total Sales Plus Tax Column	Total Sales Including Tax SUMX Version
Accessories	$756,821	$756,821
Bikes	$30,583,596	$30,583,596
Clothing	$366,954	$366,954
Total	**$31,707,371**	**$31,707,371**

Note: I have talked extensively about how calculated columns and iterators work "one row at a time." It is convenient to think of the process working in this way, and indeed that is the logical execution approach. In reality, though, the Power BI engine has been built and optimised to work very efficiently under the hood. In many circumstances, the actual physical execution is much more efficient than is implied by the "one row at a time" logical execution explanation. This is a very deep technical topic and is beyond the scope of this book. The key thing to note is that you should not think that iterators are inherently inefficient because they are working one row at a time; the Power BI engine optimisations normally make the physical execution much more efficient than is implied by the phrase "one row at a time."

Parameter 2 Can Be Any Valid DAX

The second parameter of SUMX() (and, for that matter, the syntax for calculated columns) does not have to be a simple addition; it can be any valid formula you can write. Consider the following data structure, which could exist in a typical sales table.

Order Quantity ▼	Unit Price ▼	Extended Amount ▼
3	$3.00	$9.00
2	$4.00	$8.00
1	$6.00	$6.00

Total Quantity
6

Total Sales
$23.00

This sales table stores the quantity of items sold and the unit price. In order to calculate the total sales ($23.00), you would first need to generate the Extended Amount column by multiplying Order Quantity by Unit Price (if it didn't already exist in the sales table). Then you could add up the Extended Amount column to get the total sales of $23.00. There is no other way to generate the Total Sales value; you simply must evaluate the quantity multiplied by the unit price for every row in the table and then add up the total. This is the only way to get the correct answer. However, you have a choice of how to calculate the sales total: You could load an extended amount column from the source, you could create an extended amount column as a calculated column after the source data is loaded, or you could generate the extended amount values on the fly inside SUMX() without ever permanently storing the extra column. Generally speaking, you should prefer the SUMX() approach.

In the AdventureWorks database Sales table, there is a Quantity column, a Unit Price column, and an Extended Amount column. Technically, the Extended Amount column is not needed; if you ever want to know the total of the Extended Amount column, you can generate the required calculation by using SUMX() without the need to ever store this column in your data model.

> **Note:** It is best practice to load into your data model only the columns of data you need and not to load columns that can be calculated on demand inside a measure.

Practice Exercises: SUMX()

Write the following measures for practice. Find the solutions to these practice exercises in "Appendix A: Answers to Practice Exercises" on page 252.

25. [Total Sales SUMX Version]

Multiply quantity by unit price from the appropriate columns in the Sales table. This will give you the same result as the [Total Sales] measure from before but will give you an opportunity to practice the concept that was just explained.

26. [Total Sales Including Tax SUMX Version]

Add the ExtendedAmount column together with the appropriate tax column in the Sales table.

27. [Total Sales Including Freight]

Add the ExtendedAmount column to the freight cost.

How Did It Go?

Did you get the following matrix?

Category	Total Sales SUMX Version	Total Sales Including Tax SUMX Version	Total Sales Including Freight
Accessories	$700,760	$756,821	$718,281
Bikes	$28,318,145	$30,583,596	$29,026,099
Clothing	$339,773	$366,954	$348,267
Total	**$29,358,677**	**$31,707,371**	**$30,092,647**

Make sure you are following these steps to minimise rework:

- Put the measures in the correct table by right-clicking the target table and selecting New Measure. (Do not select New Measure from the Modeling tab!)
- Give the measure a meaningful name that includes spaces.
- Apply suitable formatting immediately after writing the measure.

- Write the formula and then check to ensure that it was written correctly by adding it to a matrix to check your results.

28. [Dealer Margin]

Create a new matrix. From the `Products` table, put `Category` on Filters for this matrix and then select `Accessories` from this filter. Then put `ProductName` on Rows. You should have something like what is shown below (although what is shown here is truncated). Note that I have used a filter from the Filters pane on this visual section to apply the filter on `Products[Category]`.

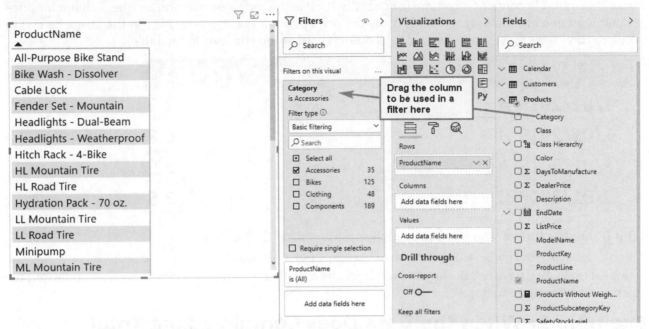

Write a measure that shows the theoretical margin the dealer gets (i.e., the difference between the product's list price and the product's dealer price). Both columns you need for this measure are in the `Products` table. Did you get the answers shown below? (Once again, the matrix in the image below is truncated; it shows only the first nine rows, though in reality it is longer.)

ProductName	Dealer Margin
All-Purpose Bike Stand	$63.60
Bike Wash - Dissolver	$3.18
Cable Lock	$10.00
Fender Set - Mountain	$8.79
Headlights - Dual-Beam	$14.00
Headlights - Weatherproof	$18.00
Hitch Rack - 4-Bike	$48.00
HL Mountain Tire	$14.00
HL Road Tire	$13.04

When to Use X-Functions vs. Aggregators

Now you know that you can use X-functions such as SUMX(), and you can also use aggregators such as SUM(), and they do similar things but take different approaches. The following examples will help you figure out when to use X-functions and when to use aggregators. These examples use simplistic tiny tables for illustration purposes only. In real life, tables of data are, of course, much larger.

Example 1: When the Data Doesn't Contain the Line Total

If your Sales table contains a column for quantity (Qty in the image below) and another column for price per unit, you need to multiply the quantity by the price per unit (Price Per Unit in the image below) to calculate total sales (because the actual total doesn't exist at the line level in the table).

Date	Product	Qty	Price Per Unit
1/01/2018	A	3	2.5
1/01/2018	B	1	6.8
2/01/2018	A	5	2.5
2/01/2018	C	3	3.5

If this is the structure of your data, you simply must use SUMX(), like this:

```
Total Sales 1 = SUMX(Sales, Sales[Qty] * Sales[Price Per Unit])
```

In this example, you have to calculate the totals for the rows first, one row at a time. This is what the iterator functions are designed to do.

Example 2: When the Data Does Contain a Line Total

If your data contains a single column with the extended total sales for that line item, you can use SUM() to add up the values:

```
Total Sales 2 = SUM(Sales[Total Sales])
```

Date	Product	Total Sales
1/01/2018	A	7.5
1/01/2018	B	6.8
2/01/2018	A	12.5
2/01/2018	C	10.5

There is no need for an iterator in this example. Note, however, that you could still use SUMX(), like this, to get the same answer:

```
Total Sales 2 alternate = SUMX(Sales, Sales[Total Sales])
```

> **Note:** In the formula above, there is only a single column for the expression parameter: Sales[Total Sales]. This is a valid DAX expression, and it will work just fine. For each row in the iteration of SUMX(), the formula just takes the line-level total for this column. At the end, it simply adds up all the values.

So Which Should You Use, SUM() or SUMX()?

There is technically no difference in the operation of the following two formulas:

```
Measure 1 = SUM(Sales[Total Sales])
Measure 2 = SUMX(Sales, Sales[Total Sales])
```

Measure 1 should be familiar to Excel users because it is virtually the same syntax used in Excel. The syntax of Measure 2 is harder to understand. But the truth is, these two formulas are evaluated in exactly the same way. Technically, Measure 1 is converted to Measure 2 prior to evaluation. Microsoft wants to make it as easy as possible for Excel users to start using DAX, so where possible, it provides simple functions with similar syntax to Excel to help you get started. (Microsoft calls this similarity and simplicity "syntax sugar.") But under the hood, Microsoft converts this simple syntax into the more advanced syntax required to get the job done.

Whether you use SUM() or SUMX() comes down to personal preference and the structure of your data. If, for example, you have an extended amount column, you can choose either option. If, however, you have only a quantity column and a unit price column, you must use SUMX().

Performance Implications

As a general rule, the more unique values loaded in a column (i.e., the higher the cardinality of the column), the worse the calculation performance will be. But don't panic. Power BI is generally super-fast at doing calculations. If you have 200 million rows of data, you might start to see a problem with a high-cardinality column, but if you have fewer than several million rows of data, it is unlikely that you will experience any measurable performance impact.

Avoiding Data You Don't Need

One important point to note before moving on is that you should definitely not load redundant data. It should be apparent that if you have a quantity column and price per unit column in a table, you can "calculate" the value of total sales any time you need by using a measure. Similarly, if you have total sales and quantity in a table, you can calculate price per unit any time you like. Generally speaking, you should not load columns of redundant data that can be calculated on the fly with a measure. Doing so increases file size and can make everything refresh and perform more slowly. The general rule is to bring in the minimum number of columns you need to do the job, and it is best to bring in the columns with the lowest numbers of unique values, where possible.

Now take a look at the cardinality of the three numeric columns below.

Date	Product	Qty	Price Per Unit	Total Sales
1/01/2018	A	3	2.5	7.5
1/01/2018	B	1	6.8	6.8
2/01/2018	A	5	2.5	12.5
2/01/2018	C	3	3.5	10.5

There are duplicate values in the Qty column and also in the Price Per Unit column, but there are no duplicates in the Total Sales column. The cardinalities of the Qty and the Price Per Unit columns are therefore lower than the cardinality of the Total Sales column. As a general rule, it is better to load the first two columns and not the third column and to use an iterating function such as SUMX() or AVERAGEX() to generate the results on the fly. This may seem counterintuitive if you think about iteration as being a slow, row-by-row evaluation (and it is understandable that you might think of it that way). However, the underlying Power BI engine is optimised to work this way. There are exceptions to this rule, but they are beyond the scope of this book.

When Totals Don't Add Up

There is another use case that requires you to use SUMX() or some other iterator. The following small table of sample data will help illustrate the problem and the preferred solution.

Customer	Spend per Visit	Number of Visits
A	50	7
B	40	3
C	100	12
D	15	4

This table shows four customers, with the average amount of money they have spent each time they have shopped as well as the number of times they have shopped. If you load this data into Power BI and then try to use aggregating functions to find the average amount spent across all customers as well as the total amount spent, you get the wrong answers, as shown below.

Customer	Total Number of Visits	Avg Spent per visit Wrong	Total Spent Wrong
A	7	$50	$350
B	3	$40	$120
C	12	$100	$1,200
D	4	$15	$60
Total	**26**	**$51**	**$1,333**

The following measures are used above:

```
Total Number of Visits = SUM(VisitData[Number of Visits])
Avg Spent per visit Wrong= AVERAGE(VisitData[Spend per Visit])
Total Spent Wrong =
     [Avg Spent per visit Wrong] * [Total Number of Visits]
```

The first measure, [Total Number of Visits], is correct because the data is additive, but the other two measures give the wrong results. This is a classic situation where you can't perform multiplication on the averages at the grand total level. Given the original sample data, the only way to calculate the correct answer is to complete a row-by-row evaluation for each customer, as shown below.

Customer	Total Number of Visits	Total Spent SUMX	Avg Spent per visit Correct
A	7	$350	$50.00
B	3	$120	$40.00
C	12	$1,200	$100.00
D	4	$60	$15.00
Total	**26**	**$1,730**	**$66.54**

The table above includes a SUMX() function to find the total spent, row by row. Only then does the matrix calculate the average spent per visit. Here is the complete set of correct formulas:

```
Total Number of Visits = SUM(VisitData[Number of Visits])
Total Spent SUMX =
    SUMX(VisitData,
        VisitData[Spend per Visit] * VisitData[Number of Visits]
    )
Avg Spent per visit Correct =
    DIVIDE([Total Spent SUMX], [Total Number of Visits])
```

Whenever you see that the totals in your visuals don't add up, you should try to figure out what is happening row by row in the visual that is not happening in the total row. Such a problem is almost always caused by the fact that the visual is doing some filtering inside the matrix that is not occurring at the total level. You should look at the visual and consider how you can simulate the row-by-row filtering that you see inside the visual in the total row. When you determine the answer, you will know how to solve the problem of totals not adding up. It normally involves using an iterating function like SUMX().

Are You Writing Measures Correctly?

It's time to practice using some new functions. Before you get into the following practice exercises, here is a refresher on the process you should use to write measures:

1. Create a new matrix on a new sheet.

2. Put a column (such as Products[Category]) on Rows.

3. In the Fields pane, right-click the table where the measure will be stored and select New Measure.

4. Give the measure a descriptive name.

5. Start typing the DAX formula. To check the syntax as you go, pause to read the IntelliSense description of the function and the syntax, as shown below.

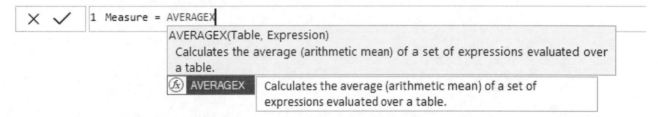

6. Write the complete formula you need for the task at hand.

7. Immediately after writing the formula, apply any formatting you want to use.

8. Add the measure to your matrix so you can see the results before moving on.

Practice Exercises: AVERAGEX()

Set up a new matrix and put Products[Category] on Rows. Then write the following measures by using AVERAGEX(). Find the solutions to these practice exercises in "Appendix A: Answers to Practice Exercises" on page 252.

29. [Average Selling Price Including Tax per Item]

You need to find the sales amount column and the tax column in the Sales table. Then use AVERAGEX() to find the average selling price, including tax. Note that there is more than one sales amount column you can use; you can choose any one of them for this exercise.

30. [Average Profit Per Item Sold]

To work out the profit per item sold, you need to work out the profit per item and then find the average. There is no column in the Sales table for profit, so you need to use AVERAGEX() to do the calculation. Profit is simply the selling price minus the cost price.

31. [Average Value of Safety Stock Per Product]

There are safety stock level and list price columns in the `Products` table. Calculate what the average value of the safety stock will be. You should put the results in a matrix, as shown below.

Category	Average Sell Price Including Tax per Item	Average Profit Per Item Sold	Average Value of Safety Stock Per Product
Accessories	$20.97	$12.15	$3,142
Bikes	$2,011.42	$756.71	$152,459
Clothing	$40.32	$14.99	$188
Components			$270,848
Total	**$524.97**	**$200.02**	**$176,772**

Note: There are other X-functions that are not covered in this book, such as `MAXX()`, `MINX()`, `COUNTAX()`, and `COUNTX()`. You can find out how to use them by typing one of them at a time into the formula bar and reading the IntelliSense.

9: DAX Topic: CALCULATE()

CALCULATE() is the most important and powerful function in the DAX language. It is important because it is the only function that has the ability to modify the natural filtering behaviour of visuals.

> **Note:** Actually, there are some other functions that can modify filter behaviour, including CALCULATETABLE(). However, those functions are typically used in DAX queries, and DAX queries are beyond the scope of this book.

I am going to teach you everything you need to know about how to use CALCULATE(). But keep in mind that CALCULATE() seems simple on the surface, but in reality there is a lot to learn, and there are traps hiding in plain sight. You will need to concentrate hard (and possibly read this chapter more than once), and you definitely need to practice writing DAX formulas using CALCULATE() in order to build your depth of knowledge and understanding.

Altering the Standard Offering

Have you ever gone into a restaurant and looked at the menu, only to discover that the standard offering is not quite what you are after? Lots of people love Caesar salad, for example, but many people do not like anchovies. Say that you're one of them, and you read the following description on the menu:

Caesar Salad: Romaine lettuce, croutons, parmesan cheese, anchovies, and egg tossed in a creamy Caesar dressing.

When you order the salad, you alter the standard menu option by saying, "I'll have the Caesar salad, no anchovies." CALCULATE() is a lot like that: It allows you to alter the standard offering that you get from a visual in order to get some variation that ends up being exactly what you want.

CALCULATE() alters the natural filtering behaviour of visuals. It modifies an expression (which can be a measure or another DAX formula) by applying, removing, or modifying filters. The syntax of CALCULATE() is:

```
= CALCULATE(expression, filter 1, filter 2, ..., filter n)
```

CALCULATE() alters the filtering behaviour of a visual by applying zero, one, or more filters prior to evaluating the expression. CALCULATE() then "reruns" the built-in filter propagation engine in Power BI—the one that makes the filters automatically propagate from the lookup tables and flow downhill to the data tables in the direction of the arrows. When CALCULATE() reruns the filter engine, if there are any filters inside the CALCULATE() function, these filters are included as part of the overall filters before the expression is evaluated. (You'll read more about how this works in Chapter 11.)

> **Note:** I just said that you can use zero, one, or more filters inside CALCULATE(). It might seem strange that you can use none at all. Why would you want to do this? Using no filters is a special use case that is covered in Chapter 11.

Simple Filters

CALCULATE() can use two types of filters: simple filters and table filters. A simple filter has a column name on the left and a value on the right, as in these examples:

```
Customers[Gender] = "F"
Products[Color] = "Blue"
'Calendar'[Date] = "1/1/2017"
'Calendar'[Calendar Year] = 2018
```

The first parameter to the CALCULATE() function is always an expression. You can use simple filters like the ones shown above as the second and subsequent parameters to CALCULATE() to alter the original meaning of the expression. Simple filters are designed to be easy to use and understand. They operate a bit like SUMIF() or SUMIFS() in Excel.

Note: Under the hood, Power BI converts a simple filter into a much more complex formula that is harder for beginners to learn and understand. Consider the following measure, using a simple filter:

```
Total Sales to Females =
    CALCULATE([Total Sales], Customers[Gender] = "F")
```

Under the hood, Power BI converts this into the following formula prior to execution:

```
Total Sales to Females =
    CALCULATE([Total Sales],
        FILTER(ALL(Customers[Gender]), Customers[Gender] = "F")
    )
```

I am sure you will agree that the first formula is easier to read and understand than the second. As mentioned earlier, Microsoft developers call this type of simple syntax "syntax sugar." The simple syntax is provided to make it easier for people to use Power BI without having to first become experts in DAX.

When you have more experience and have learnt some new table functions like ALL() (in Chapter 14) and FILTER() (in Chapter 15), you will be able to write the more advanced CALCULATE() formulas that use table filters instead of a simple filters. (Table filters are discussed later in this chapter.)

To see CALCULATE() in action (with simple syntax), set up a new matrix like the one below, with Products[Category] on Rows and Products[Total Sales] on Values. (You should be getting used to this by now!)

Category	Total Sales
Accessories	$700,760
Bikes	$28,318,145
Clothing	$339,773
Total	**$29,358,677**

Then write the following measure:

```
Total Sales of Blue Products =
    CALCULATE([Total Sales], Products[Color]="Blue")
```

In the image below, can you see how the simple filter used here, Products[Color]="Blue", has altered the initial filter behaviour coming from the matrix and given a variation to the regular measure [Total Sales]? It is as if you have changed the recipe for the standard product on the menu and received a variation of that regular menu item. Think Caesar salad without anchovies.

Category	Total Sales	Total Sales of Blue Products
Accessories	$700,760	$74,354
Bikes	$28,318,145	$2,169,056
Clothing	$339,773	$35,687
Total	**$29,358,677**	**$2,279,096**

Practice Exercises: CALCULATE() with a Single Table

It's time for you to write some simple CALCULATE() examples that filter a single table using simple syntax. Set up a new matrix with Customers[Occupation] on Rows and [Total Number of Customers] on Values. (You should have already written the [Total Number of Customers] measure for Practice Exercise 9.) You should have the matrix shown below as your starting point.

Occupation	Total Number of Customers
Clerical	2,928
Management	3,075
Manual	2,384
Professional	5,520
Skilled Manual	4,577
Total	**18,484**

Then write the following measures, using CALCULATE(). Find the solutions to these practice exercises in "Appendix A: Answers to Practice Exercises" on page 252.

32. [Total Male Customers]

Write a new measure that modifies the [Total Number of Customers] measure you wrote in Practice Exercise 9 to find a total for male customers only. You need to look for a suitable column from the Customers table to use in your filter.

33. [Total Customers Born Before 1970]

In this case, you need to enter the date < January 1, 1970, into the formula as the filter parameter. You need to use the DATE() function in order to refer to a date. Remember that you can get help from the tool-tips that IntelliSense provides when writing the measure. Just start typing =DATE inside the formula bar, and a tooltip pops up, explaining the purpose and syntax of the function, as shown below.

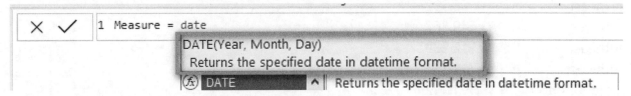

Now that you know how to write a date inside a formula, you can go ahead and write the measure [Total Customers Born Before 1970].

34. [Total Customers Born in January]

This exercise is similar to Practice Exercise 33, but this time you need to use the MONTH() function to turn the information in the Customers[BirthDate] column into a month.

35. [Customers Earning at Least $100,000 per Year]

Write a measure that counts the number of customers who earn $100,000 or more per year. Look for a suitable column to use for the filter in the Customers table.

How Did It Go?

Did you end up with the following matrix?

Occupation	Total Number of Customers	Total Male Customers	Total Customers Born Before 1970	Total Customers Born in January	Customers Earning at least $100,000 per Year
Clerical	2,928	1,488	433	132	
Manual	2,384	1,251	134	128	
Skilled Manual	4,577	2,293	234	192	
Professional	5,520	2,727	609	254	792
Management	3,075	1,592	1,543	136	1,406
Total	**18,484**	**9,351**	**2,953**	**842**	**2,198**

Using CALCULATE() over Multiple Tables

In Practice Exercises 32–35, the CALCULATE() function touches only a single table; the filtering is applied to a table, and the expression is evaluated on the same table. However, CALCULATE() can work over multiple tables, too. When you use the CALCULATE() function, it first applies the filters to the relevant tables, and then it reruns the filter propagation engine and makes sure that any new filters inside the CALCULATE() function automatically propagate from the "one" side of the relationship to the "many" side (i.e., the filters flow downhill) before the expression is evaluated. So you can apply a filter to one or more of the lookup tables, and these filters will propagate to the data tables, and any expression that evaluates over the connected data tables will reflect the filters from the lookup tables. (Are you feeling supercharged now?!)

Practice Exercises: CALCULATE() with Multiple Tables

Set up a new matrix. Put Territories[Region] on Rows and [Total Sales] on Values. Note that there are now two tables involved. The initial filter in the visual is coming from the Territories table (see #1 below), and the calculation [Total Sales] is operating over the Sales table (#2).

Region	Total Sales ②
Australia ①	$9,061,001
Canada	$1,977,845
Central	$3,001
France	$2,644,018
Germany	$2,894,312
Northeast	$6,532
Northwest	$3,649,867
Southeast	$12,239
Southwest	$5,718,151
United Kingdom	$3,391,712
Total	**$29,358,677**

With your matrix set up like this, write the following new measures. Find the solutions to these practice exercises in "Appendix A: Answers to Practice Exercises" on page 252.

36. [Total Sales of Clothing]

Use the Products[Category] column in your simple filter. The filter gets applied to the lookup table, but then the measure [Total Sales] is modified by the filter (and Total Sales comes from the Sales table), so you use CALCULATE() with multiple tables in this formula.

37. [Sales to Female Customers]

Use CALCULATE() to modify the measure [Total Sales] and create a new measure that is for sales to female customers.

38. [Sales of Bikes to Married Men]

You need to use multiple filters on two tables for this one. CALCULATE() can accept as many filters as you pass to it. Just separate the filters with commas.

How Did It Go?

Did you end up with the following matrix?

Region	Total Sales	Total Sales of Clothing	Sales to Female Customers	Sales of Bikes to Married Men
Australia	$9,061,001	$70,260	$4,634,993	$2,205,159
Canada	$1,977,845	$53,165	$1,011,320	$517,808
Central	$3,001	$157	$124	
France	$2,644,018	$27,035	$1,271,964	$726,649
Germany	$2,894,312	$23,565	$1,539,713	$694,776
Northeast	$6,532	$106	$3,836	$2,295
Northwest	$3,649,867	$58,230	$1,843,586	$982,266
Southeast	$12,239	$301	$11,938	
Southwest	$5,718,151	$74,714	$2,881,098	$1,451,036
United Kingdom	$3,391,712	$32,240	$1,615,046	$1,031,765
Total	**$29,358,677**	**$339,773**	**$14,813,619**	**$7,611,754**

Table Filters

So far you have used only simple filters inside CALCULATE(), in this format:

> *TableName[ColumnName]* = *some value*

You can also use a table filter, which is a more advanced type of filter that is passed in the form of a table that contains values that are required for the filter. This table can be either a physical table or a function that returns a table (e.g., ALL(), VALUES(), FILTER()). Importantly, both types of tables used as table filter parameters retain all relationships that exist in the data model. Table filters and the way the tables retain their relationships in the data model are complex topics that are covered in more detail in the coming chapters. For now, it is enough to know that so far you have only learnt about simple filters for CALCULATE(), and the more advanced table filters are discussed later.

10: DAX Topic: Making DAX Easy to Read

Now is a good time to pause and talk about how to lay out your DAX so it is easy to read. Consider this example:

```
Total Sales to Single Males in Australia =
    CALCULATE([Total Sales], Customers[MaritalStatus]="S",
    Customers[Gender]="M", Territories[Country]="Australia")
```

Long formulas like this one can be difficult to read. The generally accepted approach is to lay out a formula by using line breaks and spaces so it is easier to see which parts of the formula belong together. There is no single right way to do this. Here is one way that I find useful:

```
Total Sales to Single Males in Australia =
    CALCULATE([Total Sales],
        Customers[MaritalStatus] = "S",
        Customers[Gender] = "M",
        Territories[Country] = "Australia"
    )
```

In this example, I put the first parameter in CALCULATE() (which is the expression) on the first line, followed by a comma. Then I placed each filter on a new line and indented the filters so it is easy to see that they belong to the CALCULATE() function.

> **Note:** To create a new line in the formula bar, you need to press Shift+Enter on the keyboard. Then you can use the Tab key to indent the next line of the formula from the left-hand side.

The final closing parenthesis for the CALCULATE() function in this example is on a new line of its own, aligned with the C in CALCULATE() so that I know that this bracket closes the CALCULATE() function.

Using DAX Formatter

DAX Formatter is a very useful (and free) tool that you can use to help format your DAX. Marco Russo and Alberto Ferrari from SQLBI developed the free http://daxformatter.com website. You simply paste your DAX code into the website, and DAX Formatter formats the code for you. You can then cut and paste it back into the formula bar in Power BI.

When you use DAX Formatter, you have a choice about whether to include the measure name. You can omit the name if you like, but it is just as easy to copy the entire formula, including the measure name.

The image below shows the [Total Sales to Single Males in Australia] formula from DAX Formatter, including the measure name.

```
Total Sales to Single Males in Australia =
CALCULATE([Total Sales],
Customers[MaritalStatus] = "S",
Customers[Gender] = "M",
Territories[Country] = "Australia"
)
```

The image below shows the same formula after DAX Formatter has applied formatting.

```
1  Total Sales to Single Males in Australia =
2  CALCULATE (
3      [Total Sales],
4      Customers[MaritalStatus] = "S",
5      Customers[Gender] = "M",
6      Territories[Country] = "Australia"
7  )
```

Error Checking

DAX Formatter does another important job for you: It checks whether a DAX formula is valid and written correctly. If it is not, DAX Formatter does its best to find the error. To see this in action, try removing one of the commas from the DAX code above, such as the one after Gender = "M", so it looks like this:

```
Total Sales to Single Males in Australia =
    CALCULATE([Total Sales],
        Customers[MaritalStatus] = "S",
        Customers[Gender] = "M"
        Territories[Country] = "Australia"
    )
```

In this case, DAX Formatter is expecting a comma but instead finds the letter T (on the next line). As you can see in the following image, DAX Formatter describes the syntax error at the bottom of the screen and places a triangle next to the character where it found the error.

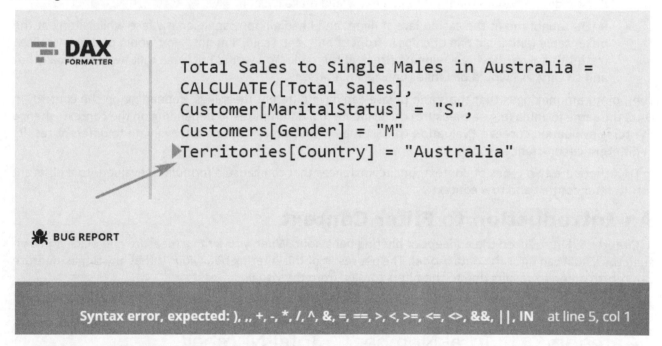

Although it was not strictly designed for debugging, DAX Formatter is a great tool for helping you debug your DAX code when you can't work out what is wrong. I use DAX Formatter all the time to help me with my DAX. I suggest you do, too.

> **Note:** Marco Russo told me that DAX Formatter was not designed to be an official error-checking tool, as I describe using it above. As a result, the error checking is not perfect, but in my view, it is worth trying this approach if you are stuck.

11: Concept: Evaluation Context and Context Transition

This chapter covers one of the hardest topics to understand and master in DAX: evaluation contexts. There are a few reasons I think this topic is confusing and hard to learn; one of them is simply that the name is confusing. What does evaluation contexts mean? A good place to start is with the word context.

What Does *Context* Mean?

You have certainly heard the term context before but possibly not as it relates to DAX. The concept of context is very important in language; the same words can mean different things in a different contexts. Take the phrase "I'm hot." Now, what does this mean? Well, it depends on the context:

- If I were running a marathon on a midsummer's day and I said "I'm hot," you would have no misunderstanding of what I meant; the context would make it clear.

- If you caught me at the casino late at night, and I had a happy smile on my face while sitting at the poker table (and a big pile of chips in front of me), and I said "I'm hot," you would probably realise I meant that I was having a winning streak at the table. You would not think that I was physically hot and sweaty, as I would be while running a marathon.

The point I am making is that the same phrase can have different meanings, depending on the context. In DAX, the same formula (e.g., a measure) can evaluate to a different result depending on the context—hence the term evaluation context. Evaluation context means that every formula can evaluate to different results in different circumstances.

In DAX there are two types of context, or circumstances that can cause a formula to evaluate to a different result: filter context and row context.

An Introduction to Filter Context

In Chapter 5, I introduced the concept of filtering behaviour. When you write a measure and place it in a visual, the visual can filter the data model. The net result of this filtering behaviour is that any single measure can return different results due to the filters coming from the visual.

The following matrix is one I first showed in Chapter 4.

Category	Total Number of Customers	Total Number of Products
Accessories	18,484	35
Bikes	18,484	125
Clothing	18,484	48
Components	18,484	189
Total	**18,484**	**397**

The Category column in this matrix (see #1 above) is a column that comes from the Products table in the data model. When the Category column is filtered by the visual, the entire Products table is filtered, too. That is why you can see a different result for the measure [Total Number of Products] in each row of the matrix. But the Products table does not filter the Customers table, either directly or indirectly. The following image shows the Model view again so you can verify this.

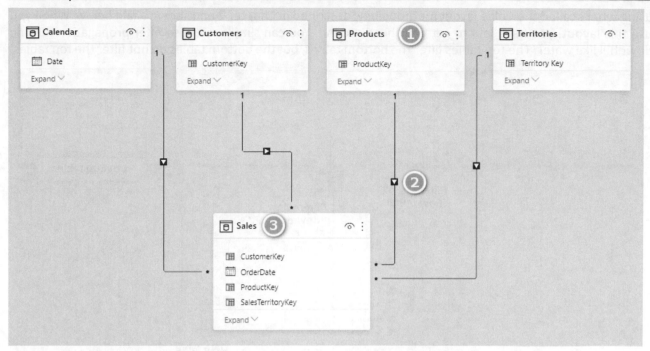

Note that the `Products` table (see #1 above) directly filters the `Sales` table (#3) through the relationship. You can verify this based on the arrow from `Products` to `Sales` (#2). But the `Sales` table does not filter the `Customers` table; there is no arrow pointing from the `Sales` table to the `Customers` table, so you know that the `Customers` table is not filtered. The implication is that the measure `[Total Number of Customers]` does not show a different result for each row in the matrix visual above.

The filtering behaviour I'm describing here and elsewhere in this book has a formal name: filter context. Filter context refers to any filtering that is applied to the data model in Power BI. Filter context can be created by a visual (e.g., a matrix) and also by the `CALCULATE()` function. The initial filter context is the natural filtering behaviour that comes from a visual or a report. The initial filter context can come from the following areas:

- Rows in a visual, such as a matrix (see #1 below)
- Columns in a matrix (#2)
- Filters in the Filters pane (#3)
- Slicers (#4)
- Any other visual on the canvas, such as a column chart (#5)

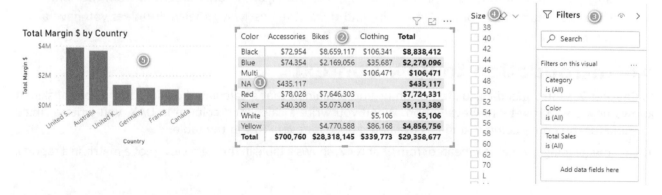

The initial filter context is the natural filtering behaviour that comes from the combination of all the filters applied in a report.

The filter context coming from a report filters the underlying tables in the data model. If the tables are joined, the filters automatically propagate from the "one" side of the relationship to the "many" side of the relationship. But the filter does not automatically propagate in the other direction, from the "many" side to the "one" side of a relationship. This is why I recommend (for Excel users anyway) laying out the data model using what I called the Collie layout methodology, described in Chapter 2 and shown again below. When you use this layout, you have less to get your head around. You can simply visualise filter propagation flowing downhill like water: The top tables filter the bottom tables, but the bottom tables do not filter the top tables.

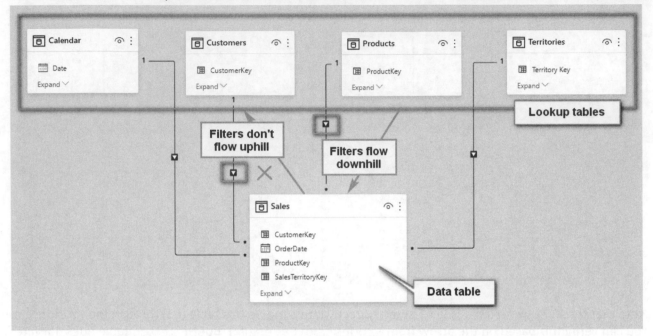

This setup provides a visual clue that the filters flow downhill through the relationships but do not flow uphill through the relationships.

In summary, filter context comes from:

- A visual in a report
- The Filters pane in a report
- The CALCULATE() function

If you don't have a visual with a filter, and you don't have a CALCULATE() function, then you don't have filter context; it's as simple as that.

> **Note:** It is possible to filter lookup tables (the tables at the top in the Collie layout methodology) based on the results in a data table (the tables below) by using DAX instead of automatic filter propagation. It is also possible to change the default direction of the filter behaviour by making changes to the relationships. But by default, filters propagate in one direction, from the "one" side to the "many" side of a relationship, and this is the best way to leave it unless you have a reason to make a change.

An Introduction to Row Context

In Chapter 7, I introduced calculated columns and explained that a calculated column has a special skill: It knows how to do row-by-row evaluation. When you write a calculated column in DAX, you write a single formula for the entire column, and it is evaluated once for every row in the table.

The following image, which is repeated from Chapter 7, shows a table in the Data view (not a matrix in a report).

ExtendedAmount	TaxAmt	Total Sales Plus Tax Column
539.99	43.1992	$583.19
159	12.72	$171.72
120	9.6	$129.60
742.35	59.388	$801.74
769.49	61.5592	$831.05
564.99	45.1992	$610.19

The third column in the table above is a calculated column with a single formula:

```
Total Sales Plus Tax Column =
        Sales[ExtendedAmount] + Sales[TaxAmt]
```

With only a single formula, there is a different result for every row in the new column in this table. This single formula works because a calculated column has a special skill of being able to complete row-by-row evaluation. It evaluates the same formula, over and over again, for every row in the table, often returning a different result for each row. There's that reference again: Every formula can return a different result, depending on the context. In the case of calculated columns, the context is called row context. Row context is simply the awareness and ability of DAX to complete row-by-row evaluation, often returning a different result each time.

As I mentioned in Chapter 8, there are some special DAX functions that also have the ability to do row-by-row evaluation (i.e., they have row context). All of the X-functions, such as SUMX() and AVERAGEX(), have row context, just as a calculated column does. (So do some other functions that are covered later in this book.)

When you think about row context, think of the function (or calculated column) stepping through the table one row at a time and selecting the single values at the intersection between the columns and row (highlighted in the image above) and then acting on the single values in each column (#1 and #2 in the image above) for a single row. Regular measures can't do this; only functions that have row context and calculated columns can perform this trick.

Do you remember the following measure formula?

```
Total Sales Plus Tax Measure =
        Sales[ExtendedAmount] + Sales[TaxAmt]
```

This measure returns an error; it is not legal syntax to write this measure in DAX. This formula contains "naked columns"—columns with no functions wrapped around them. It is not legal DAX syntax to write a measure that has naked columns. Such a measure returns an error. Every formula in DAX can return a different result depending on the context; in this case, the different result is an error because there is no row context for this formula when it is written as a measure.

Let's look again at the SUMX() measure from Chapter 8, shown below.

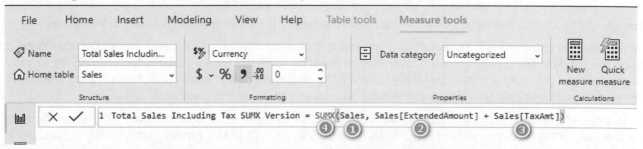

SUMX() first creates row context over the Sales table (see #1 above). It then steps through this table one row at a time. At each row, it takes the single value that is the intersection of the Sales[ExtendedAmount] column (#2) and the current row and adds it to the single value that is the intersection of the Sales[TaxAmt]

column (#3) and the current row. It does this for each row in the table (#1) and then adds up all the values (#4). These same columns from the earlier measure example now return a valid result because they exist inside a SUMX() function that has row context.

Remember that if you can't visualise what a SUMX() function is doing in the formula above, you can write a test formula as a calculated column instead so you can better visualise how it works. A calculated column and a SUMX() function essentially do the same thing; the only difference is that the calculated column permanently stores the row-by-row results in the table, and the SUMX() function does not.

> **Note:** One thing I often get asked about the formula above is "Why does the formula refer to the table name twice—once in the first parameter and again in the second parameter?" Remember that it is best practice to always fully qualify a column name by prepending the table name. Technically, the formula above would work without the table names in front of ExtendedAmount (see #2 above) and TaxAmt (#3), but including the table names is a best practice authoring technique that ensures clarity.

Row Context Does Not Automatically Create Filter Context

This is a very important point that you must understand clearly: Row context does not automatically create filter context. Row context and filter context are two concepts that are completely independent. To understand this better, you can create a new calculated column in the Products table. In the Data view, go to the Fields pane, right-click the Products table (see #1 below), and select New Column (#2).

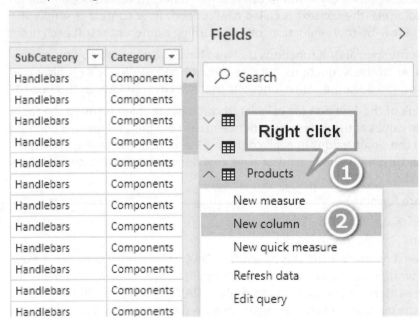

Add the following calculated column to the table but don't press Enter yet:

```
Total Sales Column = SUM(Sales[ExtendedAmount])
```

You should recognise the right side of this formula because it is part of the first formula in this book.

What value do you think will appear in every row of this new column when you press Enter? Do you expect it to be the total for the product in each row? Do you expect it to be the total for all products? Well, the answer might surprise you, and it is directly related to the point that row context does not automatically create filter context. Press Enter and take a look at the new calculated column in the Data view.

As you can see in the figure below, the value is the same for every single row in the table. There is no filtering on the Sales table (or any other table, for that matter) as a result of this formula, and hence the answer is always the same for every row. There is row context in this formula because it is a calculated column: The rows are evaluated one at a time. But that row context does not create filter context. Again, row context has nothing to do with filter context; row context and filter context are completely independent concepts. Earlier in this chapter, you learnt that there are only three places filter context can come from: a visual, the Filters pane, or a `CALCULATE()` function. In the calculated column in the example shown below, there is neither a visual nor a `CALCULATE()` function, so there simply cannot be filter context. Given that there is no filter context, the `Sales` table is completely unfiltered, and hence `SUM(Sales[ExtendedAmount])` must return the result of the unfiltered `Sales` table. This is not intuitive, but it is how it works.

StartDate	EndDate	Status	SubCategory	Category	Total Sales Column
1/07/2017	30/06/2018		Handlebars	Components	$29,358,677.22
1/07/2018		Current	Handlebars	Components	$29,358,677.22
1/07/2017	30/06/2018		Handlebars	Components	$29,358,677.22
1/07/2018		Current	Handlebars	Components	$29,358,677.22
1/07/2017	30/06/2018		Handlebars	Components	$29,358,677.22
1/07/2018		Current	Handlebars	Components	$29,358,677.22
1/07/2017	30/06/2018		Handlebars	Components	$29,358,677.22
1/07/2018		Current	Handlebars	Components	$29,358,677.22
1/07/2017	30/06/2018		Handlebars	Components	$29,358,677.22
1/07/2018		Current	Handlebars	Components	$29,358,677.22
1/07/2017	30/06/2018		Handlebars	Components	$29,358,677.22

Formula bar: `1 Total Sales Column = SUM(Sales[ExtendedAmount])`

Fields: Search, Status, SubCategory, Total All Products, Total Number of ..., Total Number of ..., Total Number of ..., Total Sales Column, Σ Weight

Creating Context Transition

It is possible to convert the row context from a calculated column into filter context through a process called context transition. To do this, simply wrap the formula from the previous section in a `CALCULATE()` function, as shown below.

Formula bar: `1 Total Sales Column = CALCULATE(SUM(Sales[ExtendedAmount]))`

StartDate	EndDate	Status	SubCategory	Category	Total Sales Column
1/07/2017	30/06/2018		Wheels	Components	
1/07/2016	30/06/2017		Caps	Clothing	
1/07/2017	30/06/2018		Caps	Clothing	
1/07/2018		Current	Caps	Clothing	$19,688.10
1/07/2018		Current	Bike Racks	Accessories	$39,360.00
1/07/2018		Current	Bike Stands	Accessories	$39,591.00
1/07/2018		Current	Bottles and Cages	Accessories	$21,177.56
1/07/2018		Current	Bottles and Cages	Accessories	$20,229.75
1/07/2018		Current	Bottles and Cages	Accessories	$15,390.88
1/07/2018		Current	Cleaners	Accessories	$7,218.60
1/07/2018		Current	Fenders	Accessories	$46,619.58

Fields: Search, Status, SubCategory, Total All Products, Total Number of ..., Total Number of ..., Total Number of ..., Total Sales Column, Σ Weight

When you do this, the row context that exists in the calculated column is transformed into an equivalent filter context. The `CALCULATE()` function then tells the Power BI filter to add a new filter on the `Products` table, and then that filter propagates through the relationship to the `Sales` table before the calculation is completed, and it does so for each row in the table. You will therefore potentially end up with a different value in each row of the column. The value returned to each row of this new column in the `Products` table is the total sales for that product.

Note: Some rows are blank because there are no sales.

You can think of the formula working like this:

```
= CALCULATE(
    SUM(Sales[ExtendedAmount]),
    Products[ProductKey] = the product represented by this row in the table
    )
```

This pseudocode is illustrative only, but it shows that the concept of context transition can work anywhere that row context exists—that is, in calculated columns as well as in iterators like SUMX() and other functions covered later in this book. This is the special use case mentioned in Chapter 9, where there are no filters at all needed inside CALCULATE() but instead CALCULATE() creates a new filter context from the row context by using context transition. You can add additional filters inside CALCULATE(), too, if you want or need to, but none are required to trigger context transition.

The Hidden Implicit CALCULATE()

Now that you know that you can use CALCULATE() to convert row context into filter context, there is one more thing you need to know. Consider this measure from earlier in the book:

```
Total Sales (the measure) = SUM(Sales[ExtendedAmount])
```

Now think back to the first version of the calculated column above. What happened when we added a new column in the Products table, as follows?

```
Total Sales Column =SUM(Sales[ExtendedAmount])
```

Do you remember? We got the value $29.4 million all the way down the new column in the Products table. Why? Because there is row context in a calculated column, but there is no filter context. The Sales table is therefore completely unfiltered, and hence SUM(Sales[ExtendedAmount]) simply must return $29.4 million for every row.

Now back to this measure:

```
Total Sales (the measure) = SUM(Sales[ExtendedAmount])
```

Notice that the formula for this measure is identical to the calculated column (the first example above but with a different name, of course). So if the formula inside the measure is identical to the formula in the calculated column, you can be excused for thinking that you could substitute the formula in the calculated column with the actual measure, adjusted as follows:

```
Total Sales Column = [Total Sales]
```

If the measure [Total Sales] has the same formula embedded, won't we get the same result? Well, actually no; we get a different result from before, as shown below.

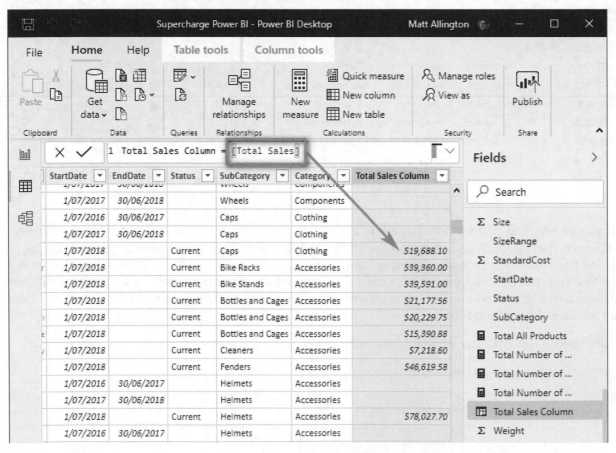

Go back and look again. Here is a summary of what you will find:

```
Total Sales Column (Ver 1) = SUM(Sales[ExtendedAmount])
```

This calculated column returns $29.4 million all the way down the column. There is row context but no filter context, so the formula must return $29.4 million for each row in the table.

This next calculated column returns the total sales for each product in the `Products` table (a different number for each product):

```
Total Sales Column (Ver 2) = CALCULATE(SUM(Sales[ExtendedAmount]))
```

There is row context, and because of the CALCULATE() function, the row context is converted to an equivalent filter context through the process of context transition; there is row context and filter context. CALCULATE() converts the row context from the `Products` table into an equivalent filter context, and this new filter context propagates to the `Sales` table for each row of the calculated column.

The following calculated column also returns the total sales for each product in the `Products` table:

```
Total Sales Column (Ver 3) = [Total Sales]
```

The calculated column `Total Sales Column (Ver 3)` returns exactly the same result as `Total Sales Column (Ver 2)`. If you take a look inside the measure `[Total Sales]`, you can't see a CALCULATE() function; the measure does not include CALCULATE(). But there is an implicit CALCULATE() that you can't see. Every measure has an implicit CALCULATE() automatically added by Power BI; that is why `Total Sales Column (Ver 3)` behaves like `Total Sales Column (Ver 2)` and not like `Total Sales Column (Ver 1)`.

> **Note:** If you've arrived at this point and don't fully understand context transition, don't worry, you are not alone. This is one of the hardest topics in this book to learn and understand well. Sleep on it for a few nights, get some practice, and then come back and reread this chapter again (along with Chapter 9, on CALCULATE()). You may need to reread this content many times before it completely sinks in. If you get confused, go back to the lay terms I used for the first nine chapters of this book: Filter behaviour is the same as filter context; row-by-row evaluation is the same as row context. When you have more experience under your belt (in, say, 6 to 18 months), you may be interested in expanding your skills and depth of knowledge further. I offer a great training course called "Demystifying DAX" that can help you go to the next level of understanding, if and when you a ready. You can learn more at http://xbi.com.au/adv-dax-training.

12: DAX Topic: IF(), SWITCH(), and FIND()

DAX has a number of useful functions that allow you to apply a test and then branch the formula based on the results from that test. You will most likely be familiar with this concept from the IF() function in Excel. This chapter covers a few functions that are useful in DAX.

The IF() Function

The IF() function in DAX, which uses the following syntax, is almost identical to IF() in Excel:

        IF(*Logical Test*, *Result if True*, [*Result if False*])

Note that the last parameter, [*Result if False*], is optional. If you omit this parameter and the result is False, the IF() formula returns BLANK(). This is very useful because a matrix or chart in Power BI will not show values if the result in the Values section is BLANK().

The SWITCH() Function

The SWITCH() function is a lot like Select Case in VBA programming. The syntax of the SWITCH() function is as follows:

        SWITCH(*expression*, *value*, *result*[, *value*, *result*]...[, *else*])

This syntax is a little confusing, so let's go through a simple example with another calculated column. To begin the example, right-click on the Customers table in the Fields pane, select New Column, and enter the following formula:

```
House Ownership =
    SWITCH(Customers[HouseOwnerFlag],
        1,"Owns their house",
        0,"Doesn't own their house",
        "Unknown"
    )
```

It is much easier to understand SWITCH() if you use DAX Formatter to improve the layout, as shown below. You can see in this figure that line 3 is the branching point. The possible values in the HouseOwnerFlag column are 0 and 1 in this instance. Lines 4 and 5 offer up pairs of input and output values. So if the value of HouseOwnerFlag is 1, the result "Owns their house" is returned. If the value of HouseOwnerFlag is 0, the result "Doesn't own their house" is returned.

```
    DAX           1    House Ownership =
    FORMATTER     2    SWITCH (
                  3        Customers[HouseOwnerFlag],
                  4        1, "Owns their house",
                  5        0, "Doesn't own their house",
                  6        "Unknown"
                  7    )
```

Line 6 is a single value, and it applies to all other possible values of HouseOwnerFlag (although there are no other values in this example).

Note: You will see a much more exciting use of the SWITCH() function in Chapter 20.

The FIND() Function

The FIND() function in DAX is almost identical to the FIND() function in Excel. In DAX, it has this format:

```
= FIND(FindText, WithinText, [StartPos], [NotFoundValue])
```

Even though this syntax suggests that [StartPos] and [NotFoundValue] are optional, in my experience (as of this writing), you actually do need to provide values for these parameters, or the result returned is #ERROR.

Example: Using IF() and FIND()

In this section, you will see how to create a calculated column in one of your lookup tables. As I have said previously, it is perfectly valid to create calculated columns in lookup tables, but wherever possible, it is a better practice to create these columns in your source data or by using Power Query. Remember why this is important:

- Calculated columns may take up more space than imported columns (but this is generally not a major issue for lookup tables).
- If you are manually creating a calculated column, it exists only in that single workbook, and you need to re-create it over and over for every other workbook where you need the column.

If it is not possible to create a column in your source data for some reason, then creating a calculated column instead is a great solution, particularly for lookup tables.

In this example, you are going to create a Mountain Products column that doesn't exist in your lookup table (Products). In this new column, any product with the word mountain in the description will be flagged as a mountain product.

Right-click the Products table in the Fields pane, select New Column, and type the following formula:

```
Mountain Products = FIND("Mountain", Products[ModelName],1, 0)
```

Switch to the Data view so you can check the results of your new column.

> **Note:** Remember that it is your responsibility to check that your formulas give the expected results, and switching to the Data view can help you validate this.

This formula searches for the word mountain in the ModelName column. Remember that because a calculated column has row context, it is possible to refer to the column in this way, and it will calculate a result for every row in the Products table and store the answer in the column.

The result is an integer representing the starting position where the word mountain is found. If the word mountain is not found, the last parameter in the formula (which is the value 0 in this case) is returned. So you get something like the Mountain Products column shown in the image below.

ModelName	Description	StartDate	EndDate	Mountain Products
LL Mountain Handlebars	All-purpose bar for on or off-road.	1/07/2017	30/06/2018	4
LL Mountain Handlebars	All-purpose bar for on or off-road.	1/07/2018		4
ML Mountain Handlebars	Tough aluminum alloy bars for downhill.	1/07/2017	30/06/2018	4
ML Mountain Handlebars	Tough aluminum alloy bars for downhill.	1/07/2018		4
HL Mountain Handlebars	Flat bar strong enough for the pro circuit.	1/07/2017	30/06/2018	4
HL Mountain Handlebars	Flat bar strong enough for the pro circuit.	1/07/2018		4
LL Road Handlebars	Unique shape provides easier reach to the levers.	1/07/2017	30/06/2018	0
LL Road Handlebars	Unique shape provides easier reach to the levers.	1/07/2018		0
ML Road Handlebars	Anatomically shaped aluminum tube bar will suit all riders	1/07/2017	30/06/2018	0

This table is not overly useful as is, but you can wrap an `IF()` statement around this formula to make it more useful. As shown below, you can use the `IF()` statement to return `True` if the number is greater than zero (i.e., if it is a mountain product) and return `False` if it is equal to zero (i.e., it is not a mountain product).

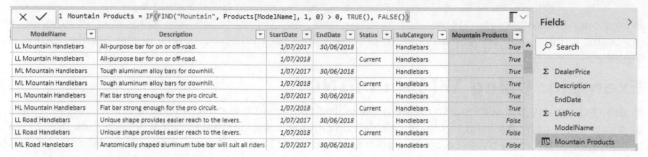

Now you have a new calculated column, and you have further enhanced your data model to make it more useful. Remember that this calculated column takes up some space in your file and disk. However, given the small number of unique values (only `True` and `False` in this case) and the fact that this column is in a lookup table, the space this particular column takes up is minimal.

> **Note:** The greater the number of unique values in a column, the more disk space and memory the column consumes. If a column is small and adds value to your model, then there is no reason not to create it.

You can now use this new column anywhere in your Power BI report to produce new insights that weren't previously visible in the data. Because this formula is a column in the data model, it can be used to filter a matrix, or it can be used in a chart, as shown below.

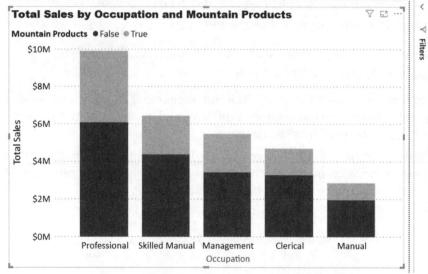

Enhancing Your Data Models

Let me just pause for a brief moment and reflect on an important point: The role of a data modeller is to build a model that adds value to the data. Raw data is useful, but a well-designed data model is gold. Your job as a data modeller is to build a data model that enhances the raw data and makes it more useful than the raw data alone. The example above does just this. There is nothing explicit in the raw data that allows you to visualise sales based on the concept of a mountain product. If you want to have this ability, you have to create the capability in the tool. In doing so, you are enhancing the raw data and building a useful (and possibly invaluable) asset that can be used and reused as needed.

13: DAX Topic: VALUES(), HASONEVALUE(), SELECTEDVALUE(), and CONCATENATEX()

Before we get to the new functions in this chapter, you need to understand the concept of virtual tables. Before we actually get to virtual tables, though, let me step back and talk first about physical tables. A physical table is a table that is loaded and materialised inside the Power BI data model. If you switch to the Model view, you can see physical tables. In the case of the standard AdventureWorks database used in this book, there are five physical tables (Calendar, Customers, Products, Territories, and Sales).

In the DAX language, there are special functions called table functions that create tables of data. These functions create "virtual" tables in that these tables are not materialised and physically stored and visible inside the Model view in Power BI. Virtual tables behave exactly like physical tables, but the tables are simply not materialised or visible to you.

Table Functions Inside CALCULATE()

The most common place (but not the only place) to use a table function in DAX is inside a CALCULATE() function. In Chapter 9 I introduced the idea that CALCULATE() can use two types of filters: simple filters and table filters. Simple filters are in this form:

> *TableName[ColumnName] = some value*

As its name suggests, a table filter takes a table as a filter input. In other words, you use an existing table (or create a virtual table on the fly) that contains the rows you want included in the filter parameter, and then CALCULATE() applies that filter to the data model before completing the evaluation of the main expression.

Using Virtual Tables

The tables you create using DAX table functions inside measures can be thought of as being virtual because they are not physically stored as part of the data model. They are created on the fly inside your DAX measure formulas and can be used to filter your formulas to just the rows of data that exist in the virtual table. Importantly, when you create a virtual table using a formula, the new virtual table has a virtual relationship to the data model, and that virtual relationship propagates the filters in exactly the same way that the permanent relationships do. (You'll hear more about this shortly.) Virtual tables are said to retain lineage with their source tables.

The VALUES() Function

VALUES() is the first function you have come to in this book that returns a (virtual) table. If you type the word VALUES into the formula bar and read the IntelliSense, you can see that this function returns a table, as shown below.

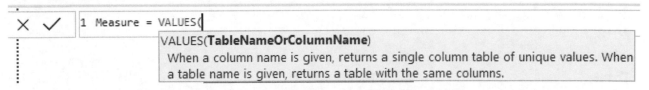

One important thing to note about VALUES() is that it respects the initial filter context coming from your visuals. So if you combine this fact that VALUES() respects the current filter context with the information provided by IntelliSense in the image above, you can see that VALUES() returns a table that contains the list of all possible values in the current filter context (i.e., after the filters have been applied from the visuals).

It's time to work through some examples to demonstrate the point.

A Calendar Example

Set up a new matrix like the one shown below by putting Calendar Year on Rows.

CalendarYear

2016
2017
2018
2019

Then write the following measure in the Calendar table:

        Total Months in Calendar = COUNTROWS(VALUES('Calendar'[MonthName]))

> **Note:** The following formula does not work here:
>
>   Total Months in Calendar wrong = COUNTROWS('Calendar'[MonthName])
>
> This formula doesn't work because COUNTROWS() expects a table as the input, but 'Calendar'[MonthName] is not a table; rather, it is a column that is part of a bigger table (the Calendar table, in this case).

Say that you wrap 'Calendar'[MonthName] inside the VALUES() function, like this:

        VALUES('Calendar'[MonthName])

The original single column that is part of the Calendar table is converted into a virtual table in its own right, and the new virtual table retains a relationship (i.e., lineage) to the original Calendar table. This new table returned by VALUES() is still a single column, but now it is technically a table with a single a column instead of simply being a single column that is part of some other table (Calendar, in this case).

So VALUES('Calendar'[MonthName]) returns a virtual single-column table of possible values that respects the initial filter context coming from the matrix. It is not possible to put this new table created by VALUES() into a measure on its own unless you wrap it inside some other formula that returns a single value (e.g., an aggregator function like COUNTROWS()). In the earlier example (shown again below), the VALUES() part of the formula creates the virtual table, and then the COUNTROWS() function counts how many rows are in the table:

        Total Months in Calendar = COUNTROWS(VALUES('Calendar'[MonthName]))

CalendarYear	Total Months in Calendar
2016	6
2017	12
2018	12
2019	12
Total	**12**

Notice that the year 2016 has only 6 months, and each of the other years has 12. This is proof that the VALUES() function respects the initial filter context from the matrix. In the AdventureWorks database, the first year of data starts on 1 July 2016, so there are only 6 months in the Calendar table for the year 2016. The initial filter for the first row in the matrix is 'Calendar'[Year] = 2016. That filter is applied first, and then the measure [Total Months in Calendar] is evaluated. VALUES() respects the filter coming from the visual prior to the calculation.

Conceptualising Virtual Tables

VALUES() can take a column or a table as its only parameter. When you use a column as the parameter, VALUES() generates a virtual single-column table that contains all the unique values that exist in that source column. The image below conceptualises this process.

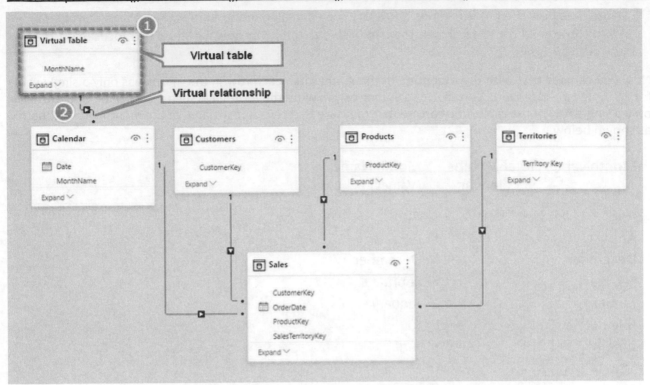

Remember that this is just an illustration of a concept to help you understand what is happening under the hood. There is no actual physical table materialised, but this image helps you conceptualise what the virtual table would look like if it were materialised in your model. In the image, the virtual table (see #1 above) has a virtual relationship (#2) to the original table it comes from; this is its lineage. The new virtual table respects the current filter context coming from the visual in the report.

Returning a Single Value

There is another very cool feature of VALUES() that is very powerful: In the special case where VALUES() returns just a single row (i.e., there is just one value), you can refer to this value directly in your formulas.

If you start with the example created above, remove CalendarYear from Rows, and put MonthName on Rows instead, you should get a matrix like the one shown below.

MonthName	Total Months in Calendar
April	1
August	1
December	1
February	1
January	1
July	1
June	1
March	1
May	1
November	1
October	1
September	1
Total	**12**

Note: See how the month names above are sorted in alphabetical order? Yes, this is a problem. I will show you how to fix this at the end of this chapter. For now, let's just stay focused on the VALUES() function.

Now you can see that with the exception of the grand total, each row in the matrix has only a single value for [Total Months in Calendar]. So as long as you write the formula in such a way that it operates over only a single row of the table, you can create a measure that returns the name of the month into the matrix, as shown below.

MonthName	Total Months in Calendar	Month Name (Values)
April	1	April
August	1	August
December	1	December
February	1	February
January	1	January
July	1	July
June	1	June
March	1	March
May	1	May
November	1	November
October	1	October
September	1	September
Total	**12**	

This use case for VALUES() works only if there is a single value in the VALUES() virtual table. If there is more than one value in the VALUES() virtual table, the formula returns an error. Therefore, to write this formula, you need to provide protection for the possible scenario where VALUES('Calendar'[MonthName]) has more than one row in the table. This is done using the function HASONEVALUE(), like so:

```
Month Name (Values) =
    IF(HASONEVALUE('Calendar'[MonthName],
        VALUES('Calendar'[MonthName])
    )
```

Remember that the structure of an IF() statement is as follows:

```
= IF(Logical Test, Result if True, [Result if False])
```

The last parameter is optional. If you leave it out, then you are accepting the default value, BLANK().

To see this more clearly, set up a matrix with the columns Products[ModelName] and Products[ProductName] on Rows and the measure [Total Number of Products COUNTROWS Version] (from Chapter 4) on Values. Your matrix should look as shown below.

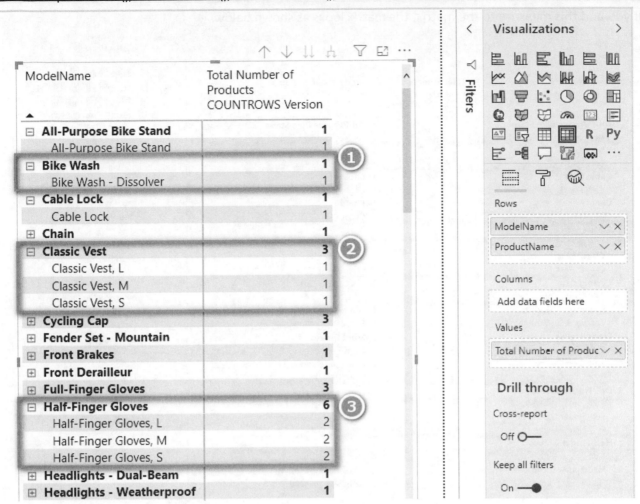

Note that there is only one product for some models (see #1 above), and there are multiple products for some other models (#2 and #3).

Now write the following measure:

```
Product Name(Values) =
    IF(HASONEVALUE(Products[ProductName]),
        VALUES(Products[ProductName])
    )
```

If you add this measure to the matrix, the matrix looks as shown below.

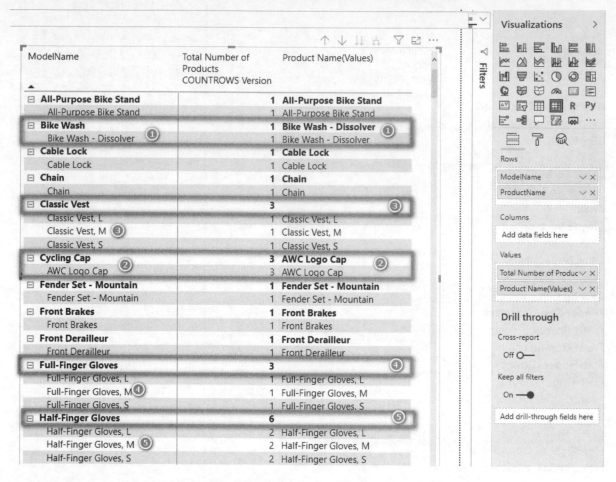

Notice that when there is only one product for a model, the product name is displayed (see #1 and #2 above). If there are multiple products for a model, a blank is returned for `ModelName` (#3, #4, and #5).

Now write the following incorrect formula, which omits `HASONEVALUE()`:

```
Product Name(Values) Wrong = VALUES(Products[ProductName])
```

If you put this measure in the matrix, you get the error shown below.

Couldn't load the data for this visual   ✕

MdxScript(Model) (32, 47) Calculation error in measure
'Products'[Product Name(Values) Wrong]: A table of multiple values
was supplied where a single value was expected.

Copy details

| Send a Frown | Close |

The key information in this error message is "A table of multiple values was supplied where a single value was expected." You can use `VALUES()` in a measure only if it returns a single value. If `VALUES()` returns more than a single value, it throws an error. The `HASONEVALUE()` function is used to protect against the specific case where `VALUES()` returns more than a single value, and the `IF(HASONEVALUE())` pattern prevents this error from occurring.

The SELECTEDVALUE() Function

Power BI has a function called SELECTEDVALUE() that is another example of the syntax sugar concept that has come up several times. Here is the syntax for this function:

```
SELECTEDVALUE(ColumnName, AlternateResult)
```

SELECTEDVALUE() was created to replace the following complex formula from the previous section:

```
Product Name(Values) =
    IF(HASONEVALUE(Products[ProductName]),
        VALUES(Products[ProductName])
    )
```

The SELECTEDVALUE() function allows you to rewrite this formula as follows:

```
Product Name Alternate = SELECTEDVALUE(Products[ProductName])
```

Under the hood, SELECTEDVALUE() performs the IF(HASONEVALUE()) test, and it returns the single value in the column if there is just one. AlternateResult is BLANK() by default.

> **Note:** The SELECTEDVALUE() function is not available in Power Pivot for Excel at the time of this writing, so you need to use the IF(HASONEVALUE()) formula instead when using Excel.

CONCATENATEX() to the Rescue

Power BI has a special DAX function called CONCATENATEX() that iterates over a list of values in a table and concatenates them together into a single value. By using this function, you can write a formula that returns the single value when there is just one value but concatenate all the values into a single value when there are multiple values. You could write the earlier VALUES() formula like this:

```
Product Name(Values) ConcatenateX =
    CONCATENATEX(
        VALUES(Products[ProductName]),
        [ProductName],
        ", "
    )
```

With this formula, you get the result shown below. I have added a slicer here to make it possible to change the number of items visible in the matrix.

ModelName

- ◼ All-Purpose Bike Stand
- ◼ Bike Wash
- ☐ Cable Lock
- ☐ Chain
- ◼ Classic Vest
- ☐ Cycling Cap
- ☐ Fender Set - Mountain
- ☐ Front Brakes
- ☐ Front Derailleur
- ◼ Full-Finger Gloves
- ☐ Half-Finger Gloves
- ☐ Headlights - Dual-Beam
- ☐ Headlights - Weatherproof
- ☐ Hitch Rack - 4-Bike
- ☐ HL Bottom Bracket
- ☐ HL Crankset
- ☐ HL Fork
- ☐ HL Headset
- ☐ HL Mountain Frame

ModelName	Total Number of Products COUNTROWS Version	Product Name(Values) ConcatenateX
⊟ **All-Purpose Bike Stand**	**1**	**All-Purpose Bike Stand**
All-Purpose Bike Stand	1	All-Purpose Bike Stand
⊟ **Bike Wash**	**1**	**Bike Wash - Dissolver**
Bike Wash - Dissolver	1	Bike Wash - Dissolver
⊟ **Classic Vest**	**3**	**Classic Vest, S, Classic Vest, M, Classic Vest, L**
Classic Vest, L	1	Classic Vest, L
Classic Vest, M	1	Classic Vest, M
Classic Vest, S	1	Classic Vest, S
⊟ **Full-Finger Gloves**	**3**	**Full-Finger Gloves, S, Full-Finger Gloves, M, Full-Finger Gloves, L**
Full-Finger Gloves, L	1	Full-Finger Gloves, L
Full-Finger Gloves, M	1	Full-Finger Gloves, M
Full-Finger Gloves, S	1	Full-Finger Gloves, S
Total	**8**	**Full-Finger Gloves, S, Full-Finger Gloves, M, Full-Finger Gloves, L, Classic Vest, S, Classic Vest, M, Classic Vest, L, All-Purpose Bike Stand, Bike Wash - Dissolver**

Here's How: Changing the Month Name Sort Order

Earlier in this chapter I placed the month names from the `Calendar` table into a matrix (shown again below). In this matrix, the month names are sorted in alphabetical order rather than in the logical calendar order.

MonthName	Total Months in Calendar	Month Name (Values)
April	1	April
August	1	August
December	1	December
February	1	February
January	1	January
July	1	July
June	1	June
March	1	March
May	1	May
November	1	November
October	1	October
September	1	September
Total	**12**	

In Power BI (and many other software tools), by default, all columns in all tables sort in alphanumeric order. It is, however, possible to change the sort order. To do so, follow these steps:

1. Go to the Data view and navigate to the `Calendar` table. (It is not really necessary to switch to the Data view, but it is a good idea to do that in this learning example so you can see what is going on.)

2. Click in the `MonthName` column (see #1 below), click the Sort by Column button (#2), and then select the `MonthNumberOfYear` column to make it the sort column (#3).

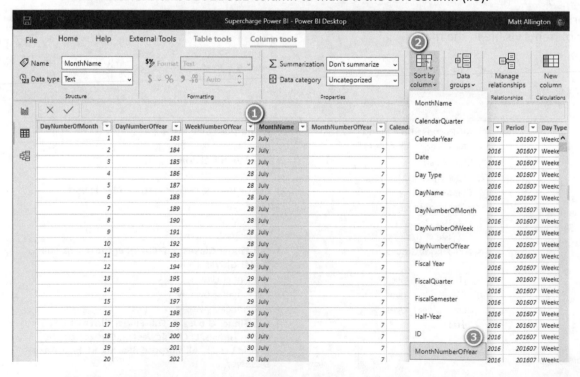

3. Return to your matrix in the Report view, and you see that the rows are sorted in logical month order, as shown below.

MonthName	Total Months in Calendar	Month Name (Values)
January	1	January
February	1	February
March	1	March
April	1	April
May	1	May
June	1	June
July	1	July
August	1	August
September	1	September
October	1	October
November	1	November
December	1	December

It is best practice to load a sort column in a lookup table for every column that needs to be sorted in an order other than alphabetic order. You should therefore always include a sort column in your Calendar table for data such as days of the week and months of the year. If you operate over a financial year that does not start in January, then you should, of course, make sure your sort column reflects that.

Note: When you create a sort column in a table, there must be a one-to-one match between the values in the sort order and the values in the column to be sorted.

Practice Exercises: VALUES()

Create a new matrix and put Products[Category] on Rows and the measure [Total Number of Products] on Values. Then write the following measures by first creating a VALUES() table and then wrapping this table inside a COUNTROWS() function, as in the example shown earlier in this chapter. Find the solutions to these practice exercises in "Appendix A: Answers to Practice Exercises" on page 252.

39. [Number of Color Variants]

40. [Number of SubCategories]

41. [Number of Size Ranges]

Use the column Products[SizeRange] for this one.

How Did It Go?

Did you end up with the following matrix?

Category	Total Number of Products	Number of Color Variants	Number of Sub Categories	Number of Size Ranges
Accessories	35	6	12	2
Bikes	125	5	3	5
Clothing	48	5	8	5
Components	189	7	14	6
Total	**397**	**10**	**37**	**11**

Note: Each of these measures is the equivalent of dragging the column name and dropping it into the Values drop zone for the matrix. When you drop a text field into the Values drop zone for a matrix in Power BI, the matrix creates an implicit measure and uses COUNT() as the aggregating method. But recall that I recommended that you avoid using implicit measures. The names created by implicit measures are not user friendly, and values are not formatted. In addition, you need DAX practice at this point, so I recommend that you write explicit DAX measures, particularly while you are learning.

The New Table Button

Business Power BI users (i.e., those who don't have a professional IT background) often find it somewhat difficult to understand the VALUES() function because you can't actually see the table it creates. So far I have shown you that even though you can't see the table, you can wrap the table inside a COUNTROWS() function so that at least you can see the number of rows in the table.

Power BI Desktop has a feature called New Table that is not currently available in Power Pivot for Excel. The New Table button is on the Modeling tab (see #1 below).

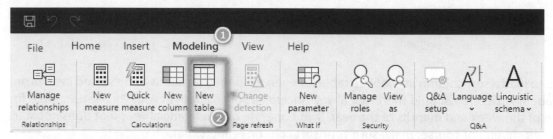

When you click the New Table button (see #2 above), you see that you can write a formula in the formula bar, as shown below.

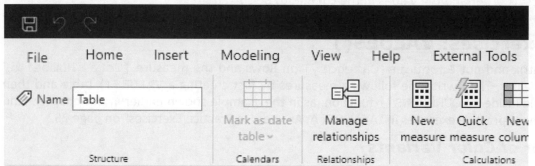

When you create a new table by using this button, you can write a formula (e.g., using VALUES()) that returns a table, and the table is added to the data model; that is, it is physically materialised into the model.

Say that you write a table with the following DAX formula:

```
Product Colors = VALUES(Products[Color])
```

You get the new table shown below in the data model (visible in the Data view).

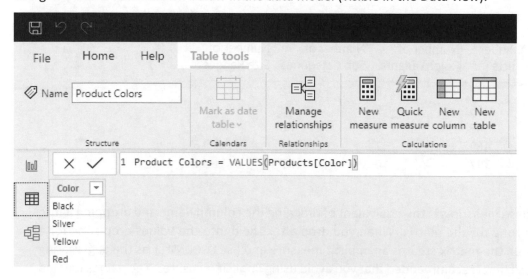

Recall that VALUES () returns all the unique values in the current filter context. A new table doesn't respond to filters from the Report view, so there is no initial filter context for a new table. The table above therefore shows a complete list of all possible values for Products[color] in the entire Products table (with no filters applied).

The New Table button is very useful for materialising any virtual table so you can "see" the contents of the table. Later in the book, when you learn about the FILTER() function, you will see how you can add your own filter to one of these tables so you can see a subset of a table with a filter applied. For now, it is just good to know that if you ever can't get your head around a virtual table, you can always materialise it by using this feature so you can take a peek, and then you can delete it when you are done.

Practice Exercises: VALUES(), Continued

For the following practice exercises, begin with the matrix from Practice Exercises 39–41 but remove the measure [Number of Size Ranges] from the matrix. Then write the following measures, each of which returns a single value (the text name) into a cell in the matrix. Each formula has the word (Values) in the name, so it is clear that the formulas are written using the VALUES() function; this is just a "note to self." In each example, make sure you wrap your VALUES() function in an IF(HASONEVALUE()) function, as in the example earlier in this chapter. Alternatively, you can use the SELECTEDVALUE() function if you prefer. Find the solutions to these practice exercises in "Appendix A: Answers to Practice Exercises" on page 252.

42. [Product Category (Values)]

43. [Product SubCategory (Values)]

44. [Product Color (Values)]

How Did It Go?

Did you end up with the following matrix?

Category	Total Number of Products	Number of Color Variants	Number of Sub Categories	Product Category (Values)	Product Subcategory (Values)	Product Color (Values)
Accessories	35	6	12	Accessories		
Bikes	125	5	3	Bikes		
Clothing	48	5	8	Clothing		
Components	189	7	14	Components		
Total	**397**	**10**	**37**			

Notice that two of these measures are blank. This is because the VALUES() formula has more than one value, and hence the IF(HASONEVALUE()) (or SELECTEDVALUE()) part of the formula returns BLANK(); this is the default if you omit the last parameter.

45. Modifying Practice Exercise 43

Try editing the IF() statement for [Product SubCategory (Values)] so that it returns the value More than 1 SubCategory instead of BLANK(). Recall that the syntax for IF() is IF(*Logical Test*, *Result if True*, *Result if False*).

46. Modifying Practice Exercise 44

Now try editing the IF() statement for [Product Color (Values)] so that it returns More than 1 Color instead of BLANK().

How Did It Go?

Did you end up with the following matrix?

Category	Total Number of Products	Number of Color Variants	Number of Sub Categories	Product Category (Values)	Product Subcategory (Values)	Product Color (Values)
Accessories	35	6	12	Accessories	More than 1 SubCategory	More than 1 Color
Bikes	125	5	3	Bikes	More than 1 SubCategory	More than 1 Color
Clothing	48	5	8	Clothing	More than 1 SubCategory	More than 1 Color
Components	189	7	14	Components	More than 1 SubCategory	More than 1 Color
Total	**397**	**10**	**37**		**More than 1 SubCategory**	**More than 1 Color**

Finally, you can add to your report a couple of slicers—for color and subcategory—from the Products table. When you click on these slicers, the values in the matrix update to reflect the filtering in the slicer(s), as shown below.

Category	Total Number of Products	Number of Color Variants	Number of Sub Categories	Product Category (Values)	Product Subcategory (Values)	Product Color (Values)
Accessories	3	1	1	Accessories	Helmets	Blue
Bikes	13	1	1	Bikes	Touring Bikes	Blue
Clothing	3	1	1	Clothing	Vests	Blue
Components	9	1	1	Components	Touring Frames	Blue
Total	**28**	**1**	**4**		**More than 1 SubCategory**	**Blue**

SubCategory
- ☐ Helmets
- ☐ Touring Bikes
- ☐ Touring Frames
- ☐ Vests

Color
- ☐ Black
- ■ Blue
- ☐ Grey
- ☐ Multi
- ☐ NA
- ☐ Red
- ☐ Silver
- ☐ Silver/Black
- ☐ White
- ☐ Yellow

14: DAX Topic: ALL(), REMOVEFILTERS(), ALLEXCEPT(), and ALLSELECTED()

The DAX functions ALL(), ALLEXCEPT(), ALLSELECTED(), and REMOVEFILTERS() are very similar in what they do. Let's start with ALL() and then look at the differences between this function and the others.

The ALL() Function

Basically, the ALL() function creates a virtual table that contains all possible unique values from the source. This can be tricky to understand because you can't see a virtual table, and if you can't see it, then how can you understand it? The easiest way to understand the way ALL() behaves as a virtual table is with a couple of examples.

ALL() Compared to VALUES()

In Chapter 13, I showed how to materialise the VALUES() function by going to the Modeling tab, clicking on the New Table button, and adding the following formula:

        Product Colors Values = VALUES(Products[Color])

VALUES() is a table function, so you can materialise a table by using the New Table button in Power BI. You can use the same technique with the ALL() function:

        Product Colors All = ALL(Products[Color])

In this case, when you use the New Table button to materialise the table, ALL() returns exactly the same table as VALUES(). But even though these two functions deliver the same table in this scenario, there is a very important difference between them. The VALUES() function respects the filter context prior to returning a table, and the ALL() function ignores (or removes) the filter context. In the case of the table materialised using the New Table button, no filter context exists, so the two functions return the same result. But if there were filter context, these two functions would behave differently.

There is a second difference between VALUES() and ALL(): ALL() can take more than one parameter, so it can combine more than one column at a time into a new table. You can see this by looking at the Intelli-Sense, as shown below.

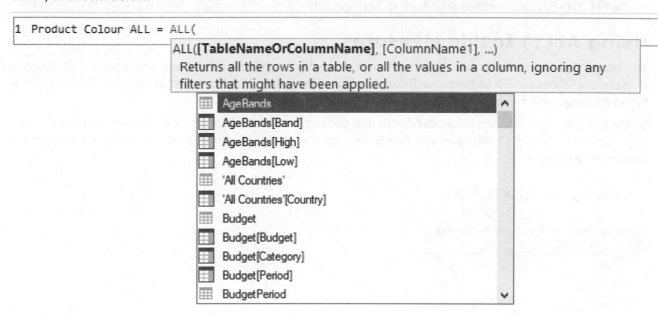

Consider the following formula:

        Product Color/Category ALL = ALL(Products[Color],Products[Category])

If you write this as a new table, you can "see" what it does. You get a new table that looks like the one in the image below (which shows only the first 12 rows of many).

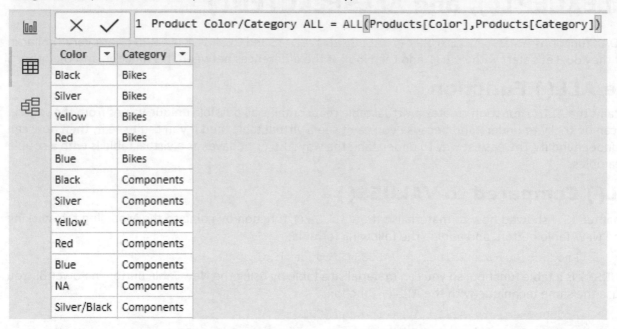

The ALL() formula above creates a table containing all the unique combinations that exist in the table from the specified columns with all filters removed.

> **Note:** In the examples above, I have materialised these tables so you can see the result, but this is just for testing purposes. Under normal circumstances, you use the ALL() function as a virtual table function inside another DAX formula. The virtual table behaves exactly as it would if it existed as a physical table inside your model, including as if it had a relationship between the new table and the source table. But because it is a virtual table, you never actually "see" the result. This is what makes table functions difficult to learn in DAX.

Using ALL() Inside Measures

The most common use of the ALL() function is as a table function inside a measure. The ALL() function is really useful because it can remove filters coming from visuals. (Remember that VALUES() respects the filters coming from a visual, and ALL() ignores or removes the filters.)

To see how ALL() works, create a new matrix and put Products[Category] on Rows and put the [Total Number of Products] measure you created earlier into the Values drop zone for the visual. You get the matrix shown below.

Category	Total Number of Products
Accessories	35
Bikes	125
Clothing	48
Components	189
Total	**397**

Technically, what is happening here is that the first row in the matrix is filtering the Products table so that only products that are of type Products[Category]="Accessories" are unfiltered in the source table (i.e., the Products table); the other products are all filtered out. You can't see that the table is filtered, but you can imagine what the underlying table in your data model would look like with a filter applied to Accessories behind the scenes. In fact, let's take a diversion and go and see what that actually looks like. Switch to the Data view, navigate to the `Products` table, and go to the `Category` column. From the drop-down arrow at the top of the column (see #1 below), you can select Accessories (#2) to place a filter on it and then click OK (#3).

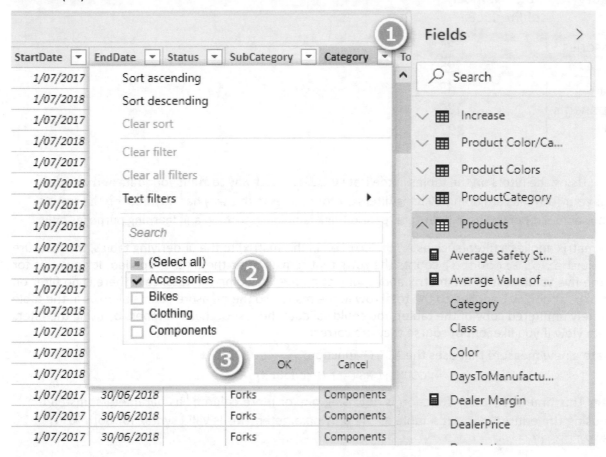

You now have a filter on the `Products` table so that it shows just the products that are accessories. After you apply this filter, you see some very important information in the bottom-left corner of the screen, as shown below.

	Description	StartDate	EndDate	Status	SubCategory	Category
	Versatile 70 oz hydration pack offers extra storage, easy-fil	1/07/2018		Current	Hydration Packs	Accessories
	High-density rubber.	1/07/2018		Current	Tires and Tubes	Accessories
	Lightweight carbon reinforced for an unrivaled ride at an	1/07/2018		Current	Tires and Tubes	Accessories
	Higher density rubber.	1/07/2018		Current	Tires and Tubes	Accessories
	Same great treads as more expensive tire with a less exper	1/07/2018		Current	Tires and Tubes	Accessories
	Incredible traction, lightweight carbon reinforced.	1/07/2018		Current	Tires and Tubes	Accessories
	Great traction, high-density rubber.	1/07/2018		Current	Tires and Tubes	Accessories
	Comparible traction, less expensive wire bead casing.	1/07/2018		Current	Tires and Tubes	Accessories
	General purpose tube.	1/07/2018		Current	Tires and Tubes	Accessories
	Conventional all-purpose tube.	1/07/2018		Current	Tires and Tubes	Accessories
	Self-sealing tube.	1/07/2018		Current	Tires and Tubes	Accessories
	Includes 8 different size patches, glue and sandpaper.	1/07/2018		Current	Tires and Tubes	Accessories
	Simple and light-weight. Emergency patches stored in han	1/07/2017	30/06/2018		Pumps	Accessories
	Designed for convenience. Fits in your pocket. Aluminum	1/07/2017	30/06/2018		Pumps	Accessories
	Durable, water-proof nylon construction with easy access.	1/07/2017	30/06/2018		Panniers	Accessories

Table: Products (397 rows, 35 filtered rows) Column: Category (4 distinct

You can see in this image that there are 397 rows in the `Products` table, but after the filter is applied, just 35 rows remain. This is exactly the number that appears in the matrix visual (shown again below for convenience).

Category	Total Number of Products
Accessories	35
Bikes	125
Clothing	48
Components	189
Total	**397**

Note: Using the filters on the tables in the Data view is a great way to audit your data and visualise what your formulas are doing. Placing filters on your tables in this way has no effect on the results in your actual reports. These filters are for auditing, debugging, testing, and learning purposes only.

After the matrix applies a filter (such as `Accessories` in this matrix) to the underlying tables, the measure `[Total Number of Products]` counts the rows that remain after the filter is applied. It does this for each of the five value cells in the matrix above, one at a time, including the total cell. There is no filter on `Products[Category]` applied to the total row in the matrix, so the measure counts all rows in the table (a completely unfiltered copy of the table). You could validate the rest of these numbers by using the filters in the Data view if you like, but of course they are correct.

Now create a new measure that uses the `ALL()` function:

```
Total All Products = COUNTROWS(ALL(Products))
```

Note: This time the `ALL()` function is not using one or more columns as parameters; instead, it is using the entire `Products` table as the only parameter. This is valid syntax for both `ALL()` and `VALUES()`.

The `ALL()` function returns a table. You cannot add a table inside a measure unless it is wrapped inside another function. You can wrap `COUNTROWS()` around any table in order to be able to find the number of rows in the table. When you have finished typing this formula, you can add the measure to your matrix, and you should get the results shown below.

Category	Total Number of Products	Total All Products
Accessories	35	397
Bikes	125	397
Clothing	48	397
Components	189	397
Total	**397**	**397**

You can see from this matrix that the new measure is always returning 397, regardless of the filters coming from the rows in the matrix. The matrix is placing a filter on the `Products[Category]` column, but the `ALL()` function is removing that filter. By the time `COUNTROWS()` kicks in, the `ALL()` function has removed all the filters coming from the visual, and hence this measure always returns the total products in the `Products` table. In this use case, you can see that `ALL()` has the ability to remove the filters coming from the initial filter context.

Using ALL() as a Table Filter Inside CALCULATE()

One common use of ALL() is as a table filter inside a CALCULATE() function so that it removes the filters that are coming from the visual. This has the effect of giving you direct access to the total row in the visual so you can use it inside another formula. Let's look at an example for clarity.

Calculating the Country Percentage of Total Sales

Say that you want to calculate the country percentage of global sales. First, you need to set up a matrix with Territories[Country] on Rows and [Total Sales] on Values, as shown below.

Country	Total Sales
Australia	$9,061,001
Canada	$1,977,845
France	$2,644,018
Germany	$2,894,312
United Kingdom	$3,391,712
United States	$9,389,790
Total	**$29,358,677**

It is then possible (as shown below) to select the matrix (see #1 below), click on the drop-down arrow next to the measure [Total Sales] (#2), and then select Show Value As (#3) and Percent of Grand Total (#4).

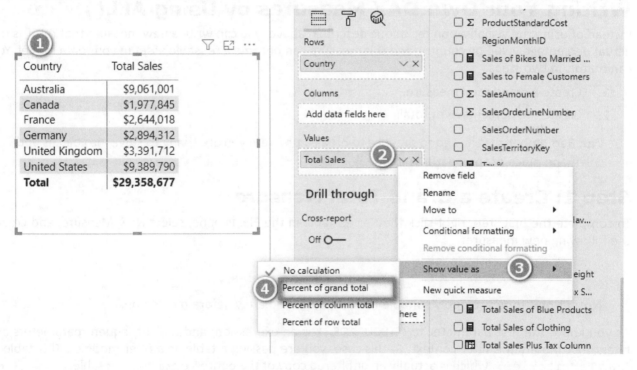

If you do this, you indeed see the country percentage of global sales, as shown below.

Country	%GT Total Sales
Australia	30.86%
Canada	6.74%
France	9.01%
Germany	9.86%
United Kingdom	11.55%
United States	31.98%
Total	**100.00%**

If this solves your problem, then you are done. But doing it this way does not give you access to the percentages for use in further calculations. For example, what if you want to write a formula that counts the number of countries that each represent more than 10% of global sales? You cannot do this calculation by using the visualisation technique shown above. If you want to use the results (percentage of global sales in this case) inside another formula, you have to write a measure.

Tip: Of course, in this case, you are trying to learn to write DAX, so I recommend that you invest the time to learn how to write the measure yourself rather than resorting to using the visualisation feature shown above. The following section explains how to write a measure by using `ALL()`.

Writing Your Own DAX Measures by Using ALL()

Instead of using the visualisation technique described above, you can write a new measure that returns the actual percentage value by country, and this measure can become a reusable asset in your data model. You can do this in two steps:

1. Create a grand total measure.
2. Create the percentage of total.

Tip: Remember that it is good practice to break a problem you are trying to solve into pieces and solve one piece of the puzzle at a time.

Step 1: Create a Grand Total Measure

To complete the first step, right-click the `Sales` table in the Fields pane, select New Measure, and create the following new measure:

```
Total Global Sales =
       CALCULATE([Total Sales], All(Territories))
```

Note: Don't forget to apply suitable formatting immediately before moving on.

As you know, the first parameter to `CALCULATE()` is an expression, and the subsequent parameters are filters that modify the filter context. In this case, you are passing a table as a filter modifier. This table is `ALL(Territories)`, which is actually an unfiltered copy of the entire `Territories` table.

After you add the new measure to the matrix, your matrix looks as shown below. Do you see that the new measure is ignoring the initial filter context coming from the matrix? `CALCULATE()` is the only function that can modify the filter context. In this case, `CALCULATE()` is replacing the initial filter context from the visual on `Territories[Country]` with a new filter context by using an unfiltered copy of the `Territories` table instead.

Country	Total Sales	Total Global Sales
Australia	$9,061,001	$29,358,677
Canada	$1,977,845	$29,358,677
France	$2,644,018	$29,358,677
Germany	$2,894,312	$29,358,677
NA		$29,358,677
United Kingdom	$3,391,712	$29,358,677
United States	$9,389,790	$29,358,677
Total	**$29,358,677**	**$29,358,677**

I call this [Total Global Sales] measure an "interim measure" because it was created to help break the problem into manageable pieces.

> **Tip:** It is a good idea to determine whether the interim measure works as expected before you move on.

Step 2: Create the Percentage of Total

After you have created the measure [Total Global Sales], it is easy to create a new measure to calculate the country percentage of global sales. Right-click the Sales table in the Fields pane, select New Measure, and create the measure as follows:

```
% of Global Sales =
    DIVIDE([Total Sales], [Total Global Sales])
```

Make sure you format this measure so that Format is set to Percentage and Decimal Places is set to 1. You end up with the matrix shown below.

Country	Total Sales	Total Global Sales	% of Global Sales
Australia	$9,061,001	$29,358,677	30.9%
Canada	$1,977,845	$29,358,677	6.7%
France	$2,644,018	$29,358,677	9.0%
Germany	$2,894,312	$29,358,677	9.9%
NA		$29,358,677	
United Kingdom	$3,391,712	$29,358,677	11.6%
United States	$9,389,790	$29,358,677	32.0%
Total	**$29,358,677**	**$29,358,677**	**100.0%**

The final step is to remove the [Total Global Sales] interim measure from the matrix.

> **Note:** You don't actually need the interim measures to be placed in the matrix in order for the [% of Global Sales] measure to work. But you should notice how much easier it is to visualise what is happening when you write an interim measure and place it in a matrix. When you do it this way, you can easily see that the [Total Global Sales] value is the same, regardless of the country in the matrix, and hence you can immediately see that you just need to divide the country sales by this total global sales amount, and it is going to work. Doing it this way is very similar to how you would do it in regular Excel, and it can be helpful to step through the DAX formulas like this to get the same experience.

The final matrix is shown below, with some conditional formatting applied to make it easier to read.

Country	Total Sales	% of Global Sales
Australia	$9,061,001	30.9%
Canada	$1,977,845	6.7%
France	$2,644,018	9.0%
Germany	$2,894,312	9.9%
United Kingdom	$3,391,712	11.6%
United States	$9,389,790	32.0%
Total	**$29,358,677**	**100.0%**

Using the New Quick Measure Option

You may already know (or may have noticed in one of the earlier images) that there is a New Quick Measure option available in Power BI. If you click the drop-down arrow next to Total Sales (see #1 below), you see the New Quick Measure option (#2).

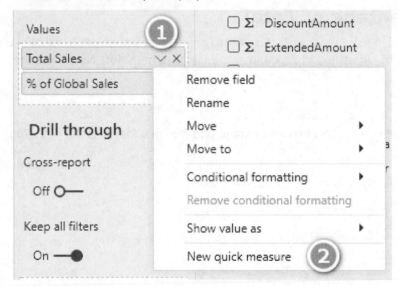

If you select the New Quick Measure option, Power BI helps you write a measure, and you don't have to have any knowledge of DAX at all. Using a new quick measure is much better than creating implicit measures (by dragging the column to the Values drop zone for the visual, as discussed earlier in this chapter). Using quick measures is better than using implicit measures for several reasons. For example, you can rename a quick measure, edit the measure, format the measure, and reuse the measure inside other measures.

The image below shows the wizard for creating a new quick measure that calculates the total for a category (without filters). All you have to do is drag a column or measure from the Fields list on the right into the relevant placeholder areas on the left. In the example below, I have added [Total Sales] to Base Value and Territories[Country] to Category.

> **Note:** Did you notice that I didn't need to tell you that [Total Sales] is a measure and Territories[Country] is a column? Remember that it is a best practice to omit the table name from a measure and always include the table name in front of a column; if you do, others in the DAX authoring community who follow best practices will understand what you mean.

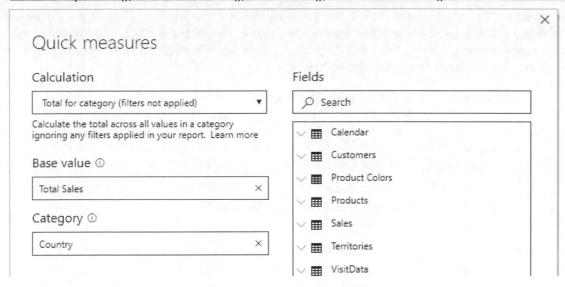

Power BI creates the quick measure shown below.

```
Total Sales total for Country =
CALCULATE('Sales'[Total Sales], ALL('Territories'[Country]))
```

This is a functioning measure, and it is almost identical to the one that was hand-written above.

> **Note:** Using the New Quick Measure option is a great help for writing complex DAX functions quickly and without a lot of knowledge about how it all works. However, I do not spend any more time talking about the feature in this book because this is a book about writing your own DAX formulas. If you want to use quick measures, then do so by all means. I don't, however, recommend that you use quick measures instead of learning how the DAX language works; rather, I recommend that you use quick measures as a tool to help you learn the DAX language.

Passing a Table or a Column to ALL()

Before we finish with ALL(), it is worth noting that the following measure would return exactly the same result as [Total Global Sales] in the matrix example in the earlier section "Step 1: Create a Grand Total Measure":

```
Total All Country Sales =
    CALCULATE(
        [Total Sales],
        ALL(Territories[Country])
    )
```

Notice that this measure passes a single column instead of the entire table to the ALL() function, just like the formula created by the quick measure. In this specific matrix, which is shown below, [Total Global Sales] and [Total All Country Sales] return the same result.

Country	Total Sales	Total Global Sales	Total All Country Sales
Australia	$9,061,001	$29,358,677	$29,358,677
Canada	$1,977,845	$29,358,677	$29,358,677
France	$2,644,018	$29,358,677	$29,358,677
Germany	$2,894,312	$29,358,677	$29,358,677
NA		$29,358,677	$29,358,677
United Kingdom	$3,391,712	$29,358,677	$29,358,677
United States	$9,389,790	$29,358,677	$29,358,677
Total	**$29,358,677**	**$29,358,677**	**$29,358,677**

However, the measure [Total All Country Sales] would not show the same result (i.e., it would not remove the filter) if there were some other column on Rows in the matrix (i.e., something other than Country). To test this, remove Territories[Country] from Rows in the matrix and replace it with Territories[Region]. You get the result shown below.

Region	Total Sales	Total Global Sales	Total All Country Sales
Australia	$9,061,001	$29,358,677	$9,061,001
Canada	$1,977,845	$29,358,677	$1,977,845
Central	$3,001	$29,358,677	$3,001
France	$2,644,018	$29,358,677	$2,644,018
Germany	$2,894,312	$29,358,677	$2,894,312
NA		$29,358,677	
Northeast	$6,532	$29,358,677	$6,532
Northwest	$3,649,867	$29,358,677	$3,649,867
Southeast	$12,239	$29,358,677	$12,239
Southwest	$5,718,151	$29,358,677	$5,718,151
United Kingdom	$3,391,712	$29,358,677	$3,391,712
Total	**$29,358,677**	**$29,358,677**	**$29,358,677**

Notice the difference between passing the entire table name to the ALL() function and passing a single column. [Total Global Sales] removes the filter from the entire Territories table, but [Total All Country Sales] removes the filter only from the Territories[Country] column of the table. In the matrix visual above, there is no filter on the Territories[Country] column of the table, and hence ALL() has no effect on the visual.

Remove [Total All Country Sales] from the matrix before proceeding.

The REMOVEFILTERS() Function

Several times so far in this book, I have discussed the concept of syntax sugar. As a recap, this is a term that describes variations to functions that Microsoft developers sometimes create to make DAX easier to learn and understand. The REMOVEFILTERS() function is an example of syntax sugar. When I first learnt DAX, I learnt that the ALL() function is the "remove filters" function. In fact, I still teach this concept to my students today. So as you may have guessed, the REMOVEFILTERS() function is actually just syntax sugar for the ALL() function that you can use when you want to remove filters in the way shown above. Personally I never use REMOVEFILTERS() because I just learnt to do it using ALL(), but of course you can use it if you like.

The ALLEXCEPT() Function

The ALL() function has a few siblings that are very similar but with a few important differences. ALLEXCEPT() allows you to remove filters from all columns in a table except the ones that you explicitly specify. Say that you want to remove filters for every column in the Products table except for the Products[Category] column. There are 21 columns in the Products table, so if you use the ALL() function, you have to specify the 20 columns from which you want to remove the filter so that ALL() can do what you want for those 20, while retaining the filter on Products[Category]. This is what it looks like:

```
Total Sales of ALL Products except Category =
    CALCULATE(
        [Total Sales],
        All(Products[color],Products[Size],Products[Weight],
            <+ 17 more that are not listed here>)
    )
```

`ALLEXCEPT()` makes it easier to write a formula to remove filters from most but not all columns in a table. You can use it to write the `ALL()` formula shown above as follows:

```
Total Sales of ALL Products except Category 2 =
    CALCULATE(
        [Total Sales],
        ALLEXCEPT(Products, Products[Category])
    )
```

When using `ALLEXCEPT()`, you must first specify the table that contains the columns to be removed and then specify the columns that are not to be removed.

The ALLSELECTED() Function

The `ALLSELECTED()` function works much like `ALL()` except in the way it works with other visuals and the Filters pane. The `ALLSELECTED()` function is useful when you want to calculate percentages, as shown above, and you have a filter applied from somewhere else in your report (say, via a slicer, the Filters pane, or cross-filtering from another visual) and you want the total in your matrix to add up to 100%.

Look at the example below. Say that you're working with the same matrix used earlier in this chapter but now with a slicer that filters on `Territories[Group]`. Notice below that `[% of Global Sales]` adds up to 38.7%; this is correct because the other countries that make up the remaining 61.3% have been filtered out using the Group slicer.

Group	Region	Total Sales	% of Global Sales
☐ Europe	Canada	$1,977,845	6.7%
☐ NA	Central	$3,001	0.0%
■ North America	Northeast	$6,532	0.0%
☐ Pacific	Northwest	$3,649,867	12.4%
	Southeast	$12,239	0.0%
	Southwest	$5,718,151	19.5%
	Total	**$11,367,634**	**38.7%**

But what if you want to see the percentage for each region in a group in the matrix, such as for each region in the group North America? This is where `ALLSELECTED()` comes in. `ALLSELECTED()` removes the filters coming from the matrix but respects the filters coming from the slicer (or any other type of cross-filtering).

Add the following interim measure to the matrix above:

```
Total Selected Territories =
    CALCULATE([Total Sales], ALLSELECTED(Territories))
```

In the image below, notice that `[Total Selected Territories]` returns the same value as the total of the region sales in the matrix.

Group ⌄	Region	Total Sales	% of Global Sales	Total Selected Territories
☐ Europe				
☐ NA	Canada	$1,977,845	6.7%	$11,367,634
■ North America	Central	$3,001	0.0%	$11,367,634
☐ Pacific	Northeast	$6,532	0.0%	$11,367,634
	Northwest	$3,649,867	12.4%	$11,367,634
	Southeast	$12,239	0.0%	$11,367,634
	Southwest	$5,718,151	19.5%	$11,367,634
	Total	**$11,367,634**	**38.7%**	**$11,367,634**

Using the same steps as before, you can now write the new measure [% of Selected Territories] and then remove the interim measure [Total Selected Territories] from the matrix. Here's how you write the new measure:

```
% of Selected Territories =
      DIVIDE([Total Sales], [Total Selected Territories])
```

If you format this new measure by using percentage and one decimal place and apply conditional formatting to the measure, the matrix that results looks as shown below.

Group
- ☐ Europe
- ☐ NA
- ■ North America
- ☐ Pacific

Region	Total Sales	% of Global Sales	% of Selected Territories
Canada	$1,977,845	6.7%	17.4%
Central	$3,001	0.0%	0.0%
Northeast	$6,532	0.0%	0.1%
Northwest	$3,649,867	12.4%	32.1%
Southeast	$12,239	0.0%	0.1%
Southwest	$5,718,151	19.5%	50.3%
Total	**$11,367,634**	**38.7%**	**100.0%**

The Value of Interim Measures

Remember that it is good practice to split a problem into pieces and solve one piece of the problem at a time. My advice is to get used to creating interim measures first and then writing the final measure that you actually need. Doing this helps you visualise each step of the process and makes it easier to get each part of the end-state formula correct before you proceed to the next step.

It is, of course, possible to write one single measure that carries out a number of steps. This is what it would look like, for example, for the process described above:

```
% of Selected Territories ONE STEP =
      DIVIDE(
          [Total Sales],
          CALCULATE([Total Sales], ALLSELECTED(Territories))
      )
```

But an all-in-one formula like this one can be difficult to write, read, and debug—particularly when you are learning to write DAX. It's not wrong; it can just be difficult when you are starting out, and life is too short to do things that are harder than they need to be.

Practice Exercises: ALL(), ALLEXCEPT(), and ALLSELECTED()

It's time for you to get some practice. Create a new matrix and put Customers[Occupation] on Rows and [Total Sales] on Values. You get the matrix shown below.

Occupation	Total Sales
Clerical	$4,684,787
Management	$5,467,862
Manual	$2,857,971
Professional	$9,907,977
Skilled Manual	$6,440,081
Total	**$29,358,677**

Then, using the principles covered in this chapter, create the following measures by first creating the interim measure you need and then creating the final measure. Find the solutions to these practice exercises in "Appendix A: Answers to Practice Exercises" on page 252.

47. [Total Sales to All Customers]

48. [% of All Customer Sales]

Add a slicer for Customers[Gender] to the report you just created and filter by male gender, as shown below.

Gender
☐ F
■ M

Occupation	Total Sales	Total Sales to All Customers	% of All Customer Sales
Clerical	$2,421,327	$29,358,677	8.2%
Management	$2,793,527	$29,358,677	9.5%
Manual	$1,463,060	$29,358,677	5.0%
Professional	$4,773,493	$29,358,677	16.3%
Skilled Manual	$3,093,651	$29,358,677	10.5%
Total	**$14,545,059**	**$29,358,677**	**49.5%**

Note that [% of All Customer Sales] doesn't add to 100%. This is correct because the other 50.5% of customers are filtered out with the slicer.

Set up another matrix with Customers[NumberCarsOwned] on Rows, Customers[Occupation] on Slicer, and [Total Sales] on Values. Your job is to create the other measure in this matrix: [% of Sales to Selected Customers]. When you are done, your matrix should look like the one below, with the last column showing the percentage of sales to customers based on the number of cars they own.

Occupation
■ Clerical
☐ Management
☐ Manual
☐ Professional
☐ Skilled Manual

NumberCarsOwned	Total Sales	% Sales to Selected Customers
0	$2,660,886	56.8%
1	$1,204,496	25.7%
2	$790,154	16.9%
3	$28,141	0.6%
4	$1,109	0.0%
Total	**$4,684,787**	**100.0%**

Remember that in this case, you want to create an interim measure first, so you actually need to create the following two measures and then remove the first of them from the matrix.

49. [Total Sales to Selected Customers]

50. [% of Sales to Selected Customers]

Next, your objective is to try to understand how sales per day varies across the week (i.e., Monday is x%, Tuesday is y%, etc.). But you also need to allow the user to select a particular date range and have the report update to show the daily sales mix for the selected date range. First, you need to make sure you set up a suitable visual so you can determine whether your measures are performing as expected. Then you should create the following two measures. The first one is an interim formula that you can remove from the matrix once you have finished the second formula.

51. [Total Sales for All Days Selected Dates]

52. [% Sales for All Days Selected Dates]

How Did It Go?

Did you end up with the following matrix?

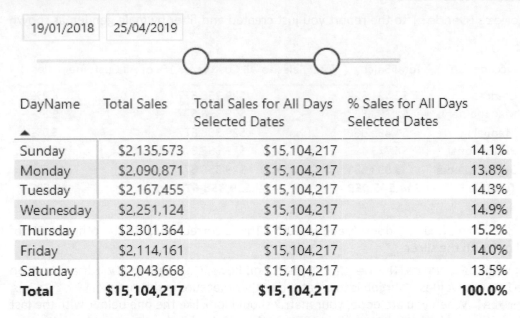

DayName	Total Sales	Total Sales for All Days Selected Dates	% Sales for All Days Selected Dates
Sunday	$2,135,573	$15,104,217	14.1%
Monday	$2,090,871	$15,104,217	13.8%
Tuesday	$2,167,455	$15,104,217	14.3%
Wednesday	$2,251,124	$15,104,217	14.9%
Thursday	$2,301,364	$15,104,217	15.2%
Friday	$2,114,161	$15,104,217	14.0%
Saturday	$2,043,668	$15,104,217	13.5%
Total	**$15,104,217**	**$15,104,217**	**100.0%**

Here's How: Using ALLEXCEPT()

I don't use ALLEXCEPT() much, and you may not either, but it is still good to work through an example of how it can be used. This section will give you some practice while also demonstrating one possible use case.

Say that you want to compare the percentage of sales across all occupations and see how it changes depending on the other customer filters. Follow these steps:

1. Set up a new matrix by placing Customers[Occupation] on Rows.
2. Add Gender and NumberCarsOwned slicers.
3. Put [Total Order Quantity] on Values.

Your setup should look as shown below. Note that the total order quantity will change as you click on the slicers.

Here I have set the NumberCarsOwned slicer to be horizontal by selecting the slicer (see #1 below), going to the Format pane (#2), selecting General (#3), and then setting Orientation to Horizontal (#4).

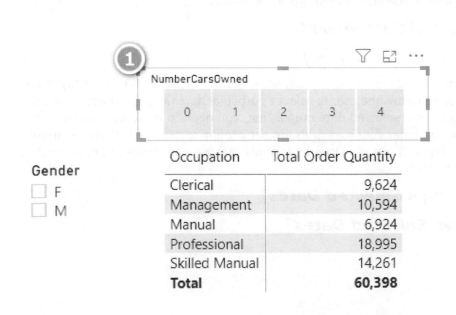

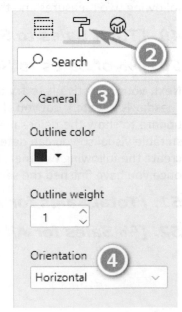

In the following practice exercises, you will create a number of measures; they are all needed to produce the final table visual, but only some of them will be visible in the final visual. As you create each measure, ensure that the results you see in your matrix make sense. Remember that writing DAX and then immediately adding it to a matrix helps you get your head around what you are doing.

NumberCarsOwned

| 0 | 1 | 2 | 3 | 4 |

Gender
■ F
☐ M

Occupation	Total Order Quantity	Total Orders All Customers	Baseline Orders for All Customers with This Occupation	Baseline % This Occupation of All Customer Orders	Total Orders Selected Customers	Occupation % of Selected Customers	Percentage Point Variation to Baseline
Clerical	7	60,398	9,624	15.9%	2,199	0.3%	-15.6%
Management	872	60,398	10,594	17.5%	2,199	39.7%	22.1%
Manual	1	60,398	6,924	11.5%	2,199	0.0%	-11.4%
Professional	1,263	60,398	18,995	31.4%	2,199	57.4%	26.0%
Skilled Manual	56	60,398	14,261	23.6%	2,199	2.5%	-21.1%
Total	**2,199**	**60,398**	**60,398**	**100.0%**	**2,199**	**100.0%**	**0.0%**

After writing the above measures, you will be able to build the final visual, shown below, with just the final measures included.

NumberCarsOwned

| 0 | 1 | 2 | 3 | 4 |

Gender
■ F
☐ M

Occupation	Total Order Quantity	Occupation % of Selected Customers	Baseline % This Occupation of All Customer Orders	Percentage Point Variation to Baseline
Clerical	7	0.3%	15.9%	-15.6%
Management	872	39.7%	17.5%	22.1%
Manual	1	0.0%	11.5%	-11.4%
Professional	1,263	57.4%	31.4%	26.0%
Skilled Manual	56	2.5%	23.6%	-21.1%
Total	**2,199**	**100.0%**	**100.0%**	**0.0%**

As you can imagine, with this matrix, it is possible to select different combinations of gender and number of cars and then compare the variation between the baseline order quantity and the order quantities for the selected filter.

Practice Exercises: ALL(), ALLEXCEPT(), and ALLSELECTED(), Continued

Based on the background just provided, you should now write the following DAX formulas, one at a time, and check to make sure each looks correct before moving to the next one. Find the solutions to these practice exercises in "Appendix A: Answers to Practice Exercises" on page 252.

53. [Total Orders All Customers]

To check this measure, click on the slicers and note that [Total Order Quantity] should change, but [Total Orders All Customers] should not change based on the slicers.

54. [Baseline Orders for All Customers with This Occupation]

This measure should also not change when you make changes to the slicers. However, note that you should get a different value for each occupation (unlike with [Total Orders All Customers] above). This measure provides the baseline for comparison.

55. [Baseline % This Occupation of All Customer Orders]

This measure converts the measure in Practice Exercise 54 into a percentage of the baseline for all orders. The description of this measure should help you work out how to write the DAX. Test the slicers again and make sure this new baseline percentage doesn't change with the slicers.

56. [Total Orders Selected Customers]

This measure should adjust depending on the selections you have in the slicers. Hint: Use `ALLSELECTED()`.

57. [Occupation % of Selected Customers]

You can use the interim measures above to create this measure. Click the slicers a few times and see which values change. This new measure should change based on the values you select in the slicers.

58. [Percentage Point Variation to Baseline]

This measure is the percentage of selected customers (Practice Exercise 57) minus the baseline (Practice Exercise 55).

Now you should have an interactive report that allows you to drill into the customer attributes gender and number of cars owned to see the impact on the mix of business compared to the baseline of all customers.

Sometimes it is useful to change the descriptions of the final measures as they appear in a matrix. For example, while `[Baseline % This Occupation of All Customer Orders]` is a good name for your measure because you know what it means, when you use this measure in a specific matrix, you might want to rename it. You can do this by selecting the matrix, going to the Values section on the right-hand side of the screen, and double-clicking the measure name you want to change. The name changes just for the particular visual that is selected (the matrix in this case).

How Did It Go?

After giving your measures new names, did you end up with something like the matrix shown below?

Gender	Occupation	Total Order	Share of Selected Customers	Baseline Share All Customers	Variation to Baseline
■ F	Clerical	7	0.3%	15.9%	-15.6%
☐ M	Management	872	39.7%	17.5%	22.1%
	Manual	1	0.0%	11.5%	-11.4%
	Professional	1,263	57.4%	31.4%	26.0%
	Skilled Manual	56	2.5%	23.6%	-21.1%
	Total	**2,199**	**100.0%**	**100.0%**	**0.0%**

Note: If you change the description of a measure in the matrix, the easiest way to change it back is to remove the measure from the visual and then add it back again. However, when you do this, you lose any conditional formatting.

15: DAX Topic: FILTER()

FILTER() is a very powerful table function in DAX. As you've seen in the last two chapters, the primary purpose of a table function is to allow you to create and use a virtual table inside your measures. It's not the only use, but it is the most common use of table functions in DAX. These virtual tables are super useful because you get all the benefits of a new table without actually having to materialise it in your physical model. When FILTER() and CALCULATE() are combined, these two functions allow you to alter the filter behaviour (aka filter context) in your formulas any way you want. Before we move to using FILTER() within CALCULATE(), I think it is worth looking at a couple of concepts that illustrate how FILTER() works.

The syntax of FILTER() is as follows:

```
= FILTER(Table, myFilter)
```

The first parameter, *Table*, is any table from your model, or a function that returns a table, such as ALL(). The second parameter, *myFilter*, is any expression that evaluates to a True/False answer.

The FILTER() function returns a table that contains zero or more rows from the original table. Stated another way, the table returned by FILTER() can contain zero rows, one row, two rows, or any other number of rows, up to and including the total number of rows in the original table. The purpose of FILTER(), therefore, is to determine which rows will be retained in the final table result after you use the *myFilter* test.

Technically speaking, FILTER() is an iterating function; it steps through every row in the table (parameter 1) and evaluates the expression to return True or False (parameter 2). But rather than think of FILTER() as being an iterating function, I want you to think about FILTER() as working like a calculated column in a table. The next section provides a detailed example and walkthrough to illustrate.

FILTER() Is Kind of Like a Calculated Column

The FILTER() function behaves kind of like a calculated column. To illustrate the point, let me first step you through a calculated column demo before coming back to FILTER(). Follow these steps:

1. Switch to the Data view and navigate to the Fields pane.

2. Add a new column by right-clicking the Customers table, selecting New Column, and entering the following:

    ```
    Test = Customers[YearlyIncome]
    ```

    As you can see in the image below, this creates a new column that simply stores the value from Customers[YearlyIncome] in the new Test column.

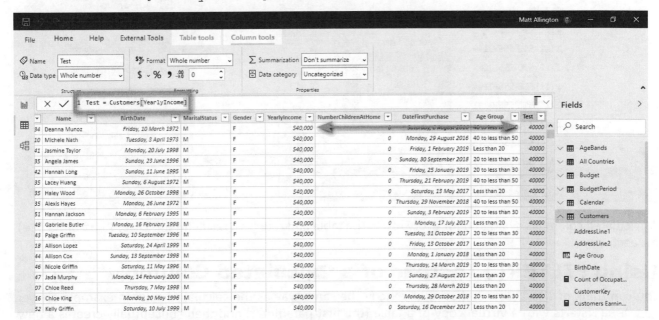

3. Now modify the formula in the calculated column as follows:

    Test = Customers[YearlyIncome] >= 80000

This revised version of the calculated column returns True or False, depending on the yearly income of each of the customers in the table. I sorted the Customers table shown below on CustomerKey so you can see some different results for different yearly incomes in this image.

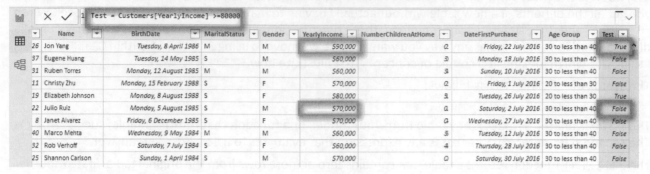

Stop and think about this for a moment: I have created a calculated column that returns True or False to indicate whether each customer has a yearly income greater than or equal to $80,000. Now that I have this new calculated column, I can use the filter buttons at the top of the column (see #1 below) to filter the entire Customers table to keep only those that are True (#2). Note the resulting information (#3) indicating that 4,382 customers have a yearly income of at least $80,000.

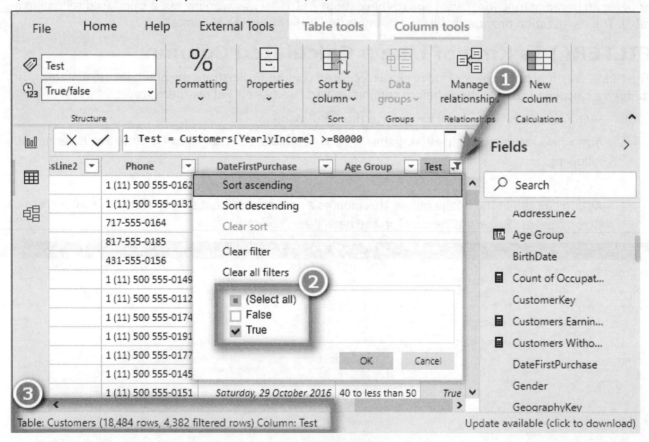

A calculated column is evaluated for every row in the table and returns a result (in this case, True or False) for each row.

Using FILTER() Instead of a Calculated Column

You can think of FILTER() behaving in exactly the same way as the calculated column example above. FILTER() starts with a virtual copy of a table (the first parameter) and then conceptually creates a new virtual calculated column that returns True or False inside that new virtual table (the second parameter). Once the virtual column has been created, FILTER() uses that column to filter only the rows of the table that return `True`, just as demonstrated above. Finally, `FILTER()` returns a virtual filtered copy of the original table that contains just the rows that evaluate to `True`.

The big advantage of the `FILTER()` function compared to the calculated column option illustrated above is that `FILTER()` does not materialise the extra columns needed to complete the task. The columns it needs are created (conceptually at least) at runtime, in memory. The virtual column is used by `FILTER()` and then released once it has been used.

Now that you understand that `FILTER()` is kind of like a calculated column, let me show you the equivalent action using the actual `FILTER()` function. Oh, but wait! `FILTER()` is a table function, and you cannot write standalone table functions in a measure, right? Just as you can't use naked columns inside a measure, you can't use naked tables; it's not allowed. A measure must return a value of some type, and it can't return a column or a table. To help you understand this, the next section takes another detour and shows the use of the New Table button again.

The New Table Button Strikes Again

When you see a `FILTER()` function, you should try to conceptualise that `FILTER()` takes a virtual copy of the `Customers` table, generates a new `True/False` virtual column (the second parameter), filters the new table using the new column to keep the values that are `True`, and removes the `True/False` column, leaving just the filtered rows in the new virtual table. To help you conceptualise this, this example shows how to use the New Table button again to actually materialise the virtual table. To "see" the `FILTER()` function version of the calculated column from above, you can create a new table by using the following formula:

```
Customers > 80000 Table =
    FILTER(Customers, Customers[YearlyIncome] >= 80000)
```

If you add this formula as a new table in Power BI and then switch to this new table in the Data view, you can "see" the table and check how many rows there are in the new table. As shown below, it is indeed a filtered copy of the original `Customers` table that contains exactly the same number of rows (and columns) as before.

	1 Customers > 80000 Table = FILTER(Customers, Customers[YearlyIncome]>=80000)

CustomerKey ▼	GeographyKey ▼	Name ▼	BirthDate ▼	MaritalStatus ▼	Gender ▼	YearlyIncome ▼
11059	27	Ashlee Andersen	1/04/1979 12:00:00 AM	S	F	80000
11069	23	Carolyn Navarro	21/09/1980 12:00:00 AM	S	F	80000
11071	24	Linda Serrano	26/06/1980 12:00:00 AM	S	F	80000
11072	17	Casey Luo	6/02/1980 12:00:00 AM	S	F	80000
11295	311	Taylor Lewis	16/05/1979 12:00:00 AM	S	F	80000
13093	631	Michelle James	15/10/1982 12:00:00 AM	S	F	80000
13456	623	Sydney Hernandez	24/07/1980 12:00:00 AM	S	F	80000
13460	55	Jasmine Walker	21/09/1979 12:00:00 AM	S	F	80000
14020	38	Kristine Dominguez	20/06/1979 12:00:00 AM	S	F	80000
14040	316	Stephanie Morris	12/05/1982 12:00:00 AM	S	F	80000
14041	70	Danielle Bell	3/04/1982 12:00:00 AM	S	F	80000
14263	15	Nina Lal	24/02/1979 12:00:00 AM	S	F	80000
14276	27	Melody Suarez	10/07/1980 12:00:00 AM	S	F	80000
14478	51	Abigail Patterson	9/08/1979 12:00:00 AM	S	F	80000
15171	23	Destiny Jones	11/05/1979 12:00:00 AM	S	F	80000

TABLE: Customers > 80000 Table (4,382 rows) COLUMN: YearlyIncome (9 distinct values)

Remember that I have materialised this table to show you what happens. What is great about `FILTER()` is that you don't need to create the table for it to work; you can use it as a virtual table inside a measure without ever having to materialise the table at all.

Using FILTER() Inside a Measure

This section shows how to use FILTER() inside a measure. Go to a new report page and set up a new matrix with Customers[Occupation] on Rows and the measure [Total Number of Customers] on Values. The matrix, shown below, indicates how many customers there are in the entire customer database for each occupation type.

Occupation	Total Number of Customers
Clerical	2,928
Management	3,075
Manual	2,384
Professional	5,520
Skilled Manual	4,577
Total	**18,484**

Now you can write a measure that uses the FILTER() function to determine how many customers in the database have an income of more than $80,000 per year. Here is the FILTER() function you used to find this information earlier:

```
= FILTER(Customers, Customers[YearlyIncome] >= 80000)
```

Remember that you can't use a table function (i.e., a naked table) in a measure unless it is wrapped inside another function. You know from the examples above that this FILTER() function returns a table that contains the customers who have a yearly income greater than or equal to $80,000, but you can't use it inside a measure unless you wrap it inside another function. FILTER() is a table function, so you can wrap it inside a COUNTROWS() function, as shown here, to count the rows in the resulting table:

```
Total Customers with Income of $80,000 or above Measure =
    COUNTROWS(
        FILTER(Customers, Customers[YearlyIncome] >= 80000)
    )
```

The result of the FILTER() portion of this measure is a new virtual table of customers that includes all the customers who have yearly income greater than or equal to $80,000. The COUNTROWS() function then counts the number of rows in this virtual FILTER() table, so it converts the table itself into a count of customers in the table. When you place this measure in the matrix, it looks as shown below. You should create this measure now for practice.

Occupation	Total Number of Customers	Total Customers with Income of $80,000 or above Measure
Clerical	2,928	
Management	3,075	1,963
Manual	2,384	
Professional	5,520	1,976
Skilled Manual	4,577	443
Total	**18,484**	**4,382**

FILTER() Respects the Initial Filter Context

You can see from the matrix above that not all occupations have customers that earn at least $80,000 per year. Both clerical and manual occupations return blank in the visual above. This highlights a very important concept that is easy to miss, so focus as I explain it to you!

The FILTER() portion of the measure above is as follows:

```
FILTER(Customers, Customers[YearlyIncome] >= 80000)
```

The first parameter of the FILTER() function is the table Customers. But it may not be the entire Customers table, depending on the circumstances. The first parameter of the FILTER() function respects the initial filter context coming from the visual. This is important, so let me say it again: The first parameter of the FILTER() function respects the initial filter context coming from the visual.

In the FILTER() portion of the formula above, it is not the entire Customers table passed to FILTER() but a filtered copy of the Customers table, filtered by the rows in the matrix. This explains why the first row in the table below returns blank for the new measure.

Occupation	Total Number of Customers	Total Customers with Income of $80,000 or above
Clerical	2,928	
Management	3,075	1,963
Manual	2,384	
Professional	5,520	1,976
Skilled Manual	4,577	443
Total	**18,484**	**4,382**

The first row of the matrix above is evaluated as follows:

1. The matrix visual places a filter on Customers[Occupation] = "Clerical". As a result, the Customers table is now filtered to the 2,928 rows that are clerical customers.

2. The first parameter of FILTER() therefore receives a filtered copy of the Customers table, filtered for Customers[Occupation] = "Clerical".

3. Before FILTER() even starts to do its stuff, the Customers table has already been filtered by the visual. Instead of the first parameter (the table) having 18,484 rows, it actually has only 2,928 rows because it is already filtered for clerical customers.

Key Points to Remember

These are the key points to take away from the examples above:

*   FILTER() returns a table. It is a virtual table, and hence you can't see it.

*   You can think of FILTER() as operating like a calculated column inside a table—but better. It is better because it can do everything a calculate column can do (in this case) but doesn't need to materialise a new column into the table. In Power BI, fewer columns is always better.

*   You can materialise a FILTER() function by using the New Table option if you want to see how it works.

*   The virtual table returned by FILTER() has a virtual relationship to its source; this is called lineage. The virtual table and virtual relationship behave in the same way that physical tables and relationships behave.

*   The virtual table returned by FILTER() can be used inside a measure without the need to materialise the table at all.

*   Materialising can be a great technique to help you visualise what is going on in DAX. You should materialise tables in order to learn and comprehend, but you should not leave such tables in your model. Delete them when you are done using them.

*   You can't use table functions (naked tables) on their own inside measures; they must be used inside other functions so that they return single values. In the example above, for example, I used COUNTROWS() to count the rows in the table.

A Caution Related to Using FILTER()

Generally, it is fine to use FILTER() on lookup tables, but it's somewhat riskier to use it on data tables, particularly if they are very large (with hundreds of millions of rows). Where to use FILTER() depends on your data, on the quality of your DAX formulas inside FILTER(), and on what you need to achieve. You will increase your depth of understanding with practice and experience. When you have a choice, aim to use FILTER() on the smallest table possible to keep your formulas working efficiently.

FILTER() Inside CALCULATE()

As mentioned at the start of this chapter, FILTER() is most commonly used as a table filter parameter inside CALCULATE(). FILTER() is a table function that operates over every row in a table to determine which rows to retain. FILTER() therefore allows a very granular level of evaluation of a table and is a very powerful tool for altering the filter context of a visual any way you want and at a level of detail, which is not always possible by using a simple filter inside CALCULATE().

Consider the following measure formula:

```
Total Customers with Income of $80,000 or above 2 =
    CALCULATE(COUNTROWS(Customers),
        Customers[YearlyIncome] >= 80000
    )
```

This measure formula returns exactly the same result as the COUNTROWS(FILTER()) version above. In this CALCULATE() version, the filter portion of the formula uses a simple filter. A simple filter has a column name on one side of the formula (in this case, Customers[YearlyIncome]) and a value on the right side (in this case, 80000).

CALCULATE() is designed to accept this type of simple syntax without using the FILTER() function. But in reality, this is just another example of syntax sugar that makes it easier for you to write measures. Under the hood, the formula using the simple syntax above is converted to the following formula:

```
Total Customers with Income of $80,000 Under the Hood =
    CALCULATE(COUNTROWS(Customers),
        FILTER(
            ALL(Customers[YearlyIncome]),
            Customers[YearlyIncome] >= 80000
        )
    )
```

Note the inclusion of ALL(Customers[YearlyIncome]) instead of just Customers as the first parameter of the FILTER() function. In Chapter 16 I provide more details on why the ALL() function is used here.

There is a limit to what CALCULATE() can do with a simple filter. It works only if you have a column name compared to a value. But what if you want to do something more complex? Let's look at another example.

Example: Calculating Lifetime Customer Purchases

Say that you want to know how many customers have purchased more than $5,000 of goods from you over all time. You can't use the simple filter syntax inside CALCULATE() in such a case because customers may have purchased from you on many occasions, and you don't have a column that contains a single value that contains the total sales for each customer over all time. If you tried to write this formula using a simple filter, it would look like this:

```
Customers with Sales Greater Than $5,000 Doesn't Work =
    CALCULATE(COUNTROWS(Customers), [Total Sales] > 5000)
```

The second parameter of this CALCULATE() function is:

```
[Total Sales] > 5000
```

This second parameter has a measure on the left side and a value on the right—and this is not allowed with a simple filter. A simple filter must have a column compared to a value, so a simple filter doesn't work in this scenario.

In this case, you cannot use the simple filter syntax for CALCULATE(); you simply must use a table function for the filter parameter instead. The following section shows how to use the FILTER() function as the filter parameter. (It's a bit confusing, I know.)

Simple Filter Syntax vs. Table Filter Syntax

As long as you are comparing a column to a value, you can use the simple syntax inside CALCULATE(). If you keep it simple, CALCULATE() is able to handle simple filtering just fine. But as soon as you get more complex than comparing a column to a value, CALCULATE() can't do it on its own, and it needs help. In such a case, CALCULATE() calls in the big guns and gets its friend FILTER() to help out with the more complex formula. CALCULATE() delegates to the FILTER() function the job of working out which rows to keep. FILTER() does the work and provides the filtered table back to CALCUATE(). The two functions work well together like this.

The formula above does not work with the simple syntax, but you can rewrite it as follows with table filter syntax:

```
Customers with Sales Greater Than $5,000 =
    CALCULATE(
        COUNTROWS(Customers),
        FILTER(Customers, [Total Sales] >= 5000)
    )
```

It is worth understanding how FILTER() works in this example because there is a slight difference from the earlier example that involved Customers[YearlyIncome] >= 80000.

The FILTER() portion of the CALCULATE() function is evaluated first. With CALCULATE(), the filter portion is always evaluated first (for both simple filters and table filters).

Let's start by looking at just the FILTER() portion of the above formula:

```
FILTER(Customers, [Total Sales] >= 5000)
```

I am going to use the same calculated column approach I used earlier in this chapter to help you see what FILTER() does here. Remember that you can think of FILTER() as creating a calculated column in the table of choice. (Thinking about it this way will help you understand what's happening.)

In the image below, I have added to the Customers table the new calculated column Test = [Total Sales].

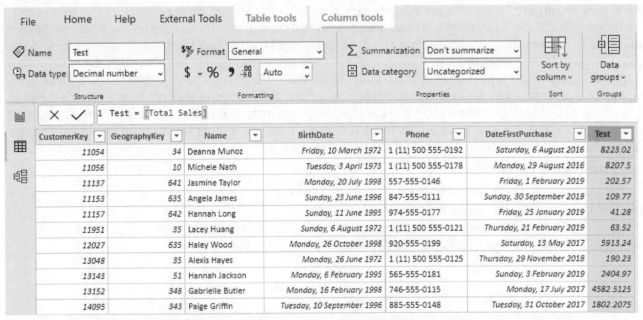

Here you can see that Deanna Munoz has sales of $8,333.02, Hanna Long has sales of $41.28, etc. Intuitively, you should feel very comfortable with this calculated column because it works as expected. But if you think more deeply about this, you see that there is actually a lot going on here. The measure `[Total Sales]` contains the following formula:

```
Total Sales = SUM(Sales[ExtendedAmount])
```

This measure is adding up the `ExtendedAmount` column in the `Sales` table, but the calculated column is not in the `Sales` table; it is in the `Customers` table. This formula works exactly as you would expect, but the reason it works is quite complex. You need to learn why it works if you want to be a DAX superhero.

Context Transition Revisited

To see what I mean when I say there is a lot going on here, go back to the calculated column above and replace the measure `[Total Sales]` with the formula `SUM(Sales[ExtendedAmount])`. When you do this, you get the result shown below—which is probably not what you expect!

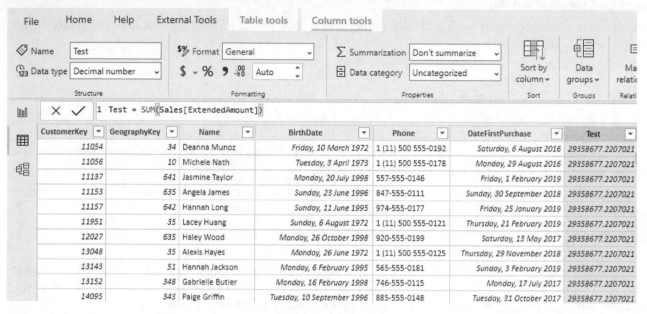

Why does `[Total Sales]` return the total sales of the customer when `SUM(Sales[ExtendedAmount])` does not?

This is very important: This occurs because of an implicit `CALCULATE()` inside the measure `[Total Sales]`. The hidden `CALCULATE()` inside a measure causes context transition: The row context from the calculated column is converted to an equivalent filter context. Because of the context transition, the single row in the `Customers` table is converted into a filter, and this filter then propagates down through the relationship from the `Customers` table to the `Sales` table and, hence, the `Sales` table is filtered, too. Only sales for this one customer remain in the filtered state when the measure is evaluated. If you use the formula `SUM(Sales[ExtendedAmount])` in the calculated column instead of using a measure in the calculated column, there is no `CALCULATE()`, either implicit or explicit. Do you remember this from the end of Chapter 11? (Go back and read it again if you need to brush up.)

This is the original calculated column:

```
Test = [Total Sales]
```

You turn this into a `True`/`False` expression, as follows:

```
Test = [Total Sales] >=5000
```

After you make this change, the table looks as shown in the image below.

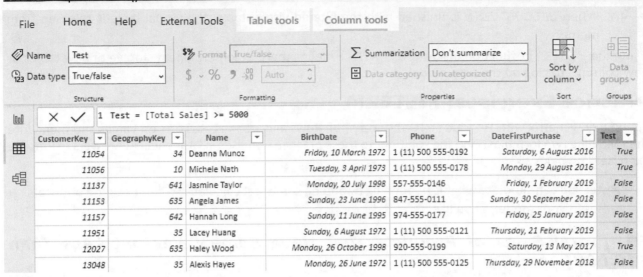

You can now see the new calculated column that returns either `True` (for sales of $5,000 or more) or `False` for each customer. If you put a filter on this new column to keep only the `True` customers (see #1 below), you can see that there are 1,732 customers who have sales of at least $5,000 (#2).

But remember that this is just an illustration to help you learn. This is not really the way to solve this problem as you definitely do not want to create a new column every time you need to do a new calculation. Instead, you need to use `FILTER()`. `FILTER()` is a function that can add a virtual calculated column to any table without the need to materialise the new column.

Here is the full `FILTER()` version of the measure again:

```
Customers with Sales Greater Than $5,000 =
    CALCULATE(
        COUNTROWS(Customers),
        FILTER(Customers, [Total Sales] >= 5000)
    )
```

This formula works as follows:

1. The `FILTER()` function creates a new virtual table with a virtual `True/False` calculated column.

2. The `FILTER()` function applies a filter to keep only the values that are `True`.

3. `FILTER()` returns the filtered virtual table so that `CALCULATE()` can use it to filter the model. You can't see the table, but you can simulate how it works by using the calculated column technique shown earlier or by using the New Table button to materialise the `FILTER()` portion of a formula.

4. When CALCULATE() is finished with the filtered virtual table, the virtual table is released from memory.

Using the FILTER() function inside CALCUATE() means there is no permanent storage of new tables or new columns to clog up the data model.

Practice Exercises: FILTER()

Set up a new matrix with Products[Category] on Rows and [Total Sales] on Values and then write the following two formulas. Find the solutions to these practice exercises in "Appendix A: Answers to Practice Exercises" on page 252.

> **Note:** You can simulate what is happening by adding some test calculated columns to the physical tables in your model if you like.

59. [Total Sales of Products That Have Some Sales but Less Than $10,000]

What you need to do here is use FILTER() to filter the Products table to determine whether each product has some sales and also whether the total of those sales is less than $10,000.

Note that you can use the double ampersand operator (&&) as follows if you need more than one condition in your filter expression:

    Condition1 && Condition2

Alternatively, you can use two separate FILTER() functions.

60. [Count of Products That Have Some Sales but Less Than $10,000]

You should end up with a matrix like the one below.

Category	Total Sales	Total Sales of Products That Have Some Sales but Less Than $10,000	Count of Products That Have Some Sales but Less Than $10,000
Accessories	$700,760	$31,431	4
Bikes	$28,318,145		
Clothing	$339,773	$5,106	2
Total	**$29,358,677**	**$36,538**	**6**

Next, add the ProductName column to Rows in the matrix (see #1 below) and then drill down (#2). Remove [Total Sales]. You can see from doing this how useful and flexible such measures can be in a model.

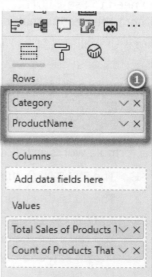

Category	Total Sales of Products That Have Some Sales but Less Than $10,000	Count of Products That Have Some Sales but Less Than $10,000
⊟ **Accessories**	**$31,431**	**4**
Bike Wash - Dissolver	$7,219	1
Patch Kit/8 Patches	$7,307	1
Road Tire Tube	$9,480	1
Touring Tire Tube	$7,425	1
⊟ **Clothing**	**$5,106**	**2**
Racing Socks, L	$2,427	1
Racing Socks, M	$2,679	1
Total	**$36,538**	**6**

More on Context Transition

Context transition is covered in Chapter 11 and again earlier in this chapter, in relationship to using calculated columns to simulate how the FILTER() function works. The concept of context transition is hard to learn, and it is especially difficult to understand when it occurs inside a virtual table like FILTER() because you can't see what is happening. This section walks through the process.

The FILTER() measure from earlier in this chapter is as follows:

```
Customers with sales greater than $5,000 =
    CALCULATE(COUNTROWS(Customers),
        FILTER(Customers, [Total Sales] >= 5000)
    )
```

The measure [Total Sales] contains the following formula:

```
[Total Sales] = SUM(Sales[ExtendedAmount])
```

If you substitute SUM(Sales[ExtendedAmount]) for [Total Sales] in the original formula above, you get the following:

```
Customers with sales greater than $5,000 Version2 =
    CALCULATE(COUNTROWS(Customers),
        FILTER(Customers, SUM(Sales[ExtendedAmount]) >= 5000)
    )
```

You should go ahead and create this formula so it is clear what is happening. The following image shows both versions of the formula placed in a matrix.

Category	Total Sales	Total Customers That Have Purchased	Customers with Sales Greater Than $5,000	Customers with sales greater than $5,000 Version2
Accessories	$700,760	15,114		18,484
Bikes	$28,318,145	9,132	1,712	18,484
Clothing	$339,773	6,852		18,484
Total	**$29,358,677**	**18,484**	**1,732**	**18,484**

The new formula returns all customers in the table instead of the correct number of customers with sales of at least $5,000. This is because of the hidden implicit CALCULATE() that has been mentioned a few times already. Technically speaking, when you write the following measure:

```
Total Sales = SUM(Sales[ExtendedAmount])
```

what is actually happening under the hood is the following formula:

```
Total Sales = CALCULATE(SUM(Sales[ExtendedAmount]))
```

Power BI adds a hidden CALCULATE() function and wraps it around every measure formula you write. You can't see this CALCULATE(), but it is there. We call this "invisible" CALCULATE() an implicit CALCULATE().

Okay, let's get back to the problem at hand: Go back into the new measure you just created and wrap the SUM() function inside CALCULATE() as follows:

```
Customers with Sales Greater Than $5,000 Version2 =
    CALCULATE(COUNTROWS(Customers),
        FILTER(Customers,
            CALCULATE(SUM(Sales[ExtendedAmount])) >= 5000
        )
    )
```

When you manually place CALCULATE() like this, it is called an explicit CALCULATE(). When you make this change, you get an expected result, as shown below.

Note: In this image, I have swapped the column `Products[Category]` with `Territories[Country]` to show an alternate view of the data. The measures work regardless of which column you have on Rows in the matrix.

Country	Total Sales	Total Customers That Have Purchased	Customers with Sales Greater Than $5,000	Customers with sales greater than $5,000 Version2
Australia	$9,061,001	3,591	719	719
Canada	$1,977,845	1,571	42	42
France	$2,644,018	1,810	163	163
Germany	$2,894,312	1,780	158	158
United Kingdom	$3,391,712	1,913	280	280
United States	$9,389,790	7,819	370	370
Total	**$29,358,677**	**18,484**	**1,732**	**1,732**

The point is that without the CALCULATE() function wrapped around SUM(Sales[ExtendedAmount]), something stops working. It doesn't matter if there is an implicit CALCULATE() that you can't see (inside another measure) or if there's an explicit CALCULATE() that you add yourself. You simply must have a CALCULATE() if you want this formula to work.

Remember that I said in Chapter 11 that row context does not automatically create filter context. In that case, I was talking about the row context in a calculated column, but as you now know, it is exactly the same in the FILTER() function. If you don't have this extra CALCULATE(), the filter that is first applied to the Customers table will not propagate to the Sales table as described above. It is the second CALCULATE() (either implicit or explicit) that causes the filter on the Customers table to propagate through the relationship to the Sales table before the rest of the FILTER() expression is evaluated for each row in the table.

Note: The only way to make this formula work is if you use a second CALCULATE() function (implicit or explicit) wrapped around SUM(Sales[ExtendedAmount]). This topic can take some time to get your head around and often doesn't really sink in until you have some real-world experience. If you are not getting it, don't worry. Just remember that sometimes an extra CALCULATE() can make the difference between a formula working and not working as expected. When you are good and ready, I recommend that you reread Chapter 11 and this chapter, working the examples along the way, until the idea is clear in your mind.

Virtual Table Lineage Revisited

I introduced the topic of lineage and visualising virtual tables in Chapter 13. I revisit the concept here to cement the learning.

Let's jump back to the version of the measure we've been working on in this chapter:

```
Customers with Sales Greater Than $5,000 =
    CALCULATE(COUNTROWS(Customers),
        FILTER(Customers, [Total Sales] >= 5000)
    )
```

I recommend that you think about the new table returned by FILTER() in the above formula as being a virtual table in your model. A virtual table created by a table function in DAX retains a link to the rest of the data model; this is called lineage. I like to visualise an imaginary temporary table being created above the real table in the data model, as illustrated below.

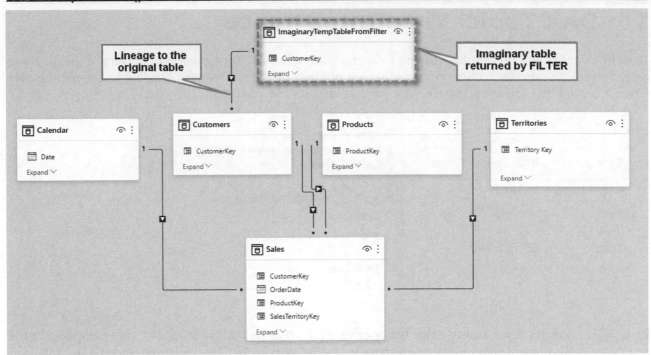

This new temporary table contains a subset of rows, as determined by FILTER(), but, importantly, it has a relationship back to the original table (lineage). Therefore, when this new temporary table is used inside CALCULATE() (as is the case here), CALCULATE() propagates the filters from the filtered copy of the table through the relationships, and any other tables that are connected downstream are filtered, too.

Remember that the image above is just an illustration of what is happening under the hood. The imaginary table is never materialised, and you can't see it, but it behaves as if it were part of the data model, as illustrated here.

> **Note:** Don't confuse lineage as described here with what happens when you use the New Table button in Power BI. The concept of lineage applies only with virtual tables used inside DAX formulas such as measures and calculated columns. At the end of the execution of a DAX formula, a virtual table ceases to exist, and the lineage is gone. On the other hand, the New Table button creates a new (physical) table that is stored in the data model. This new table does not retain lineage to the table it came from. If you want a table created by using the New Table button to filter your data model, you need to connect the new table by creating a physical relationship in the physical model.

16: DAX Topic: Time Intelligence

Time intelligence is a very important and powerful feature in DAX. Time intelligence refers to the ability to write formulas that refer to time periods that are not part of a visual without needing to change the date filters. Consider the following matrix, which shows sales for the year 2018.

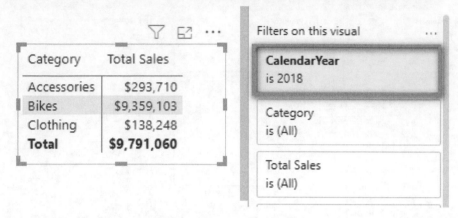

What if you wanted to see the sales for the prior year (2017) as well as the change in sales compared to the prior year? You could, of course, change the filter to see the sales for 2017, or you could place `CalendarYear` on Columns and then filter out the years that you are not interested in, as shown below.

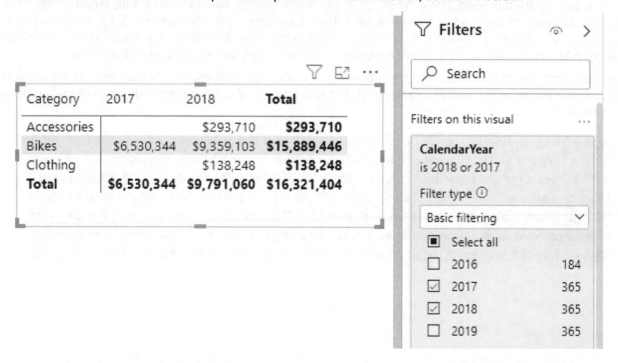

But doing it this way may not be the best approach; you can't get the same result in other matrixes without repeating the process, and besides, you can't calculate the change compared to the prior year this way.

Using Time Intelligence Functions

The general approach for time intelligence functions is to create measures that operate relative to a point in time. As an example, a measure such as `[Total Sales Last Year]` would show the sales from last year compared to a point in time: the year you have selected in the visual. Relative time intelligence functions are very useful as you can display the comparison periods without having to change the date selections in the matrix. This makes everything easier to do, and it also means you can build visuals, like the one shown below, that would not otherwise be possible.

CalendarYear	Total Sales	Change in Sales vs Prior Yesr
2016	$3,266,374	$3,266,374
2017	$6,530,344	$3,263,970
2018	$9,791,060	$3,260,717
2019	$9,770,900	-$20,161
Total	**$29,358,677**	**$9,770,900**

The DAX language includes many inbuilt time intelligence functions, and you can also write custom time intelligence functions of your own when needed. There are almost infinite use cases for time intelligence, and it would be impractical for the inbuilt functions to cater to every single use case. The inbuilt time intelligence functions therefore work only under certain circumstances. Here are a few of the rules for using inbuilt time intelligence functions:

- You must have a `Calendar` table that contains a contiguous range of dates that covers every day in the period you are analysing.

- The `Calendar` table must be at the day level of granularity.

- Every date must exist once and only once in the `Calendar` table.

- You can't skip any dates. (For example, you can't skip weekend dates just because your data doesn't include weekends.)

- The `Calendar` table must start at the beginning of the year of your first data point and extend to the end of the year of your last data point.

- Inbuilt time intelligence works only on a standard calendar (where the months are January, February, etc.).

- You can customize a standard calendar for different financial years. (For example, you can set the end date for a calendar to be June 30 or any other date instead of December 31.)

If for some reason these rules can't be met (e.g., if you have an ISO calendar, a 445 calendar, a weekly calendar, etc.), you can't use the inbuilt time intelligence functions to extract the results. If inbuilt time intelligence won't work in a particular situation, you can instead write your own custom time intelligence functions from scratch, typically using `CALCULATE()` and `FILTER()`. The DAX for this tends to be a bit complex, but don't worry, you can learn it, and I explain it later in this chapter.

Nonstandard Calendars

In some cases, you may need to use a nonstandard calendar for your reports. A standard calendar would not work in situations like the following:

- When you are building a data model using weekly or monthly data, so you use a weekly or monthly calendar instead of a daily calendar.

> **Note:** You could load your weekly or monthly data and still use a daily calendar—and this would work with inbuilt time intelligence as long as all the other criteria were still met. To make it work, your weekly or monthly data would use a single date to represent the time period (e.g., end-of-week date, end-of-month date), and you would then join this date to the standard `Calendar` table. I consider this to be a hack and not best practice, but it can work. I recommend that you instead learn to do it properly, using custom time intelligence, as described later in this chapter.

- If you use an ISO or 445 calendar for your accounting periods. This is very common in the retail industry, where businesses want to have regular trading periods with full weeks from Monday to Sunday. In a 445 calendar, there are 2 months that consist of 4 calendar weeks followed by 1 month with 5 calendar weeks. This helps smooth the months so they all start on a Monday and finish on a Sunday (for example) while also having 91 days in each quarter (91 × 4 quarters = 364 days).

- With 13 4-week periods instead of calendar months.

- With a calendar that uses times as well as dates (e.g., an hourly calendar).

There are so many variations that it is impossible to mention them all here, and it is also impossible for Power BI to cater to every possibility with inbuilt functions. So the rule is, if you have a standard calendar, you can use the inbuilt functions. If you don't have a standard calendar, you need to write your own custom time intelligence using `CALCULATE()` and `FILTER()`.

Here's How: Turning Off Auto Date/Time

Power BI has a feature called Auto Date/Time that helps beginners report on day, month, quarter, and year periods without the need to load their own calendar table. I personally do not like this feature. It automatically creates a hidden calendar table for every date column in your data. Each calendar table is standalone, which means these calendars don't work together. In addition, even though these tables are hidden from view, there can be so many of them that they can make your data models very large very quickly. Besides, you are learning to write DAX, so why not learn to do this reporting properly, with a dedicated calendar table? I recommend that you turn off the Auto Date/Time feature. To do so, follow these steps:

1. Select File, Options and Settings, Options.

2. Navigate to the Global section and choose Data Load (see #1 below).

3. Uncheck Auto Date/Time for New Files (#2).

4. If you already have a workbook that has Auto Date/Time turned on, turn it off by going to the Current File section and selecting Data Load (#3).

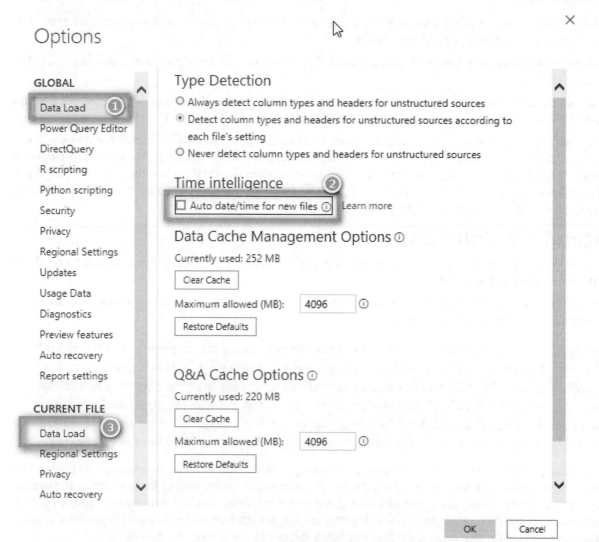

Inbuilt Time Intelligence

Before using the inbuilt time intelligence functions, you need to ensure that a few prerequisites are covered.

Using a Contiguous Date Range

In the sample data that you have been working with, the `Calendar` table already contains all the days of the year for the period that covers the `Sales` table. It is easy to ensure that all the dates are there. Just create a new matrix, put `'Calendar'[CalendarYear]` on Rows, and drop any string-based column (such as `MonthName`) into the Values section. After adding `MonthName` to the Values section (see #1 below), click the drop-down arrow and change the settings so that Values displays `Count of MonthName` (#2).

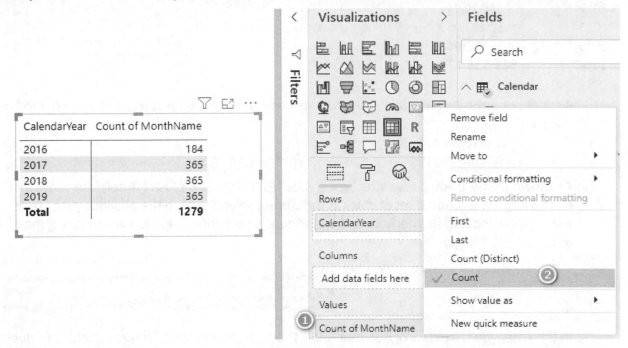

You're right: I did tell you not to create implicit measures. However, I often use implicit measures when doing quick tests on my data. This is one of those cases where it is fine to use them. Implicit measures are not wrong; it is just that you can't reuse them inside other formulas, and you have little control over the name and the formatting of an implicit measure. In this case, you don't need to reuse this measure, so it is fine to use it. As you can see above, this measure shows that the `Calendar` table has half a year for 2016 plus a full year for each of the following three years. After confirming the data in the `Calendar` table in this way, you can just remove this implicit measure from the visual as you don't need it anymore.

> **Note:** Technically, the rule is that the `Calendar` table should extend to full years covering all the dates in your model. In my experience, you can be a bit loose with this rule and choose not to extend backward and forward to always have complete years. But you do this at your own risk. If you want to be sure your model will work, you should extend your `Calendar` table to cover full years.

Here's How: Using SAMEPERIODLASTYEAR()

Let's look at an inbuilt time intelligence function you can use to easily write the [Total Sales Last Year] measure discussed earlier. Follow these steps:

1. Set up your matrix like the one below, with 'Calendar'[CalendarYear] on Rows and [Total Sales] on Values.

CalendarYear	Total Sales
2016	$3,266,374
2017	$6,530,344
2018	$9,791,060
2019	$9,770,900
Total	**$29,358,677**

2. Right-click on the Sales table in the Fields pane, select New Measure, and write the following measure:

```
Total Sales LY =
    CALCULATE([Total Sales], SAMEPERIODLASTYEAR('Calendar'[Date]))
```

As shown below, if you pause after typing SAMEPERIODLASTYEAR (, IntelliSense says that this function will return a set of dates in the current selection from the previous year. This is very helpful, indeed! (Remember that IntelliSense is your friend, and it is worth taking the time to read what it says.)

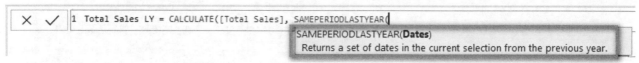

In this case, you should recognise that SAMEPERIODLASTYEAR() returns a table of values and that the table is being used inside CALCULATE() as an advanced filter.

Note: Notice in the IntelliSense that SAMEPERIODLASTYEAR() takes a single Dates parameter as its only input. All inbuilt time intelligence functions ask for this Dates parameter, and it always refers to the Date column in the Calendar table.

How Does SAMEPERIODLASTYEAR() Work?

In Chapter 15 I explained that CALCULATE() can take a table as an advanced filter input, and you can imagine the new table being connected to the data model. The table inside CALCULATE() then filters the rest of the tables in the data model (in this case, the Calendar table and the Sales table) before CALCULATE() completes the calculation. It is exactly the same with SAMEPERIODLASTYEAR(), as shown here:

```
Total Sales LY =
    CALCULATE([Total Sales], SAMEPERIODLASTYEAR('Calendar'[Date]))
```

In this instance, SAMEPERIODLASTYEAR() returns a table of dates that are the same dates coming from the matrix for the currently selected year, but SAMEPERIODLASTYEAR() time shifts the original dates back by one year.

Consider the cell highlighted in the matrix below. The function SAMEPERIODLASTYEAR() first reads the filter context from the current matrix to see which dates apply for "this year." In this case, the filter is on CalendarYear, and the filter for this cell is 2018 (see #1 below). So the dates for "this year" are all dates from January 1, 2018, through December 31, 2018. The SAMEPERIODLASTYEAR() function then takes the dates from the current filter context in the matrix, removes the current filters, time shifts the dates back one year, and returns a table of dates from January 1, 2017, through December 31, 2017.

CalendarYear	Total Sales	Total Sales LY
2016	$3,266,374	
2017	$6,530,344	$3,266,374
2018 ①	$9,791,060	$6,530,344
2019	$9,770,900	$9,791,060
Total	**$29,358,677**	**$19,587,777**

You can imagine the new table created by SAMEPERIODLASTYEAR() as a temporary table sitting above the Calendar table and retaining a relationship to the original Calendar table, as shown below. (Remember that this is logically how it works; you can't actually see this table.)

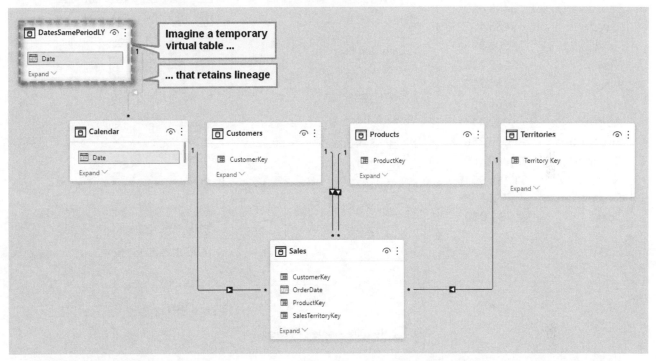

This table is then passed to CALCULATE(), and CALCULATE() uses this temporary table and propagates the filters through the relationships in the model. The temporary table (the table of dates from SAMEPERIODLASTYEAR()) filters the Calendar table, which then filters the Sales table before the calculation for [Total Sales LY] is evaluated.

> **Tip:** Read the paragraph above a couple of times if you need to until you have it clearly in your head.

Calculating Year-to-Date Sales

A very common business need is to calculate figures on a year-to-date (YTD) basis. Fortunately, there is an inbuilt DAX function for this. Before you write any YTD formula, it is a good idea to set up a matrix that will give you immediate feedback if your formula is performing as expected. As you do, it is important to set up the matrix so that you have a continuous date range. Set up a new matrix like the one shown below before proceeding. Note the filter on `CalendarYear = 2018`.

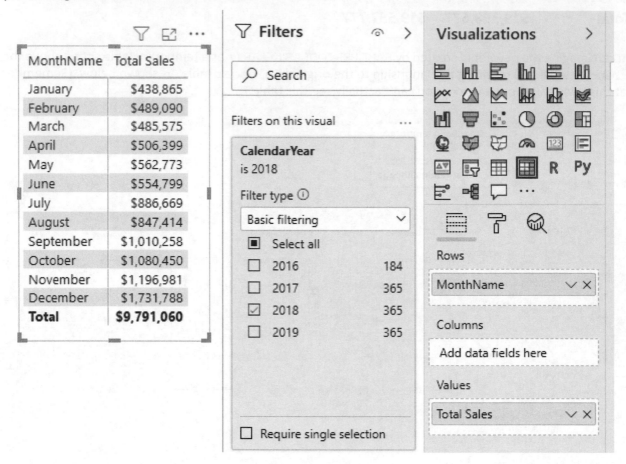

Note that the periods in the matrix are contiguous (i.e., the months of the year 2018). If you didn't have a filter on `CalendarYear = 2018` but instead had `CalendarYear = ALL`, the matrix would show the total sales for January across all years, for February across all years, etc. This would not be a contiguous range, and hence the formula would not work.

You can right-click on the `Sales` table in the Fields pane, select New Measure, and write the following measure:

```
Total Sales YTD = TOTALYTD([Total Sales], 'Calendar'[Date])
```

Then you can apply appropriate formatting to the measure and add the measure to your matrix.

When you are done, it is very easy to check whether the formula is working correctly. As shown in the image below, you can add a new slicer (see #1 below), and you can multi-select the months January, February, and March in the slicer by pressing the Ctrl key while clicking these months. You can then compare the value for March YTD (#2) with the summed total of January, February, and March (#3).

(1)

MonthName
■ January
■ February
■ March
☐ April
☐ May
☐ June
☐ July
☐ August
☐ September
☐ October
☐ November
☐ December

MonthName ▲	Total Sales	Total Sales YTD
January	$438,865	$438,865
February	$489,090	$927,956
March	$485,575	$1,413,530
Total	**$1,413,530**	**$1,413,530**

(3)   (2)

Note: Remember that is very important that you test your measures after you write them. As a data modeller, you are responsible for ensuring that the measures you write return the expected results.

This is a really good example of the benefit of writing measures in the context of a matrix. The immediate feedback you get allows you to check whether your formula is correct. Once you have written a formula, you can apply some conditional formatting to your matrix, as shown below, to get another visual clue about whether everything is working well.

MonthName	Total Sales	Total Sales YTD
January	$438,865	$438,865
February	$489,090	$927,956
March	$485,575	$1,413,530
April	$506,399	$1,919,930
May	$562,773	$2,482,702
June	$554,799	$3,037,501
July	$886,669	$3,924,170
August	$847,414	$4,771,584
September	$1,010,258	$5,781,842
October	$1,080,450	$6,862,291
November	$1,196,981	$8,059,273
December	$1,731,788	$9,791,060
Total	**$9,791,060**	**$9,791,060**

Practice Exercises: Time Intelligence

When writing [Total Sales YTD], you may have noticed from the IntelliSense tooltip that there are two other functions that are very similar to TOTALYTD(): TOTALMTD() and TOTALQTD(). In the following exercises you'll get some practice using these two functions. Before you complete these two exercises, make sure you set up a matrix like the one below that will give you feedback about whether your formula is correct. Set up the matrix like this:

1. Place CalendarYear and MonthName on Filters.

2. Filter for CalendarYear = 2018 and MonthName = January.

3. Put 'Calendar'[DayNumberOfMonth] on Rows.

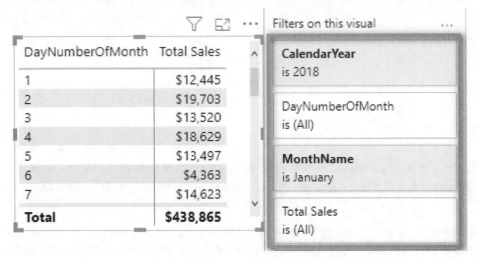

Write formulas for the following measures. Find the solutions to these practice exercises in "Appendix A: Answers to Practice Exercises" on page 252.

61. [Total Sales Month to Date]

62. [Total Sales Quarter to Date]

How Did It Go?

Did you set up a matrix with suitable values on Rows, as I showed with [Total Sales YTD] earlier in this chapter? Placing MonthName on rows will not work for Practice Exercise 61. Instead, you need to put a column such as DayNumberOfMonth in the matrix if you want to be able to see that the formula is working correctly. For Practice Exercise 62, you can place MonthName on Rows.

Your matrixes should look like the ones below after you add the measures.

DayNumberOfMonth	Total Sales	Total Sales Month to Date
1	$12,445	$12,445
2	$19,703	$32,148
3	$13,520	$45,668
4	$18,629	$64,297
5	$13,497	$77,794
6	$4,363	$82,157
7	$14,623	$96,780
Total	**$96,780**	**$96,780**

Note that for this matrix, I added a filter that sets WeekNumberOfYear to 1 to show only the values for the first week in January. The total MTD on Day 7 is equal to the total sales for the 7 days.

Your `Total QTD` values should look as shown below with the filter on `CalendarYear = 2018`.

MonthName	Total Sales	Total Sales Quarter to Date
January	$438,865	$438,865
February	$489,090	$927,956
March	$485,575	$1,413,530
April	$506,399	$506,399
May	$562,773	$1,069,172
June	$554,799	$1,623,971
July	$886,669	$886,669
August	$847,414	$1,734,082
September	$1,010,258	$2,744,340
October	$1,080,450	$1,080,450
November	$1,196,981	$2,277,431
December	$1,731,788	$4,009,218

Changing Financial Year-Ending Dates

Many of the inbuilt time intelligence functions allow you to specify a different end-of-year date if required to complete the calculation correctly. In such a case, there is an optional parameter where you specify the year-end date, as shown here:

```
Total Sales FYTD =
        TOTALYTD([Total Sales], 'Calendar'[Date], "YearEndDateHere")
```

Here's an example for a financial year ending June 30:

```
Total Sales FYTD =
        TOTALYTD([Total Sales], 'Calendar'[Date], "30/6")
```

> **Note:** This example uses a non-U.S. date format. For the U.S. date format, it looks like this:
>
> ```
> Total Sales FYTD USA =
>         TOTALYTD([Total Sales], 'Calendar'[Date], "6/30")
> ```

Notice that there is no need to specify a year when referring to the year-end date. It is simply day and month. In my experience, this year-end date can be pretty much any text string you like that clearly communicates the date, such as "30-Jun" or "30 June" or even "June 30".

Practice Exercises: Time Intelligence, Continued

Write formulas for the following measures. Find the solutions to these practice exercises in "Appendix A: Answers to Practice Exercises" on page 252.

63. [Total Sales FYTD 30 June]

64. [Total Sales FYTD 31 March]

How Did It Go?

Did you set up a matrix like the one below? (To make it easier to spot the pattern, you can apply conditional formatting as shown here by selecting Conditional Formatting, Data Bars.)

CalendarYear	Total Sales FYTD 30 June	Total Sales FYTD 31 March
2017		
January	$3,863,120	$3,863,120
February	$4,413,937	$4,413,937
March	$5,058,072	$5,058,072
April	$5,721,764	$663,692
May	$6,395,321	$1,337,248
June	$7,072,084	$2,014,012
July	$500,365	$2,514,377
August	$1,046,367	$3,060,379
September	$1,396,834	$3,410,846
October	$1,812,224	$3,826,236
November	$2,147,319	$4,161,331
December	$2,724,633	$4,738,645
2018		
January	$3,163,498	$5,177,510
February	$3,652,588	$5,666,601
March	$4,138,163	$6,152,175
April	$4,644,563	$506,399
May	$5,207,335	$1,069,172
June	$5,762,134	$1,623,971
July	$886,669	$2,510,640
August	$1,734,082	$3,358,053
September	$2,744,340	$4,368,312
October	$3,824,790	$5,448,761
November	$5,021,771	$6,645,742
December	$6,753,559	$8,377,530

Setting Calendar Columns Not to Aggregate

If you look at the Fields pane for the `Calendar` table, you will find a ∑ (sigma) icon before some column names, as shown below.

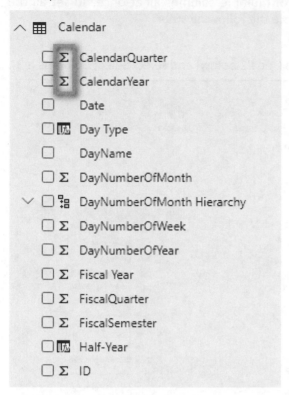

The sigma icon indicates that these columns are set to autosummarize. The sigma symbol generically refers to summing, but in Power BI, it can refer to any of the summarization options available. If you select one of the columns with a sigma next to it and navigate to the Column Tools tab (see #1 below), you can change the column behaviour by setting Summarization to Don't Summarize (#2).

When you make this change from within the Report view, you must change the columns one at a time. This is tedious, and there is a better way, as explained next.

Here's How: Changing Summarization for Multiple Columns at Once

It is possible to change the default aggregation behaviour of multiple columns all at once. To set all the `Calendar` table columns so they do not summarize, complete the following steps:

1. Navigate to the Model view (see #1 below).

2. In the Fields pane, right-click on the `Calendar` table (see #2 below) and select Select Columns (#3).

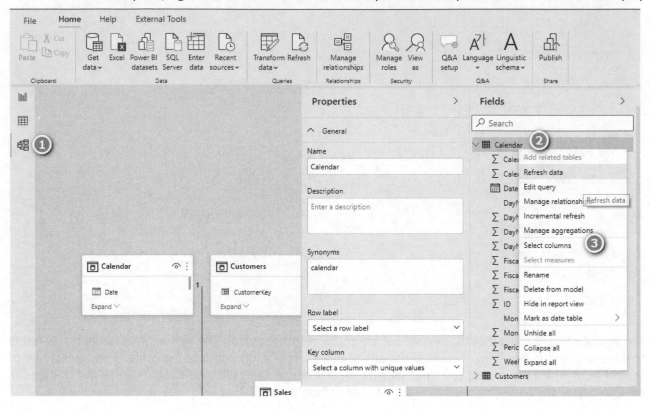

3.   Expand the Advanced pane under Properties (see #1 below).

4.   From the Summarize By drop-down menu (see #2 below), select None (#3).

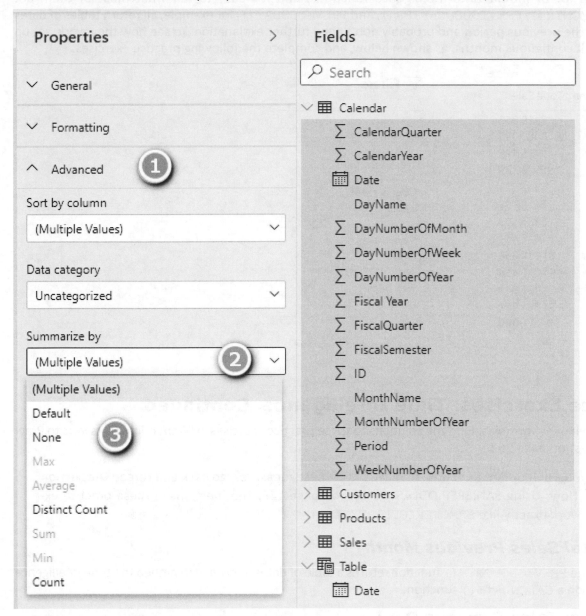

This is how you can change the summarization for all the columns at once.

Note: There are other things you can do by taking a similar approach in the Model view. For example, you can change the numeric formatting of columns and measures, and you can move columns and measures into subfolders. It is worth doing some exploration while you are here to see what is possible.

Practicing with Other Time Intelligence Functions

There are a lot of inbuilt time intelligence functions, and it's easy to tell what most of them do. PREVIOUSMONTH(), PREVIOUSQUARTER(), and PREVIOUSDAY(), for example, all return tables of dates referring to the previous period and probably don't need further explanation. To see how they work, set up a matrix with contiguous months, as shown below, and complete the following practice exercises.

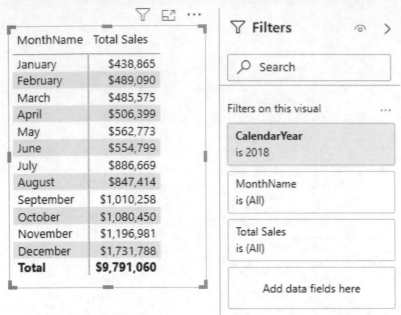

Practice Exercises: Time Intelligence, Continued

Write the following formulas. Find the solutions to these practice exercises in "Appendix A: Answers to Practice Exercises" on page 252.

> **Tip:** If you don't understand how to build any of these measures, go back and reread the section "Here's How: Using SAMEPERIODLASTYEAR()" on page 148. The functions in these practice exercises work exactly like SAMEPERIODLASTYEAR().

65. [Total Sales Previous Month]

Given that the PREVIOUSMONTH() function returns a table of dates, you need to embed the time intelligence formula inside a CALCULATE() function.

66. [Total Sales Previous Day]

You need to set up a suitable matrix that gives you immediate feedback about whether your formula is working. Put 'Calendar'[DayNumberOfMonth] on Rows and make sure you filter for a single month.

67. [Total Sales Previous Quarter]

As with Practice Exercise 66, you need to set up a suitable matrix for context. You can work out how to do this one yourself.

Using the DATEADD() Inbuilt Function

The DAX inbuilt time intelligence function DATEADD() can be used to give exactly the same results as some of the formulas already covered in this chapter. The following example shows how to use DATEADD():

```
Total Sales Previous Quarter 2 =
    CALCULATE([Total Sales],
        DATEADD('Calendar'[Date],MAX('Calendar'[Date]),-1,QUARTER)
    )
```

The syntax for DATEADD() can be difficult to understand when you are learning DAX, and the use of MAX() in the formula can be particularly challenging to grasp, but don't worry: I cover that next. Many of the functions I have covered so far in this chapter are actually syntax sugar for DATEADD(). Microsoft developers have really tried hard to provide simple ways of writing DAX, even for those who have minimal knowledge of how the language works. Instead of having to learn about CALCULATE() and DATEADD(), you can leverage the power of DAX time intelligence by using simple functions like the ones at the start of this chapter. But CALCULATE() is lurking under the hood. CALCULATE() and its cousin CALCULATETABLE() are the only DAX functions that can change filtering behaviour. If there are changes to filtering and you can't see a CALCULATE() in the function, then you are working with a syntax sugar formula. SAMEPERIODLASTYEAR(), PREVIOUSMONTH(), PREVIOUSDAY(), and PREVIOUSQUARTER() are all syntax sugar versions of the DATEADD() function.

Writing Your Own Time Intelligence Functions

As mentioned earlier in this chapter, writing your own time intelligence functions is a bit harder than using the inbuilt functions, particularly when you are new to the concepts. When you use an inbuilt time intelligence function, DAX works out the dates needed to complete the time shift for you. When you write your own time intelligence functions, it is up to you to determine how to select the new set of dates required to complete the time shift. When you get the hang of it, you will find it quite straightforward (and that will be a good sign of how much progress you are making in understanding DAX).

There are a couple of strange things in the syntax that you need to get your head around before you can fully understand what you're doing with custom time intelligence. I explain these things now, and you will be writing your own custom time intelligence functions in no time at all.

These are the two concepts you need to get your head around:

- Concept 1: Thinking "whole of table" when thinking about filter context
- Concept 2: Knowing how to use MIN() and MAX()

The following sections cover these concepts and provide examples that will help you cement what you learn.

Concept 1: Thinking "Whole of Table" When Thinking About Filter Context

Consider the single row highlighted in the matrix below. (This is the same matrix from the earlier examples.)

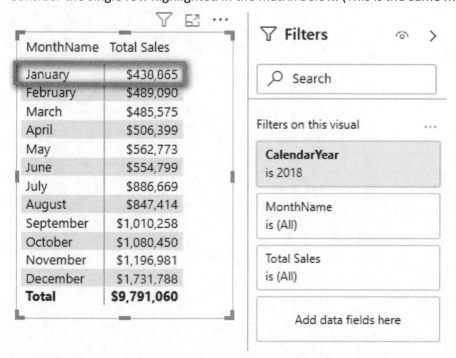

This matrix is filtered for `'Calendar'[CalendarYear]=2018` in the visual card shown above. Also, the highlighted row, January, is also filtered by `'Calendar'[MonthName]="January"`, which appears in the Rows drop zone for the matrix. When these two filters are combined, the single cell/value for `[Total Sales]` is filtered for the period January 2018. So there are only 31 days that are used in the `Calendar` table in the data model for this one row in the matrix visual. With this in mind, it is possible to imagine this filter applied on the back end.

> **Tip:** Practice using your imagination to think about what tables would look like with filters applied. (For example, in the example above, the `Calendar` table would have only 31 days visible with the filters `'Calendar'[CalendarYear]=2018` and `'Calendar'[MonthName]="January"` applied.) This is all happening in computer memory, on the fly. You can't see this filtering happening, but it is important that you be able to visualise it happening in your mind. Thinking about the filtering behaviour that is occurring under the hood will make it easier to write custom time intelligence formulas—as well as other DAX formulas.

When thinking about the filtering that is being applied, you should think about the whole table, not just the two columns with filters applied. It is clear that there is only one month visible (January) and only one year visible (2018), but it is also true that there are 31 `DayNumberOfMonth` values visible (those from 1 through 31), and there are 5 different `WeekNumberOfYear` values (1 through 5). It is possible to reference any and all of these other columns and values in your DAX formulas after the initial filter context is applied, even though these other columns are not directly being filtered.

As you can see in the next image, after you filter the `Calendar` table based on Month = January and Year = 2018, there are only 31 rows remaining in the filtered version of the table. All other columns in the table are now filtered, too. There is no direct filter placed on the `Date` column, and yet you can see in the image that the dates have inherited the filter because it is part of the `Calendar` table; as a result, only the dates 1/1/2018 through 31/1/2018 remain. This is true for every other column in the table, too. You can reference any columns from any tables in your DAX formulas, even if they are not directly filtered, and with that knowledge, you can write very powerful DAX indeed. But you need to be able to think "whole of table" to be able to understand how it works and what result you will get.

Date	DayNumberOfWeek	DayName	MonthName	MonthNumberOfYear	CalendarQuarter	CalendarYear
1/01/2018	2	Monday	January	1	1	2018
2/01/2018	3	Tuesday	January	1	1	2018
3/01/2018	4	Wednesday	January	1	1	2018
4/01/2018	5	Thursday	January	1	1	2018
5/01/2018	6	Friday	January	1	1	2018
6/01/2018	7	Saturday	January	1	1	2018
7/01/2018	1	Sunday	January	1	1	2018
8/01/2018	2	Monday	January	1	1	2018
9/01/2018	3	Tuesday	January	1	1	2018
10/01/2018	4	Wednesday	January	1	1	2018
11/01/2018	5	Thursday	January	1	1	2018
12/01/2018	6	Friday	January	1	1	2018
13/01/2018	7	Saturday	January	1	1	2018
14/01/2018	1	Sunday	January	1	1	2018
15/01/2018	2	Monday	January	1	1	2018
16/01/2018	3	Tuesday	January	1	1	2018
17/01/2018	4	Wednesday	January	1	1	2018
18/01/2018	5	Thursday	January	1	1	2018
19/01/2018	6	Friday	January	1	1	2018
20/01/2018	7	Saturday	January	1	1	2018
21/01/2018	1	Sunday	January	1	1	2018
22/01/2018	2	Monday	January	1	1	2018
23/01/2018	3	Tuesday	January	1	1	2018
24/01/2018	4	Wednesday	January	1	1	2018
25/01/2018	5	Thursday	January	1	1	2018
26/01/2018	6	Friday	January	1	1	2018
27/01/2018	7	Saturday	January	1	1	2018
28/01/2018	1	Sunday	January	1	1	2018
29/01/2018	2	Monday	January	1	1	2018
30/01/2018	3	Tuesday	January	1	1	2018
31/01/2018	4	Wednesday	January	1	1	2018

Concept 2: Knowing How to Use MIN() and MAX()

It is very common to use the MIN() and MAX() functions inside FILTER() when you write custom time intelligence functions.

> **Note:** You can also use FIRSTDATE() and LASTDATE() if you prefer, although for reasons beyond the scope of this book, it is better to use MIN() and MAX() in this case.

You'll learn more details in the examples that follow, but for now there is one key concept about MIN() and MAX() that you should understand, and it is very important (so focus!): Whenever you use an aggregation function around a column in a DAX formula, it will always respect the initial filter context coming from the visual.

To see how this works, let's go back to the matrix from before, shown again below for convenience.

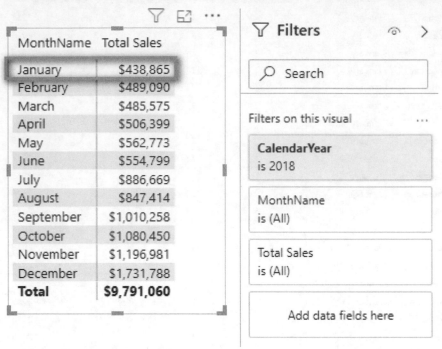

You know that the matrix has filtered the `Calendar` table so that only 31 days remain. Consider the following formulas:

```
= MIN('Calendar'[Date])
= MAX('Calendar'[Date])
```

Given that `MIN()` and `MAX()` always respect the current filter context, what would be the results of these DAX formulas for the highlighted row in the matrix above? Answer in your head before moving on. It might help to imagine the filtered version of the table in your head.

The answer for the first formula, of course, is January 1, 2018—the first date in the filter context. It's not the first date in the `Calendar` table but the first date in the current filter context. And the answer for the second formula is January 31, 2018—the last date in the filter context. This is really important because the `'Calendar'[Date]` column was not part of the filter, but that column is indeed filtered by the visual. (This is a good example of thinking "whole of table.")

So you can think of `MIN()` and `MAX()` as tools that can "harvest" the value from the current filter context, in any available column across the whole table (and any other table for that matter), and you can use the harvested values in your DAX formulas. Remember this fact about `MIN()` and `MAX()` when you get into the examples below.

Because my earlier about `MIN()` and `MAX()` is so important, I want to repeat it: Whenever you use an aggregation function around a column in a DAX formula, it will always respect the initial filter context coming from the visual.

> **Note:** One of the differences between DAX and Excel is that you can use `MIN()` and `MAX()` over non-numeric columns. If you were to write `MIN('Calendar'[DayName])`, the result would be `Friday`, the first day of the week when the `DayName` column is sorted alphabetically.

Writing Custom Time Intelligence Functions

This section shows how to write a custom version of `[Total Sales YTD]`, using `CALCULATE()` and `FILTER()`. I strongly encourage you to write this formula yourself for practice. There is a lot that can (and will) go wrong when you type your own custom time intelligence functions, and you need lots of practice to get it right. There are square bracket sets, sets of parentheses, new line spacing to make it easier to read, commas to be added in the right places, etc. So make sure you actually write the following formula on your own computer. Go ahead and type in this formula now:

```
Total Sales YTD Manual =
        CALCULATE([Total Sales],
        FILTER(ALL('Calendar'),
        'Calendar'[CalendarYear] = MAX('Calendar'[CalendarYear])
        && 'Calendar'[Date] <= MAX('Calendar'[Date])
        )
    )
```

Also make sure to set up a matrix like the one you used earlier so that you can get immediate feedback about whether your formula is correct.

This formula needs a bit of explanation. You can see below that lines 4 through 8 are all part of a `FILTER()` function because you can see that the `)` on line 8 is left aligned to the `F` in `FILTER()` on line 4.

> **Note:** I have used http://daxformatter.com below to make it easier to refer to the lines in the formulas. I mentioned DAX Formatter in Chapter 10, and you can see here that it is a great tool for helping you read DAX formulas.

```
1   Total Sales YTD Manual =
2   CALCULATE (
3       [Total Sales],
4       FILTER (
5           ALL ( 'Calendar' ),
6           'Calendar'[CalendarYear] = MAX ( 'Calendar'[CalendarYear] )
7               && 'Calendar'[Date] <= MAX ( 'Calendar'[Date] )
8       )
9   )
```

This `FILTER()` function returns a table to the function `CALCULATE()`. `CALCULATE()` then applies a filter for this table of dates and propagates this filter to the `Sales` table prior to evaluating `[Total Sales]`. Let's look more closely at lines 6 and 7 in the `FILTER()` function. Line 6 reads:

```
'Calendar'[CalendarYear] = MAX('Calendar'[CalendarYear])
```

Okay, I hear you saying, "How can the calendar year be equal to the `MAX()` of the calendar year?" What is really happening is that there is a column name on the left side of the equals sign, and there is a `MAX()` function on the right side. Remember from earlier in this chapter that a `MIN()` or `MAX()` in a formula like this always respects the current filter context. So the way to read line 6 of this formula is as follows: "Add a filter to the table so that the column `'Calendar'[CalendarYear]` is equal to the maximum value in my current filter context coming from my matrix."

For example, in the matrix below, the maximum date of the highlighted row is March 31, 2018, and hence `MAX('Calendar'[CalendarYear]) = 2018`.

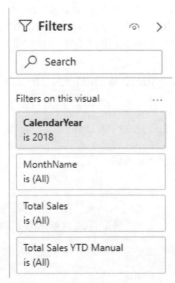

MonthName	Total Sales	Total Sales YTD Manual
January	$438,865	$438,865
February	$489,090	$927,956
March	$485,575	$1,413,530
April	$506,399	$1,919,930
May	$562,773	$2,482,702
June	$554,799	$3,037,501
July	$886,669	$3,924,170
August	$847,414	$4,771,584
September	$1,010,258	$5,781,842
October	$1,080,450	$6,862,291
November	$1,196,981	$8,059,273
December	$1,731,788	$9,791,060
Total	**$9,791,060**	**$9,791,060**

Filters

Search

Filters on this visual

CalendarYear
is 2018

MonthName
is (All)

Total Sales
is (All)

Total Sales YTD Manual
is (All)

See how you need to think "whole of table" here? The initial filter context is applied over the month of March 2018, but the MAX() formula is working over the CalendarYear column. To imagine this filter context acting on the table in your data model, mentally apply the filters: There were 31 rows left in the Calendar table, and for each of these rows, the value in 'Calendar'[CalendarYear] was 2018. As a result (in this case), the MIN() of 'Calendar'[CalendarYear] would also return 2018—as would SUM() and AVERAGE(), for that matter. So line 6 is really saying "Filter my table where 'Calendar'[CalendarYear] equals the current filter context year," which is 2018 in this case. If you stopped here, the formula would return the total sales for the current year, which is not what is needed to solve this problem. You only want to keep the sales up until the end of March for the highlighted row in the matrix.

Let's move on. Line 7 starts with the double ampersand operator (which means AND and says, in this case, to do both line 6 and line 7) and then says:

```
'Calendar'[Date] <= MAX('Calendar'Date])
```

The same applies here as with line 6. MAX('Calendar'[Date]) reads the initial filter context from the matrix and hence returns the value March 31, 2018, for the highlighted row in the matrix. Therefore, this part of the formula adds an AND condition so that the underlying table is filtered for 'Calendar'[CalendarYear] = 2018 and also for the condition 'Calendar'[Date] is on or before March 31, 2018. As you can deduce, this is all the dates year to date.

> **Note:** If you need to visualise what is going on here, go to the Data view and manually apply these filters to the 'Calendar'[Year] and 'Calendar'[Date] columns in the Data view table. Doing so can help you build your understanding.

Let's keep going. As you go to the next row in the matrix visual, the calendar year stays the same, but the month-end date moves to the end of the next month. So the number of days that are included increases as you work down the rows in the matrix.

> **Note:** it is important to point out that you could not use MIN() in line 7 as you could do in line 6; this time, it has to be MAX(). If you used MIN(), you would get March 1, 2018, as the last date, and the year-to-date result would give you a total up to the start of March instead of up to the end of March; you would be missing almost a full month of sales. It is important to think about what your formulas need and make sure to provide the right formulas to achieve the desired outcome.

Now let's go back to ALL('Calendar'). Line 5 of the formula refers to ALL('Calendar') instead of just the Calendar table (which you have used previously). ALL(), as discussed in Chapter 14, is the "remove filter" function. (If necessary, go back to Chapter 14 and refresh your memory about ALL() before moving on.)

It is important to use the ALL() function here because you know that the matrix applies the current filter context before doing the calculation. Probably the easiest way to explain why you need the ALL() function is to look at what would happen if you didn't use ALL().

Consider again the highlighted row in the matrix above (March 2018). You know that the initial filter context for this row of the matrix is for all 31 days in the month of March 2018. You can imagine that the Calendar table is filtered behind the scenes so that only these 31 days of March 2018 are visible.

Now let's look at why the [Total Sales YTD Manual] formula does not work without the ALL() function. You should write the following formula and add it to your matrix, as shown below. (Don't miss the opportunity to practice now!)

```
1  Total Sales YTD Doesn't Work =
2  CALCULATE (
3      [Total Sales],
4      FILTER (
5          'Calendar',
6          'Calendar'[CalendarYear] = MAX ( 'Calendar'[CalendarYear] )
7              && 'Calendar'[Date] <= MAX ( 'Calendar'[Date] )
8      )
9  )
```

MonthName	Total Sales	Total Sales YTD Doesn't Work
January	$438,865	$438,865
February	$489,090	$489,090
March	$485,575	$485,575
April	$506,399	$506,399
May	$562,773	$562,773
June	$554,799	$554,799
July	$886,669	$886,669
August	$847,414	$847,414
September	$1,010,258	$1,010,258
October	$1,080,450	$1,080,450
November	$1,196,981	$1,196,981
December	$1,731,788	$1,731,788
Total	**$9,791,060**	**$9,791,060**

You can see in this matrix that this formula is giving the sales for the current month rather than YTD in each row of the matrix. The reason it doesn't work is related to the initial filter context discussed earlier. For the `March 2018` row, the initial filter context applied a filter so that only the 31 days of March 2018 were "visible" in the `Calendar` table (behind the scenes). So how can the formula possibly return sales for all days "year to date," including the sales from January and February, if only March remains due to the existing filters? The dates in January and February were already filtered out by the initial filter context coming from the matrix, so you can't get the sales for these months to somehow reappear for the new formula if you write the formula this way.

If you want to include sales from January and February in the row next to the actual sales for March, you must first remove the filter created by the matrix. This is what `ALL()` does when it is wrapped around the `Calendar` table in line 5: It removes the filter context that comes from the matrix that is applied to the `Calendar` table. You first remove the filters (using `ALL()`) and then reapply the filters you want to use in lines 6 and 7 so that you end up with all the dates YTD.

> **Note:** Custom time intelligence always uses some form of `ALL('Calendar')` to remove the initial filter context. The `FILTER()` function therefore operates over an unfiltered copy of the `Calendar` table. But the `MIN()` and `MAX()` functions operate with the initial filter context before the `ALL()` function removes it.

> **Tip:** Go back and read this section again if necessary until you understand it well.

Using ID Columns for Time Intelligence

Good calendar tables contain ID columns to uniquely identify the time periods you wish to use in your reports, particularly if you want to write custom time intelligence functions. A good example of this is a month ID column. I'm not talking about month number of year here. Month number of year would start at 1, increase by 1 for each month until it reaches 12, and then start again from 1 in the next year. When I talk about ID columns, I am talking about columns for unique IDs. For example, a month ID column would start at 1 for the first month in the calendar, progress through 12 to complete the first year, and then continue counting through 13, 14, 15, and so on, incrementing by 1 for every month in the calendar table. ID columns like this are super helpful when you're writing custom time intelligence functions, particularly with a non-standard calendar, such as an ISO calendar or a 445 calendar. The benefit of such an ID column is that it gives you a nice clean numeric column to move back and forward through time inside your formulas using DAX. To illustrate this point, in this section I show how to write a formula that calculates a rolling 6-month sales total. As always, I also set up a matrix to help illustrate the learning.

In the image below, you can see that I have `CalendarYear` and `MonthName` on Rows and the `[Total Sales]` measure and `Max of Month ID` implicit measure on Values (see #1 below). To create the implicit measure `Max of Month ID`, I simply dragged the `Month ID` column to the Values section and changed the aggregation to Maximum (see #2).

> **Note:** This is another good example of when to use implicit measures to help understand data. Again, I don't recommend using implicit measures as a substitute for writing DAX for a final report, but it is a quick way to help visualise what you are doing while writing formulas.

The image below shows how the month ID increments for every month in the visual—excluding the total rows for years, of course (#3).

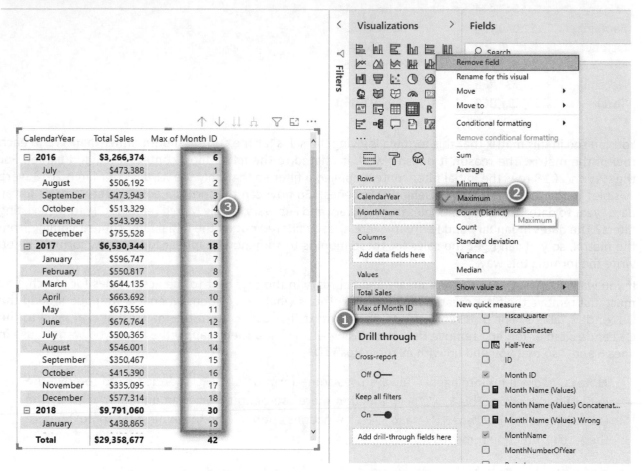

In the image above, you can see that the month ID for December 2017 is 18. To write a formula showing sales for the 6 months prior to December 2017, you would need everything from July 2017 through December 2017 inclusive. Another way to say this is that you would need everything from month ID 13 through month ID 18 inclusive. See how much easier it is to get your head around the problem when you lay out a good visual to help?

Do you remember the trick using the `MAX()` function in DAX to "harvest" a value from a table? The image above uses an implicit measure that is the equivalent of writing `MAX([Month ID])` in DAX and that returns the month ID for each month. With this in mind:

- `MAX([Month ID])` gives the last month needed in the total (December 2017 in this case, or Month ID 18)

- `MAX([Month ID])` – 5 gives the starting month needed in the total (July 2017 in this case, or Month ID 13)

Using this information, you can write the following formula:

```
Rolling 6 Months Sales =
    CALCULATE([Total Sales],
        FILTER(ALL('Calendar'),
        'Calendar'[Month ID] >= MAX('Calendar'[Month ID])-5
        && 'Calendar'[Month ID] <= MAX('Calendar'[Month ID])
        )
    )
```

The results look as shown below.

CalendarYear	Total Sales	Rolling 6 Months Sales
⊟ **2016**	**$3,266,374**	**$3,266,374**
July	$473,388	$473,388
August	$506,192	$979,580
September	$473,943	$1,453,523
October	$513,329	$1,966,852
November	$543,993	$2,510,846
December	$755,528	$3,266,374
⊟ **2017**	**$6,530,344**	**$2,724,633**
January	$596,747	$3,389,732
February	$550,817	$3,434,357
March	$644,135	$3,604,549
April	$663,692	$3,754,912
May	$673,556	$3,884,475
June	$676,764	$3,805,711
July	$500,365	$3,709,329
August	$546,001	$3,704,514
September	$350,467	$3,410,846
October	$415,390	$3,162,544
November	$335,095	$2,824,083
December	$577,314	$2,724,633

This example shows how useful it can be to add ID columns to a `Calendar` table. Doing so allows you to write very powerful and otherwise complex custom time intelligence formulas.

Using DATESINPERIOD()

Before moving on, I would like to point out that there is actually an easier way to write the rolling 6-month sales measure shown above—by using an inbuilt time intelligence function. I am not deliberately trying to show you hard ways to solve problems. I am trying to cover different techniques to solve common problems and to help you learn and understand DAX. The concept of using ID columns as demonstrated above is very powerful indeed, and it will come in handy for times when you can't use the inbuilt functions (for whatever reason).

Here is the inbuilt time intelligence version of the same formula used in the preceding example, just so you know:

```
Rolling 6 Months Sales 2 =
    CALCULATE (
        [Total Sales],
        DATESINPERIOD ('Calendar'[Date], MAX ('Calendar'[Date]), -6, MONTH)
    )
```

This formula uses the inbuilt time intelligence function `DATESINPERIOD()` to work out the dates over the past 6 months, using syntax that is pretty easy to understand. Note that I still use `MAX('Calendar'[Date])` to find the last date needed in the calculation and to go back in time 6 months from that date. Now you know how `MAX()` works inside formulas.

Practice Exercises: Time Intelligence, Continued

It's time for some more practice. Write the following formulas. First set up an appropriate matrix so that you will get immediate feedback about whether each formula is correct. (By now you should have an idea what type of matrix would help in this case.) Find the solutions to these practice exercises in "Appendix A: Answers to Practice Exercises" on page 252.

68. [Total Sales Moving Annual Total]

With this DAX formula, you need to create a rolling 12-month total of sales. It will always show you 12 months' worth of sales, up to the end of the current month. Think about the problem using English words first and then convert that to DAX, using the techniques you have learnt here. I show my tips for writing this measure later in this chapter, but you should give it a go now, before you see those tips.

Hint: Dates in DAX work as they do in Excel. For example, if you have a date, you can subtract 365 to get the same date last year (though not for leap years, of course). You could also use the `DATESINPERIOD()` function I just covered to solve this problem. However, you should try this practice exercise as a custom time intelligence function first.

69. [Total Sales Rolling 90 Days]

This is the same as the formula for Practice Exercise 68, but instead of delivering a rolling 12-month total, you should deliver a rolling 90-day total. Try to complete this practice exercise from scratch using custom time intelligence, without referencing Practice Exercise 68. It is good practice to try thinking like the DAX engine.

Tips for Writing a Moving Annual Total

This section walks through how to create the formula in Practice Exercise 68. Start by setting up a new matrix with `Years` and `Months` on Rows and `[Total Sales]` on Values, as shown below.

CalendarYear	Total Sales
⊟ **2016**	**$3,266,374**
July	$473,388
August	$506,192
September	$473,943
October	$513,329
November	$543,993
December	$755,528
⊟ **2017**	**$6,530,344**
January	$596,747
February	$550,817
March	$644,135
April	$663,692
May	$673,556
June	$676,764
July	$500,365
August	$546,001
September	$350,467
Total	**$29,358,677**

Then write this formula:

```
Total Sales Moving Annual Total =
    CALCULATE([Total Sales],
        FILTER(ALL('Calendar'),
            'Calendar'[Date] > MAX('Calendar'[Date]) - 365
            && 'Calendar'[Date] <= MAX('Calendar'[Date])
        )
    )
```

Note: This is not the only way to write this formula. Just as in Excel, there are often multiple ways to write a formula in Power BI. If you have something different and it works, that's great. Also note that this formula may not work with leap years, depending on how your business handles the extra day. (Some businesses ignore the extra day and actually have 6 × 364-day years followed by 1 × 371-day extraordinary year, so it depends.)

Now check your formulas against the matrix, as shown below. You can check Moving Annual Total at the end of December 2017 (see #1 below) against the matrix-calculated total (#2) to validate that the formula is working.

CalendarYear	Total Sales	Total Sales Moving Annual Total
2017	**$6,530,344**	**$6,530,344**
January	$596,747	$3,863,120
February	$550,817	$4,413,937
March	$644,135	$5,058,072
April	$663,692	$5,721,764
May	$673,556	$6,395,321
June	$676,764	$7,072,084
July	$500,365	$7,099,061
August	$546,001	$7,138,871
September	$350,467	$7,015,395
October	$415,390	$6,917,456
November	$335,095	$6,708,557
December	$577,314	$6,530,344
2018	**$9,791,060**	**$9,791,060**
January	$438,865	$6,372,462
February	$489,090	$6,310,736
Total	**$29,358,677**	**$9,770,900**

One thing to note is that the first FILTER() line in the formula says greater than, and the last FILTER() line says less than or equal to. It is easy to get these things wrong when writing formulas, but you should not worry about this because it is easy to check and verify. As long as you set up a matrix so that you can test the formulas you are writing, you can just take a guess and then change it if you need to (i.e., if you got it wrong). In this example, if you used greater than or equal to, you would end up with 366 days, which is incorrect.

But What About the First Year?

Technically, the [Total Sales Moving Annual Total] result really doesn't make sense in the first 11 months of the sales data because you didn't have a full year of sales until the end of June 2017. There are many ways to solve this problem by using the IF() function. Here is one solution:

```
Total Sales MAT Improved =
    IF(MAX('Calendar'[Date])>=DATE(2017,7,1),
        CALCULATE([Total Sales],
            FILTER(ALL('Calendar'),
                'Calendar'[Date] > MAX('Calendar'[Date]) - 365
            && 'Calendar'[Date] <= MAX('Calendar'[Date])
            )
        )
    )
```

Tip: By now you may have realised that it is easiest to copy one formula and then edit the copied version to create a new formula. Indeed, this is a good idea, but try to keep the copying and changing to a minimum while you are learning. It's a good idea to get as much DAX writing practice as you can. When you really know how to do it, using copy and paste is a great way to work more quickly.

Total Sales MAT DATESINPERIOD() Version

For completeness, this section shows the inbuilt time intelligence function that can calculate the same formula as above. Here is the function:

```
Total Sales MAT Improved 2 =
IF (
    MAX ('Calendar'[Date]) >= DATE (2017, 7, 1),
    CALCULATE (
        [Total Sales],
        DATESINPERIOD ('Calendar'[Date], MAX ('Calendar'[Date]), -1, YEAR)
    )
)
```

This inbuilt version has the benefit of automatically handling the leap year in a standard way: When it compares two years and one of them is a leap year, the leap year has 366 days, and the other year has 365 days automatically assigned and managed.

Researching DAX Functions

There are many time intelligence functions that you can use to write time-based DAX formulas. A key piece of advice as you learn how to use all the time intelligence functions (and, indeed, all other DAX functions) is to do a quick online search and read the relevant information in the documentation. To do this, do a web search for the function name followed by the word DAX. In the image below, for example, I have searched for "dateadd dax."

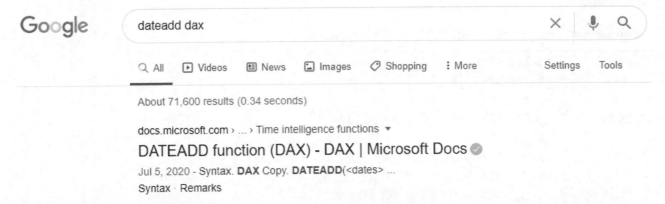

The first result returned is normally the official Microsoft documentation site. When you click on this Microsoft link, you see something like the following.

DATEADD

07/05/2020 • 2 minutes to read •

Returns a table that contains a column of dates, shifted either forward or backward in time by the specified number of intervals from the dates in the current context.

Syntax

```
DAX                                                                          Copy

DATEADD(<dates>,<number_of_intervals>,<interval>)
```

Parameters

Term	Definition
dates	A column that contains dates.
number_of_intervals	An integer that specifies the number of intervals to add to or subtract from the dates.
interval	The interval by which to shift the dates. The value for interval can be one of the following: year, quarter, month, day

Return value

A table containing a single column of date values.

In many cases, the official documentation is not as useful as other websites. But there is some very important information that you can get from Microsoft documentation: the syntax, parameters, and return value. You can find the syntax and parameters by typing a formula directly into the Power BI formula bar, but sometimes the IntelliSense help doesn't clearly tell you the return value—and this is where doing a web search can help. The return value is a key piece of information that helps you understand how to use a function. In the case of

DATEADD() above, the return value is a table, and hence you would use DATEADD() inside CALCULATE() to do a time shift. So you might write something like this:

```
Total Sales LY DATEADD =
        CALCULATE([Total Sales], DATEADD('Calendar'[Date],-1,Year))
```

This formula works on various different time horizons, including quarters as well as years, as shown below. (You might realise that this is basically the same as the SAMEPERIODLASTYEAR() example shown earlier in this chapter.)

CalendarYear	Total Sales	Total Sales LY DATEADD
⊟ 2016	$3,266,374	
3	$1,453,523	
4	$1,812,851	
⊟ 2017	$6,530,344	$3,266,374
1	$1,791,698	
2	$2,014,012	
3	$1,396,834	$1,453,523
4	$1,327,799	$1,812,851
⊟ 2018	$9,791,060	$6,530,344
1	$1,413,530	$1,791,698
2	$1,623,971	$2,014,012
3	$2,744,340	$1,396,834
4	$4,009,218	$1,327,799
⊟ 2019	$9,770,900	$9,791,060
1	$4,283,630	$1,413,530
2	$5,436,429	$1,623,971
Total	**$29,358,677**	**$19,587,777**

As another example, when you do a quick search for "firstdate," you find the Microsoft documentation site right away.

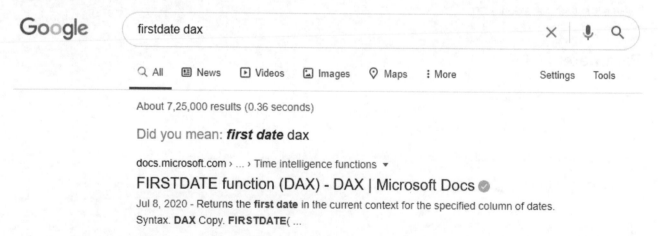

If you click through to the Microsoft documentation site, you can see that the returned value is a special table that has a single column and a single row, as shown below.

FIRSTDATE

07/08/2020 • 2 minutes to read • ∧ 🌑

Returns the first date in the current context for the specified column of dates.

Syntax

DAX	🗍 Copy
`FIRSTDATE(<dates>)`	

Parameters

Term	Definition
dates	A column that contains dates.

Return value

A table containing a single column and single row with a date value.

Note in the image above that `FIRSTDATE()` returns a table. Because it is a table, it can be used as the filter parameter inside `CALCULATE()` —for example to return the total sales on the first date from the `Calendar` table—as shown here:

    Total Sales First Date = CALCULATE([Total Sales],FIRSTDATE('Calendar'[Date]))

But `FIRSTDATE()` is a very special function. In addition to returning a table, it can also be used on its own inside a measure, as follows:

    First Date = FIRSTDATE('Calendar'[Date])

This syntax is normally not valid. Under normal circumstances, you cannot use a table function inside a measure in this way. This measure is valid, however, and can be placed into a matrix, as shown below.

CalendarYear	Total Sales	Total Sales LY DATEADD	First Date
⊟ **2016**	**$3,266,374**		**01/07/2016**
3	$1,453,523		01/07/2016
4	$1,812,851		01/10/2016
⊟ **2017**	**$6,530,344**	**$3,266,374**	**01/01/2017**
1	$1,791,698		01/01/2017
2	$2,014,012		01/04/2017
3	$1,396,834	$1,453,523	01/07/2017
4	$1,327,799	$1,812,851	01/10/2017
⊟ **2018**	**$9,791,060**	**$6,530,344**	**01/01/2018**
1	$1,413,530	$1,791,698	01/01/2018
2	$1,623,971	$2,014,012	01/04/2018
3	$2,744,340	$1,396,834	01/07/2018
4	$4,009,218	$1,327,799	01/10/2018
⊟ **2019**	**$9,770,900**	**$9,791,060**	**01/01/2019**
1	$4,283,630	$1,413,530	01/01/2019
Total	**$29,358,677**	**$19,587,777**	**01/07/2016**

The resulting date is returned as a scalar value for each cell in the matrix. In the first example, FIRSTDATE() returns a table as a filter parameter inside CALCULATE(). In the second example, FIRSTDATE() returns a scalar value and can be used as a measure. This is unique behaviour in DAX.

Other Time Intelligence Functions

Here is a list of some of the time intelligence functions that you might want to explore:

```
DATESINPERIOD(date_column, start_date, number_of_intervals, intervals)
DATESBETWEEN(column, start_date, end_date)
DATEADD(date_column, number_of_intervals, interval)
FIRSTDATE(date_column)
LASTDATE(date_column)
LASTNONBLANKDATE(date_column, [expression])
STARTOFMONTH(date_column)
STARTOFQUARTER(date_column)
STARTOFYEAR(date_column [,YE_date])
ENDOFMONTH(date_column)
ENDOFQUARTER(date_column)
ENDOFYEAR(date_column)
PARALLELPERIOD(date_column)
PREVIOUSDAY(date_column)
PREVIOUSMONTH(date_column)
PREVIOUSQUARTER(date_column)
PREVIOUSYEAR(date_column)
NEXTDAY(date_column)
NEXTMONTH(date_column)
NEXTQUARTER(date_column)
NEXTYEAR(date_column [,YE_date])
DATESMTD(date_column)
DATESQTD(date_column)
DATESYTD(date_column [,YE_date])
TOTALMTD(expression, dates, filter)
TOTALQTD(expression, dates, filter)
```

A Free Quick Reference Guide

I have produced (and I maintain for new functions) a quick reference guide of all DAX functions in PDF format that you may like to download and use. The DAX Reference Guide PDF is not meant to replace the online Microsoft documentation but to supplement it. As shown below, the PDF is fully indexed, and you can jump to the relevant sections by clicking on the hyperlinks in the table of contents.

You can download the DAX Reference Guide for free by visiting my online shop at http://xbi.com.au/on-line-shop and then navigating to the Books section.

DAX Functions Quick Reference Guide
Table of Contents

DAX Function Quick Reference List

In addition to the full Quick Reference Guide mentioned above, I have included a DAX function quick reference list in "Appendix B - DAX Quick Reference List" on page 260. It contains all the valid DAX functions along with the syntax, categorised in the same groupings as above. This DAX function quick reference list doesn't contain detail about how each function is used, however awareness of the existence of a function can be half the challenge. This simple list should help with that.

17: DAX Topic: Variables in DAX

This chapter introduces a new concept in DAX called variables. Variables have been a feature of DAX since 2015. If you have any programming experience, then you will probably already have a good sense of what you may be able to do with variables. Even if you have not done any programming, you may be able to remember learning some simple algebra at school. Here is a simple example for you to consider.

Assume the following:

```
X = 5
Y = 3
```

What is the value of $X + Y$?

The answer, of course, is 8. $X + Y = 8$ in this case because X has been assigned the value of 5, and Y has been assigned the value of 3. This is exactly how variables work in DAX. You first assign a value (or a table) to a variable, and then you can use the variable inside the rest of your DAX formulas.

Rules for Using Variables

Here are a few simple rules related to using variables in DAX:

- You assign a variable by using the VAR keyword with the following syntax:

  ```
  VAR variableName = <something>
  ```

- You can create as many variables as you want in a formula. You must define them all before using the RETURN keyword.

- There is no comma after each defined variable. (You will see this below.)

- After you define at least one variable name, you must use the keyword RETURN to complete the formula.

- Variables can be values or tables.

- A variable name cannot begin with an integer as the first character, but you can use integers as subsequent characters in a name (e.g., 1stYear is not allowed, but Year1 is fine).

- Variable names cannot contain special characters (e.g., %)

- Variable names cannot be reserved words, such as function names.

- Once a variable has been assigned a value, that value cannot change prior to the RETURN keyword.

- Variables are local in scope to the formula. You cannot refer to a variable declared in one measure from within a different measure.

Tip: You should use meaningful, descriptive names for your variables. Doing so makes your formulas easier to read and understand.

Total Sales MAT Revisited

Let's jump back to this measure from Chapter 16:

```
Total Sales MAT Improved =
    IF(MAX('Calendar'[Date])>=DATE(2017,7,1),
        CALCULATE([Total Sales],
            FILTER(ALL('Calendar'),
                'Calendar'[Date] > MAX('Calendar'[Date]) - 365
                && 'Calendar'[Date] <= MAX('Calendar'[Date])
            )
        )
    )
```

Now let's look at the same formula written using variables. Take a good look at the formula below and see what you think. (I have formatted it in DAX Formatter to make it easier to read and so I can refer to the line numbers.) What are your observations about this variable version of the formula?

```
 1   Total Sales MAT Improved with Variables =
 2   VAR StartMAT =
 3       DATE ( 2017, 7, 1 )
 4   VAR unfilteredCalendar =
 5       ALL ( 'Calendar' )
 6   VAR endDate =
 7       MAX ( 'Calendar'[Date] )
 8   VAR startDate = endDate - 365
 9   VAR Result =
10       IF (
11           MAX ( 'Calendar'[Date] ) >= StartMAT,
12           CALCULATE (
13               [Total Sales],
14               FILTER (
15                   unfilteredCalendar,
16                   'Calendar'[Date] > startDate
17                       && 'Calendar'[Date] <= endDate
18               )
19           )
20       )
21   RETURN
22       result
```

Here are the key points I want you to take away from this latest version of the formula using the VAR syntax:

- Variables make the formula easier to read and understand.
- Good variable names effectively self-document the logic of the formula and make it easier to understand.
- A variable can be assigned a constant (line 3), a table (line 5), or a value that can vary depending on the filter context (line 7).
- A variable is reused inside the formula to create other variables (line 8).

Now notice line 9 in the formula above. Why did I assign the result to a variable and then return the variable at the end? Why didn't I simply replace line 9 with RETURN? Well, when you write a variable formula this way, it is very easy to later go back and check each of the component input variables for debugging purposes. With the formula written this way, I can easily replace line 22 with one of the other variable names (e.g., startDate) to check what that variable is doing. This is a very powerful debugging technique.

Performance Impacts of Variables

One thing that is not obvious about the use of variables is that they can improve the overall performance of your formulas. For example, let's look again at the [Margin %] measure from Chapter 4 and consider expanded versions with and without using variables. Here is the version without variables:

```
Margin % full = DIVIDE([Total Sales] - [Total Cost],[Total Sales])
```

The variable version is shown below.

```
1    Margin % Variables =
2    VAR TotalSales = [Total Sales]
3    VAR TotalCost = [Total Cost]
4    VAR TotalMargin = TotalSales - TotalCost
5    VAR Result =
6         DIVIDE ( TotalMargin, TotalSales )
7    RETURN
8         Result
```

The first version of this formula is calculating the [Total Sales] measure twice: once in the numerator (to calculate the margin) and then in the denominator (to work out the percentage). The second version of the formula calculates [Total Sales] only once and assigns it to a variable (line 2). As illustrated here, sometimes variables can help improve the performance of your formulas.

> **Note:** The Power BI engine is constantly being updated and improved. The developers are always finding new ways to make the engine more efficient. It is possible (even likely) that some uses of variables that would appear to make a formula more efficient may actually not make improvements at all due to the developers' great work to improve the engine. Even so, it is still a great idea to use variables to write your formulas as doing so makes the formulas easier to use.

Variables Are Immutable

If you have a programming background, you are very familiar with the concept of variables. But a word of caution here: Variables in DAX are really more akin to the constants in other programming languages than they are to variables. Variables in DAX are immutable; this means that once a variable has been assigned a value, that value cannot change. So in most programming languages, you could write the following:

```
X = 5
X = X +1
```

In doing so, you would change the value of X from 5 to 6.

This is not possible in DAX. Once a value has been assigned to a variable in DAX, that value cannot be changed; the variable retains the same value until after RETURN keyword is used.

Here is another example, similar to one from Chapter 9:

```
Total Sales to Females =
    CALCULATE([Total Sales], Customers[Gender] = "F")
```

You could write this same formula using variables in a number of ways. One option is shown below.

```
1    Total Sales to Females =
2    VAR TotalSales = [Total Sales]
3    VAR Result =
4        CALCULATE ( TotalSales, Customers[Gender] = "F" )
5    RETURN
6        Result
```

Because variables are immutable, this formula using variables will not give the correct result. This example shows a value being assigned to the variable TotalSales in line 2. It is therefore incorrect to try to change the value of the variable in line 4. As a result, this formula will return simply total sales and not total sales to females.

18: DAX Topic: RANKX() and TOPN()

This chapter introduces the functions RANKX() and TOPN(). These functions are similar in the types of problems they solve, but technically they are very different. In this chapter, I use two scenarios to explain these functions:

- Which are the best-selling products?
- What are the sales from the top 10 best-selling products?

RANKX() vs. TOPN()

RANKX() is a function that returns a scalar value—that is, a number that can be displayed in the Values section of a visual. TOPN(), on the other hand, is a table function. TOPN() returns a table containing the top number of specified rows (N) in a table, as determined by a rule of your choice (e.g., Total Sales, Total Profit). As you should be well aware by now, a function that returns a value can be used on its own as a measure, but a naked table cannot be used on its own as a measure. Although you can't use a naked table on its own as a measure, you can use the table as an input to some other function, typically as a filter parameter inside CALCULATE().

A naked table is not allowed as a measure because it returns a table, not a value. Consider these examples:

```
Invalid Measure 1 = TOPN(10,Products)
Invalid Measure 2 = FILTER(ALL(Products),Products[Category]="Bikes")
```

Both of these formulas return tables, and so it is not valid to use them like this as measures. To be a valid measure, a formula must return a single value. But this doesn't mean you can't use table functions in measures. These next three measures all contain table functions, but they all return values:

```
Valid Measure 1 = RANKX(ALL(Products),[Total Sales])
Valid Measure 2 = CALCULATE([Total Sales], TOPN(10,Products))
Valid Measure 3 = COUNTROWS(FILTER(ALL(Products),Products[Category]=
    "Bikes"))
```

You can use table functions in measures as long as the functions are part of an overall formula that returns a value. It's awesome to use table functions this way!

RANKX()

The syntax for RANKX() is as follows:

> RANKX(*table*, *expression*, [*value*], [*order*], [*ties*])

In this syntax, there are two mandatory parameters and three optional parameters. I cover the mandatory parameters here, and you can explore the optional parameters yourself when you are ready.

Even though RANKX() is not a table function, it does take a table as the first parameter. Most functions in DAX that take a table as the first parameter operate with row context. There are some exceptions, however, such as UNION().

So you can more easily learn and comprehend this, I have set up a table in Power BI and placed Products[ProductKey], Products[ProductName], and [Total Sales] into the table visual. I have also sorted on [Total Sales] descending by clicking on the Total Sales column title in the table visual. The following image shows what it looks like.

ProductKey	ProductName	Total Sales
312	Road-150 Red, 48	$1,205,877
310	Road-150 Red, 62	$1,202,299
313	Road-150 Red, 52	$1,080,638
314	Road-150 Red, 56	$1,055,590
311	Road-150 Red, 44	$1,005,494
361	Mountain-200 Black, 42	$979,961
353	Mountain-200 Silver, 38	$979,036
363	Mountain-200 Black, 46	$961,601
359	Mountain-200 Black, 38	$954,716
357	Mountain-200 Silver, 46	$930,316
355	Mountain-200 Silver, 42	$909,436
573	Touring-1000 Blue, 46	$421,980
580	Road-350-W Yellow, 40	$418,444
362	Mountain-200 Black, 46	$411,869
561	Touring-1000 Yellow, 46	$410,060
581	Road-350-W Yellow, 42	$399,733
369	Road-250 Red, 48	$395,823
583	Road-350-W Yellow, 48	$394,630
376	Road-250 Black, 48	$383,606
Total		**$29,358,677**

Note that the total is $29.4 million. Every product is displayed in this table, but there is a way to filter this visual so that it shows just the top 10 products. If you want to filter a visual in Power BI to the top N items, you need to follow these steps:

1. Expand the Filters pane (see #1 below).
2. Select the visual and then navigate to the section Filters on This Visual (#2).
3. Find the item you want to rank, which in this case is ProductKey (#3).
4. Change Filter Type (#4) from Advanced Filtering to Top N (#5).

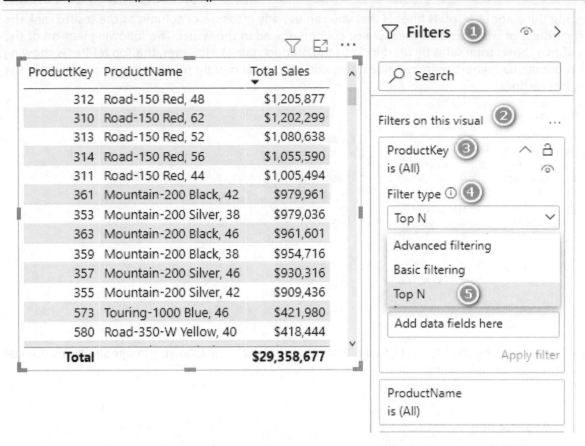

5. Specify how many items you want to keep (see #1 below) and how you will rank the top items. For example, to rank them based on the measure [Total Sales], add the measure [Total Sales] to the By Value section of the filter (#2).

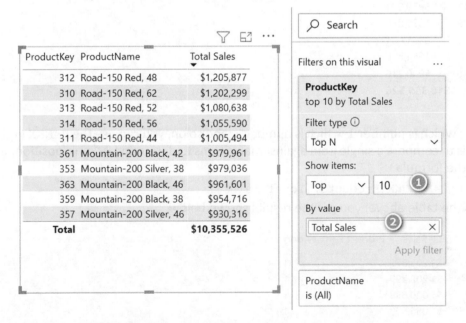

This example uses the filter capabilities of the visual to display just the top N values. This is not the same as the TOPN() function in DAX. The difference between the method just described and the TOPN() function can be confusing. Basically, TOPN() is a function that returns a table that can be used in a DAX formula. (I cover the TOPN() function later in this chapter.)

A Top N filter exists inside most visuals in Power BI. With this filter, you specify how many items you want to keep in the visual, and you specify how you will select the top items.

One interesting thing about a Top N filter is that you can use any measure or column as the test to rank the products, regardless of whether that measure or column is used in the visual. The following version of the visual from above shows total sales by product key (and product name). However, the Top N filter is showing the top 10 products by highest margin percentage, and the actual margin percentage is not shown in the visual at all. Interesting!

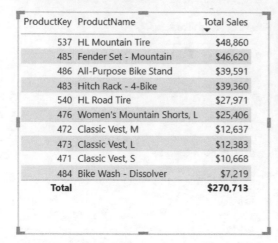
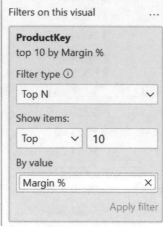

ProductKey	ProductName	Total Sales
537	HL Mountain Tire	$48,860
485	Fender Set - Mountain	$46,620
486	All-Purpose Bike Stand	$39,591
483	Hitch Rack - 4-Bike	$39,360
540	HL Road Tire	$27,971
476	Women's Mountain Shorts, L	$25,406
472	Classic Vest, M	$12,637
473	Classic Vest, L	$12,383
471	Classic Vest, S	$10,668
484	Bike Wash - Dissolver	$7,219
Total		**$270,713**

Now let's look again at using the RANKX() function with this data set. The following image shows my original filtered list of the top 10 best-selling products.

ProductKey	ProductName	Total Sales
312	Road-150 Red, 48	$1,205,877
310	Road-150 Red, 62	$1,202,299
313	Road-150 Red, 52	$1,080,638
314	Road-150 Red, 56	$1,055,590
311	Road-150 Red, 44	$1,005,494
361	Mountain-200 Black, 42	$979,961
353	Mountain-200 Silver, 38	$979,036
363	Mountain-200 Black, 46	$961,601
359	Mountain-200 Black, 38	$954,716
357	Mountain-200 Silver, 46	$930,316
Total		**$10,355,526**

To rank all these products to see which is number 1, which is number 2, and so on, you can use the RANKX() function. The role of RANKX() is to compare a single item against many items to determine its rank/position. Here is an incorrect version of the formula:

```
Product Rank Wrong = RANKX(Products,[Total Sales])
```

When you add this measure to the table above, you get the results shown below.

ProductKey	ProductName	Total Sales	Product Rank Wrong
312	Road-150 Red, 48	$1,205,877	1
310	Road-150 Red, 62	$1,202,299	1
313	Road-150 Red, 52	$1,080,638	1
314	Road-150 Red, 56	$1,055,590	1
311	Road-150 Red, 44	$1,005,494	1
361	Mountain-200 Black, 42	$979,961	1
353	Mountain-200 Silver, 38	$979,036	1
363	Mountain-200 Black, 46	$961,601	1
359	Mountain-200 Black, 38	$954,716	1
357	Mountain-200 Silver, 46	$930,316	1
Total		**$10,355,526**	1

Now, I want you to stop reading for a moment, look at the formula and the table above, and see if you can work out what is wrong. Why is each product returning the same value, 1?

> **Note:** Analysing the results in a visual and working out how the answer is calculated are core skills of a competent DAX user. You should practice whenever you get a chance. Before you read further, do your best to figure out what is wrong above.

Okay, let me explain. First of all, whenever you see measures not doing what you expect them to do, you should first and foremost suspect that unexpected filtering behaviour is causing the issue. This is not always the case, but in my experience, filtering behaviour causes most of the problems most of the time.

Let's go through the debugging process with this example. Start at the first line in the visual above (product 312). The job of RANKX() is to rank the total sales (parameter 2) of this product (product 312) against the products in the Products table. Seems simple enough, right? Well yes, but then again no. The following test measure can help illustrate the point:

```
Test= COUNTROWS(Products)
```

It can be difficult to learn how to deal with virtual tables in DAX. Because you can't see virtual tables, it is hard to be clear on what they are doing. Wrapping COUNTROWS() around a table function in a test measure can really help your understanding in this area. To illustrate, I have placed the [Test] measure in the table visual below.

> **Tip:** Writing test measures is a great way to learn how DAX operates.

Before you peek below, what do you expect the result to be in each row of the visual? After you've thought about it and made your guess, take a look and see.

ProductKey	ProductName	Total Sales	Product Rank Wrong	Test
312	Road-150 Red, 48	$1,205,877	1	1
310	Road-150 Red, 62	$1,202,299	1	1
313	Road-150 Red, 52	$1,080,638	1	1
314	Road-150 Red, 56	$1,055,590	1	1
311	Road-150 Red, 44	$1,005,494	1	1
361	Mountain-200 Black, 42	$979,961	1	1
353	Mountain-200 Silver, 38	$979,036	1	1
363	Mountain-200 Black, 46	$961,601	1	1
359	Mountain-200 Black, 38	$954,716	1	1
357	Mountain-200 Silver, 46	$930,316	1	1
Total		**$10,355,526**	**1**	**10**

Is this what you were expecting? If yes, then great: You are on your way to being great at DAX! If no, then don't worry; I am covering this point now to help you learn. The thing about table parameters inside functions is that they are affected by the filters coming from your visuals. Remember that this is the measure being used here:

```
Product Rank Wrong = RANKX(Products,[Total Sales])
```

Look at the first parameter, which is the Products table. Because the formula says Products, you can be excused for assuming that it is all the products in the table, but actually it is the Products table after it has been filtered by the visual. That is why the measure returns 1 for the first 10 rows of the table and 10 at the total level. With this in mind, let's look at the first row in the visual again.

The first row in the visual is product key 312, the "Road-150 Red, 48" bike. The RANKX() measure for the first row in the visual has the Products table as the first parameter and [Total Sales] as the second. But not all products are in the Products table. The table contains just one product, product key 312—the only product left in the table after it has been filtered by the visual. So RANKX() is trying to rank the sales of the first item in the visual (product 312) against a table containing only one product—the very same product filtered by the visual (product 312). The net result is that the product in the visual always ranks first when ranked against itself. The same is true for every row in the visual.

Ranking a product against itself doesn't solve the problem. Instead, you need to rank each product in the visual against all products in the data model. Here is the formula you need for this:

```
Product Rank = RANKX(ALL(Products),[Total Sales])
```

You use the ALL() function to remove the filters from the Products table and then rank the single product filtered by the visual against all other products in the table, ensuring that the Products table is not filtered by the visual. The image below shows the correct ranking.

ProductKey	ProductName	Total Sales	Product Rank Wrong	Product Rank
312	Road-150 Red, 48	$1,205,877	1	1
310	Road-150 Red, 62	$1,202,299	1	2
313	Road-150 Red, 52	$1,080,638	1	3
314	Road-150 Red, 56	$1,055,590	1	4
311	Road-150 Red, 44	$1,005,494	1	5
361	Mountain-200 Black, 42	$979,961	1	6
353	Mountain-200 Silver, 38	$979,036	1	7
363	Mountain-200 Black, 46	$961,601	1	8
359	Mountain-200 Black, 38	$954,716	1	9
357	Mountain-200 Silver, 46	$930,316	1	10
Total		**$10,355,526**	**1**	**1**

Filter Context Revisited

I made a very important point above, and I want to restate it and expand on it here. Table parameters used inside functions are affected by filters coming from visuals. When you see a table function as a parameter in a function placed in a visual, it is not the entire table that is used; it is a copy of the table that is filtered by the visual. If you want an unfiltered copy of the table, you have to remove the filters first by wrapping the table inside ALL().

Measures and aggregation functions are also impacted by the filters coming from your visuals. The image below shows one of the custom time intelligence formulas from Chapter 16.

```
1  Total Sales MAT Improved =
2  IF (
3      MAX ( 'Calendar'[Date] ) >= DATE ( 2017, 7, 1 ),
4      CALCULATE (
5          [Total Sales],
6          FILTER (
7              ALL ( 'Calendar' ),
8              'Calendar'[Date]
9                  > MAX ( 'Calendar'[Date] ) - 365
10                 && 'Calendar'[Date] <= MAX ( 'Calendar'[Date] )
11         )
12     )
13 )
```

Notice the use of MAX() in lines 3, 9, and 10. Each use of MAX() above is not finding the max of the entire column but the max of a column that is filtered by the visual. But wait! The MAX() functions on lines 9 and 10 are inside a FILTER() function that has ALL() as the first parameter. Doesn't this mean that the MAX() functions that are part of the second parameter inside FILTER() are operating over the unfiltered copy of the table? In short, no. The `FILTER()` function above is stepping through an unfiltered copy of the `Calendar` table (parameter 1), but that has nothing to do with the `MAX()` functions inside the `FILTER()` function (parameter 2).

The `[Total Sales]` measure on line 5 is also filtered by the visual (and the measure is also filtered by the filter function inside `CALCULATE()`, of course).

Finally, the `Calendar` table on line 7 is also filtered by the visual, but in this case, the `ALL()` function removes that filter coming from the visual, so `ALL('Calendar')` is an unfiltered copy of the `Calendar` table.

Alberto Ferrari has a great quote that he attributes to one of his past DAX students: "DAX is simple, but it's not easy." DAX has a few simple rules that you need to learn related to filter behaviour and row-by-row evaluation (filter context and row context). Learning the rules is easy. Mastering how the rules interact inside formulas takes practice and experience.

Let's get back to `RANKX()`. Now that the formula is working and you understand how it works, let's look at how it behaves in two use cases. First, the image below shows what happens when you sort the visual on `ProductKey` instead of `[Total Sales]` descending.

ProductKey	ProductName	Total Sales	Product Rank
310	Road-150 Red, 62	$1,202,299	2
311	Road-150 Red, 44	$1,005,494	5
312	Road-150 Red, 48	$1,205,877	1
313	Road-150 Red, 52	$1,080,638	3
314	Road-150 Red, 56	$1,055,590	4
353	Mountain-200 Silver, 38	$979,036	7
357	Mountain-200 Silver, 46	$930,316	10
359	Mountain-200 Black, 38	$954,716	9
361	Mountain-200 Black, 42	$979,961	6
363	Mountain-200 Black, 46	$961,601	8

This image does not show Excel; it does not show a list of products with the numbers 1 through 10 next to each product. `RANKX()` is a function that operates (in this case) over any product that is passed to it in a visual, and it tells you how that one product ranks against its peers, regardless of the display order. You can also see this by adding `ProductName` to a slicer and adding `[Product Rank]` to a card, as shown below. Then, when you select a product from the slicer, the card indicates where that product ranks.

This visual example is interesting. The column `Products[ProductName]` is not even used inside the `RANKX()` formula, but clicking a slicer using this column works. Why? Because of filtering behaviour. The column `Products[ProductName]` is filtering the entire `Products` table. When there is a single product name filtered, there is only a single product key that remains. The column `Products[ProductKey]` is used in the `RANKX()` formula, so it works. DAX is simple, but it's not easy.

TOPN()

Fortunately, the TOPN() function is a lot more straightforward than RANKX(). The syntax is as follows:

> TOPN(*n_value*, *table*, [*order by 1*], [*order by 2*], ...)

In this section I show you how to use the two mandatory parameters, and you can research the optional parameters yourself.

TOPN() is a table function, so the most common usage is as a filter parameter inside a CALCULATE() function. To calculate sales of the top 10 best-selling products, for example, the formula would be as follows:

```
Sales from Top 10 Products =
    CALCULATE ([Total Sales],
        TOPN (10, Products,[Total Sales])
    )
```

When you place this formula in a card, with no filters on any table, you get the same number from earlier in this chapter (the total sales for the top 10 products in the table visual).

Note in the formula above that this time ALL(Products) is not used inside TOPN(). It is not needed there because there are no filters in the visuals. This is neither right nor wrong; how you handle it depends on what you want to do. Because of the way the formula is written, you can use this new measure in a table like the one below.

Category	Total Sales from Top 10 Products
Accessories	$502,863
Bikes	$10,355,526
Clothing	$224,078
Total	**$10,355,526**

Because there is no ALL() around the Products table, the measure is impacted by any filter coming from the visual. In the table visual above, you can now see the total sales of the top 10 products by category. If you used ALL(Products) inside the measure, the measure would ignore any filters coming from the visual, and instead it would always return the sales from the top 10 products, regardless of the filters coming from the Products table in the visual.

19: DAX Topic: **RELATED()** and **RELATEDTABLE()**

The functions RELATED() and RELATEDTABLE() are typically used in calculated columns to reference relevant records in other tables, although they can be used in measures, too. They are a bit like VLOOKUP() functions for tables that have a relationship. As mentioned briefly in Chapter 11, row context exists in a single table, and it does not follow a relationship to impact other tables. So there may be a relationship between two tables, but row context cannot use this relationship—unless you use RELATED() or RELATEDTABLE() to trigger its use. Basically, RELATED() and RELATEDTABLE() allow row context to leverage an existing relationship so it can access columns in related tables.

When to Use **RELATED()** vs. **RELATEDTABLE()**

To understand when to use the RELATED() and RELATEDTABLE() functions, you need to understand what each one returns. As you know, you can use IntelliSense in the formula bar to find out what each of these functions returns.

You can see below that RELATED() returns a single value from another table. In particular, it returns a single value from the "one" side of another related table. RELATED() always works from the "many" side of a relationship to the "one" side of the relationship.

As shown below, RELATEDTABLE() returns a table. It works in the other direction from RELATED().

Remember from Chapter 2 that relationships between tables in Power BI are normally of the type one to many. Also remember from Chapter 2 that best practice (especially for people coming from an Excel background) is to lay out tables in the Model view with the lookup tables at the top (the "one" side of the relationships) and the data tables at the bottom (the "many" side of the relationships), as shown below.

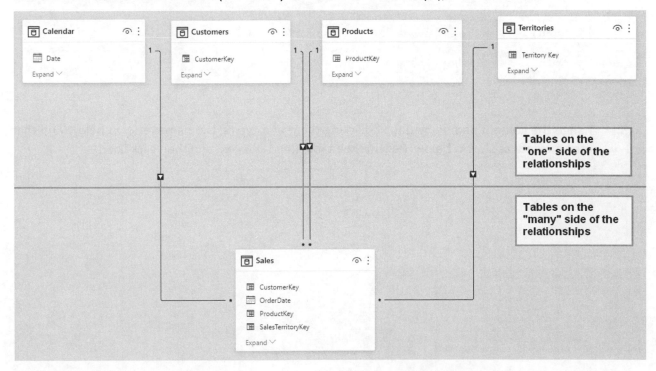

The RELATED() and RELATEDTABLE() functions allow you to refer to columns in another connected table. So if you want to add a custom column in a table on the "one" side of the relationship—that is, add a new column in a lookup table (a table above the line in the image above)—it is highly likely that there will be multiple rows on the "many" side of the relationship. When writing a formula in a calculated column on a lookup table, you must use the RELATEDTABLE() function because it fetches a table of values, including all the matching values in the data table. Conversely, if you are writing a calculated column in a table on the "many" side of the relationship (i.e., a data table), there will be only one matching row in the lookup table, and hence you use RELATED() to return that single value.

The RELATED() Function

This section provides an example of bringing a value from a column in a lookup table into a table on the "many" side of the relationship. For the sake of this example, assume that your business has a new management layer, and you want to add a new level of reporting to cover this new management layer. In effect, you need to enhance the Territories table to add a new geographic region. To achieve this, you could do the following:

1. Create a new table that contains the logic of the new management layer.

2. Import the new table into the data model.

3. Join the new table to the existing Territories table.

4. Create a new calculated column in the Territories table (on the "many" side of the relationship) and bring in the new management layer from the new table into the Territories table as a new column.

This will all make more sense as you work through the following example, which also shows how you can manually add new tables of data in Power BI.

Here's How: Manually Adding Data to Power BI

This section shows how to add data directly into Power BI without having to use another tool, such as Excel:

1. On the Home tab in Power BI Desktop, click Enter Data.

2. Click the * shown below to add a new column.

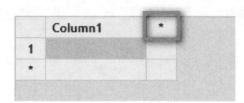

3. Change the column names by double-clicking them and typing the names shown below and then enter the data as shown below. Rename the table Hemisphere and then click Load.

Create Table

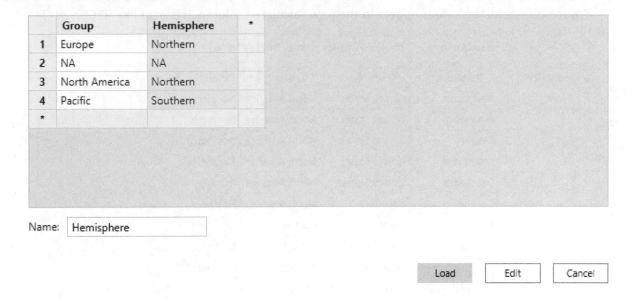

	Group	Hemisphere	*
1	Europe	Northern	
2	NA	NA	
3	North America	Northern	
4	Pacific	Southern	
*			

Name: Hemisphere

| Load | Edit | Cancel |

4. Switch to the Model view and rearrange the tables so that the new table is sitting above the current `Territories` table, as shown below. This new lookup table is a lookup table to another lookup table and will be on the "one" side of the new relationship. Power BI should automatically join the tables.

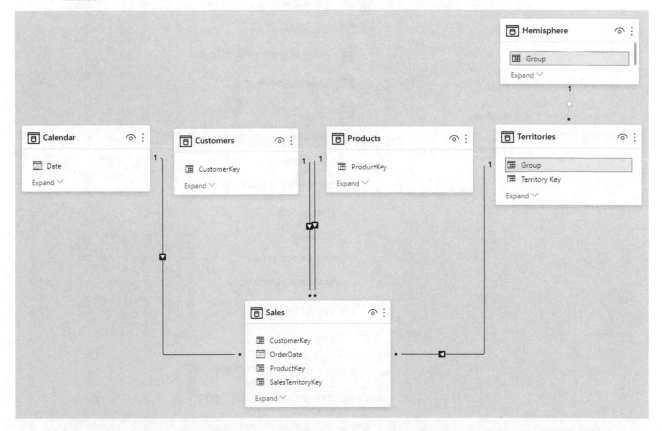

Note: The `Territories` table now has two roles. It is now acting as a lookup table to the `Sales` table and as a data table to the new `Hemisphere` table.

5. Bring the data that resides in the `Hemisphere[Hemisphere]` column into a new calculated column inside the `Territories` table. Switch to the Data view, right-click on the `Territories` table in the Fields pane, select New Column, and then type in the formula shown below. After you press Enter, you see all the values appear in the new calculated column. It is a lot like `VLOOKUP()`!

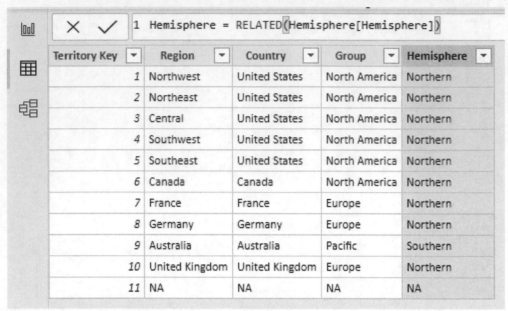

Territory Key	Region	Country	Group	Hemisphere
1	Northwest	United States	North America	Northern
2	Northeast	United States	North America	Northern
3	Central	United States	North America	Northern
4	Southwest	United States	North America	Northern
5	Southeast	United States	North America	Northern
6	Canada	Canada	North America	Northern
7	France	France	Europe	Northern
8	Germany	Germany	Europe	Northern
9	Australia	Australia	Pacific	Southern
10	United Kingdom	United Kingdom	Europe	Northern
11	NA	NA	NA	NA

Formula bar: `1  Hemisphere = RELATED(Hemisphere[Hemisphere])`

6. Finally, to hide the `Hemisphere` table from the client tools, in the Data view, right-click the table in the Fields pane (see #1 below) and select Hide in Report View (#2).

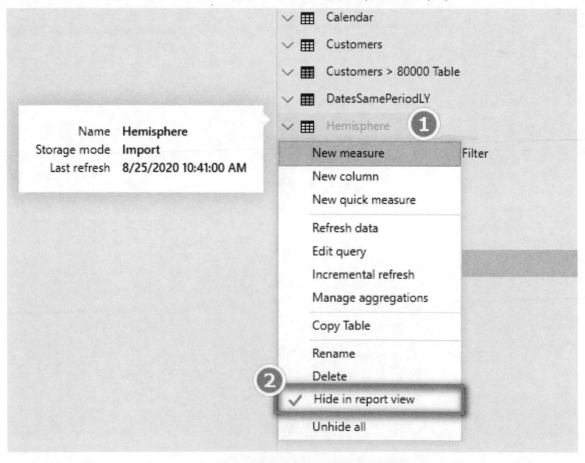

It is good practice to bring data from an add-on table like this Hemisphere table into the main Territories table as an additional column rather than use the data in an additional lookup table. It is possible to leave the Territories table untouched and use the columns from the Hemisphere table in your matrix. But the problem is that this can be confusing to users. It doesn't make business sense to have all the geographic information in the Territories table except for the hemisphere information, which is in the Hemisphere table. So for consistency and simplicity for the end user, it is better to bring all the "like data" into the same table.

> **Note:** Better practice is to bring data from an add-on table into a new column when you load the data using Power Query, but you can also do it as shown here. And best practice is to change the Territories table back at the source to include the new Hemisphere column in the source Territories table. However, the person responsible for making changes to the source table may not do it according to your time frame (if at all); this approach allows you to do it yourself right away.

The **RELATEDTABLE()** Function

As discussed earlier, RELATEDTABLE() is used to reference a table on the "many" side of a relationship. A simple example is to add a new calculated column to count the number of sales for each product. Once again, I generally don't recommend that you do this (because you can do it in a measure), but there may be valid reasons to do it in some cases.

To see how to use RELATEDTABLE(), add the following calculated column in the Products table:

```
= COUNTROWS (RELATEDTABLE (Sales))
```

As you know, RELATEDTABLE() returns a table, and COUNTROWS() counts the rows in that table. This calculated column in the Products table therefore takes the row context in the calculated column and leverages the relationship with the Sales table to count the rows in the Sales table for just the single product. As a result, you end up with a new column that indicates the number of items sold (over all time) for each product in the Products table. (The quantity for each line in the Sales table is always 1 in this sample data.)

> **Note:** You do not need to use CALCULATE() with RELATEDTABLE() to force context transition and convert the row context to filter context. In this case, RELATEDTABLE() works on its own; this is another example of syntax sugar.

One valid use case for RELATEDTABLE() would be if you want to create a slicer to filter on products that sell slowly, moderately, and quickly. If you want to use a slicer, you must write your DAX as a calculated column. (Remember that you can't place measures in slicers.) You could first create a calculated column and then use a banding technique, as discussed in the next chapter, to group products into slow-, moderate-, and fast-moving categories. (Park this thought for now and come back after you have read Chapter 20 if you want to try out this technique.)

20: Concept: Disconnected Tables

So far as you have worked through this book, you have loaded tables into the data model and then connected them to other tables. This is a fundamental technique with Power BI that allows you to work across multiple tables without using VLOOKUP(). However, you are not required to join tables together in the data model, and indeed there are some instances when it doesn't make sense to do so. This chapter discusses two techniques that do not involve connecting tables using relationships:

- What-if analysis
- Banding

Using What-If Analysis

Power BI is not Excel, and you can't just type any number into a cell and see that number impact the rest of your report. However, with Power BI's what-if parameters, you can accept user interaction with a report, and that interaction then flows through to other calculations. Let's look at an example that demonstrates how to use the Power BI what-if parameters.

Say that your profit result is directly impacted by your sales result. You have some sales data and want to see what impact an increase in sales will have on your total profit result. You could write a new measure and hard code a sales increase such as 10%, as shown below.

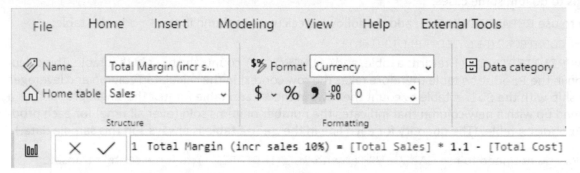

The resulting matrix would look as shown below.

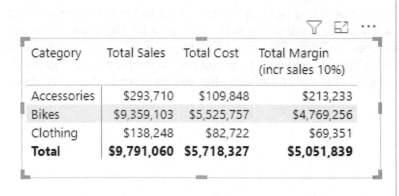

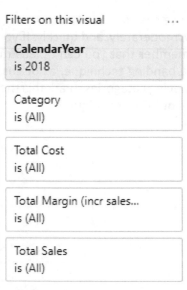

But what if you wanted to see what it looks like for a 5% increase in sales, or 15%, or some other percentage? Well, you could change this measure every time you want to see a different growth percentage, but that works only when you are using Power BI Desktop. You cannot edit measures after a workbook is published to PowerBI.com. And it would be inefficient to create lots of new measures, one for each possible value of sales growth that you want to consider. A better approach is to use the what-if analysis capability provided by Power BI.

Here's How: Using What-If

To use what-if parameters in Power BI, follow these steps:

1. Create a new blank page in your Power BI workbook.

2. Navigate to the Modeling tab and click New Parameter, as shown below.

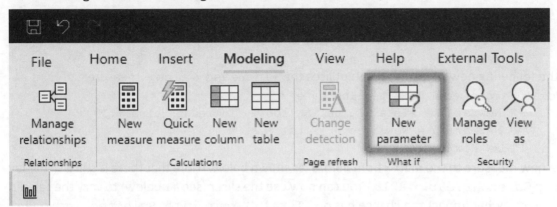

3. Enter minimum and maximum values that will be used inside the what-if analysis, along with the increment. The figure below shows a range of integers from 0 to 15 and an increment of 1 for a parameter named Increase.

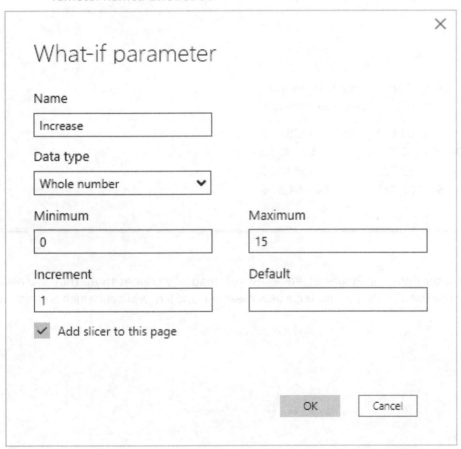

4. Click OK.

5. Notice that there is a new table (including the new measure [Increase Value] in the Fields pane (see #1 below) and also a new slicer (#2) on the report.

6. Write the following new measure, which utilises the [Increase Value] measure:

```
Total Margin with Selected Increase =
    VAR NewSales = [Total Sales] * (100 + [Increase Value])/100
    VAR NewMargin = NewSales - [Total Cost]
    RETURN NewMargin
```

7. Add the new measure to the matrix from before, as shown below. (Note that there is still a visual-level filter on CalendarYear = 2018.) You can now use the slicer (see #1 below) to vary the sales increase and see what impact the change has on [Total Margin with Selected Increase].

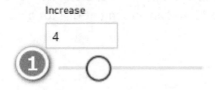

Category	Total Sales	Total Cost	Total Margin with Selected Increase
Accessories	$293,710	$109,848	$195,610
Bikes	$9,359,103	$5,525,757	$4,207,710
Clothing	$138,248	$82,722	$61,056
Total	**$9,791,060**	**$5,718,327**	**$4,464,376**

How It Works

When you click the New Parameter button in Power BI, Power BI automatically creates three things: a new table of possible values that can be used by the parameter, a new measure, and a new slicer (which is optional but is created by default).

The New Table

Select the new `Increase` table that was just created from the Fields pane (see #1 below). This new table is a calculated table that uses the formula shown below (#2).

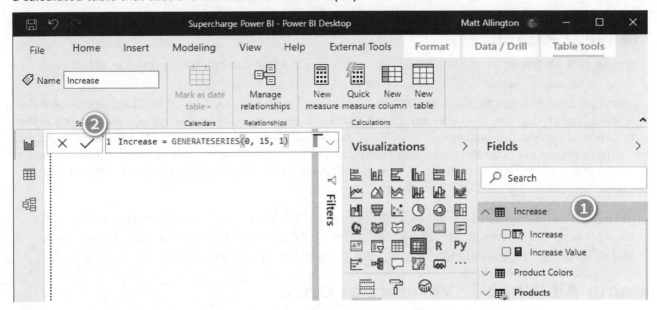

It is pretty easy to work out the syntax of the function `GENERATESERIES()` just by looking at the formula above. `GENERATESERIES()` is a DAX function in Power BI Desktop that you can use any time you want to create a new table of values with a constant increment between values.

If you switch to the Model view, you see the new table. (You may need to select Fit to Screen to be able to see it.) The table is not currently joined to any other table; it is a disconnected table. You can just position it somewhere so it is easy to see on the screen, as shown below.

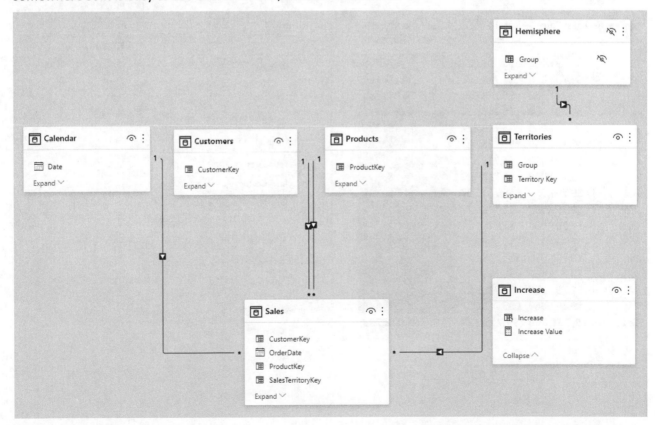

The New Slicer

If you switch back to the Report view, you can see the new slicer that was automatically created. This slicer uses the only column in the table, Increase[Increase], as the input field. The slicer allows a user to select a single value to represent the increase in sales required for analysis.

The New Measure

If you now click on the [Increase Value] measure, you see that the measure formula is as follows:

```
Increase Value = SELECTEDVALUE(Increase[Increase])
```

This measure uses the function SELECTEDVALUE(). Recall from Chapter 13 that this function returns the single value selected in the filter context, or it is blank if there is more than one value selected. This is the secret sauce of this what-if parameter: The SELECTEDVALUE() function "harvests" the selection from the user (when the user clicks on the slicer) and then passes that selected value to the formula. If the user hasn't selected a single value, it returns BLANK() by default (though this can be changed via an optional final parameter in the SELECTEDVALUE() function).

> **Note:** The behaviour of slicers tends to change as Microsoft improves and further develops Power BI. At this writing, there are a number of different configuration choices for slicers. You can click the drop-down arrow in the top-right corner of a slicer to change the way the slicer is displayed.

Seeing All What-If Variants at Once

In addition to using the slicer to see one of the what-if numbers at a time, you can use the Increase[Increase] column on Rows in a matrix to see all the possible values at once. For example, you can modify the matrix from earlier as shown below. In this example, Products[Category] has been removed from Rows, and Increase[Increase] has been added to Rows in its place (see #1 below). This example also shows the selection from the slicer cleared so you can see the full list of values. Finally, some conditional formatting has been added to make the changes in the measure more obvious.

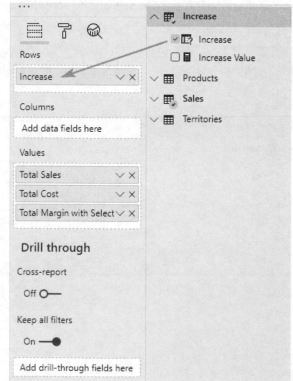

Increase	Total Sales	Total Cost	Total Margin with Selected Increase
0	$9,791,060	$5,718,327	$4,072,733
1	$9,791,060	$5,718,327	$4,170,644
2	$9,791,060	$5,718,327	$4,268,554
3	$9,791,060	$5,718,327	$4,366,465
4	$9,791,060	$5,718,327	$4,464,376
5	$9,791,060	$5,718,327	$4,562,286
6	$9,791,060	$5,718,327	$4,660,197
7	$9,791,060	$5,718,327	$4,758,107
8	$9,791,060	$5,718,327	$4,856,018
9	$9,791,060	$5,718,327	$4,953,929
10	$9,791,060	$5,718,327	$5,051,839
11	$9,791,060	$5,718,327	$5,149,750
12	$9,791,060	$5,718,327	$5,247,660
13	$9,791,060	$5,718,327	$5,345,571
14	$9,791,060	$5,718,327	$5,443,482
15	$9,791,060	$5,718,327	$5,541,392
Total	**$9,791,060**	**$5,718,327**	**$4,072,733**

Practice Exercise: Harvester Measures

In Chapter 9, you created the following DAX formula:

```
Total Customers Born Before 1970 =
    CALCULATE([Total Number of Customers],
        Customers[BirthDate] < DATE(1970,1,1)
    )
```

In the next practice exercise, you will write a measure that allows you to change the "before year" by using the what-if feature.

Write the following new DAX formula. Find the solution to this practice exercise in "Appendix A: Answers to Practice Exercises" on page 252.

70. [Total Customers Born Before Selected Year]

Using the technique described above, create a new matrix (on a new page) that allows the user to select from a list of years in a slicer by using a new what-if parameter. Change the measure [Total Customers Born Before 1970] from being hard coded to 1970 so that the year can be selected from the slicer.

This is quite a difficult problem, and you will have to think back on what you have learnt in previous chapters to make it work. You should try to do it yourself. If you get stuck, read the start of the worked-through solution below and then try again to solve the problem.

Here's How: Solving Practice Exercise 70

There is a trick to this practice exercise. The original measure you created uses a simple filter in CALCULATE(). If you replace the year value 1970 from the first formula with the what-if measure [Year Value], you get the error message shown below.

```
1 Total Customers Born Before Selected Year Error =
2 CALCULATE([Total Number of Customers], Customers[BirthDate] < DATE('Year'[Year Value],1,1))
```
⚠ A function 'CALCULATE' has been used in a True/False expression that is used as a table filter expression. This is not allowed.

The problem is that you cannot use measures in a "simple" CALCULATE() formula. If you want to use measures (as you do in this case), you must use the FILTER() function inside CALCULATE(). So instead of writing this:

```
Customers[BirthDate] < DATE ( [Year Value], 1, 1 )
```

you need to write a FILTER() function that filters the Customers table to replace the line above.

Go back and give it a go: See if you can write the correct formula by using the FILTER() function. If you still need more help, read on to see the correct formula.

Here is the worked-through solution for Practice Exercise 70:

1. Create a new what-if parameter using values such as 1900 through 2000. Give the parameter a name such as Year. If you create a parameter called Year, the what-if parameter automatically creates a new measure called [Year Value].

2. Write the following measure and then add it to your matrix:
```
Total Customers Born Before Selected Year =
    CALCULATE([Total Number of Customers],
        FILTER(Customers,
            Customers[BirthDate] < DATE([Year Value], 1, 1)
        )
    )
```

You should end up with something that looks as shown below.

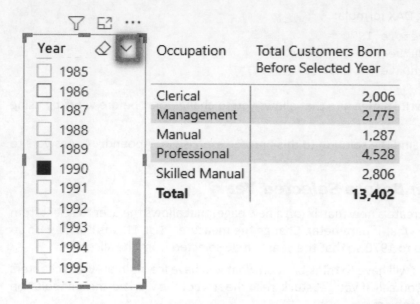

Occupation	Total Customers Born Before Selected Year
Clerical	2,006
Management	2,775
Manual	1,287
Professional	4,528
Skilled Manual	2,806
Total	**13,402**

Note: I have changed the slicer layout here to be a list of values. You can change a slicer's layout by using the drop-down arrow in the top-right corner of the slicer, as shown above.

When you click on a year in the slicer, the [Year Value] measure updates, and the results for [Total Customers Born Before Selected Year] update to show the value for the year selected in the slicer.

The SWITCH() Function Revisited

In Chapter 12, I introduced you to the SWITCH() function. One really cool feature of SWITCH() is that you can create a switch measure that allows you to toggle between multiple other measures. For example, take a look at the image below.

The left side of the image shows Total Sales selected in the slicer (see #1 above). When Total Sales is selected, the chart updates to show total sales (#2). When the user selects Total Cost (#3), the chart changes to show total cost (#4). This toggle effect is really engaging for the report user and makes it possible to create very complex and useful interactive reports.

Here's How: Creating a Morphing Switch Measure

To create a morphing switch measure, you need to create a disconnected table and a harvester measure by completing these steps:

1. On the Home tab in Power BI, click Enter Data.

2. Enter three rows of data, as shown below. Name the table `DisplayMeasure` and click Load.

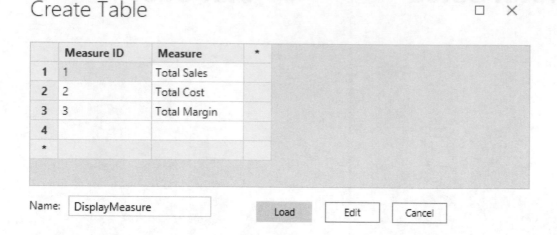

3. Navigate to the Data view, click the new `DisplayMeasure` table in the Fields pane, go to the Modeling tab, and change the sort order of the `Measure` column to sort by the `Measure ID` column instead. (Do you remember how? If not, review Chapter 13.)

4. Right-click the `DisplayMeasure` table in the Fields pane, select New Measure, and add this new measure:

   ```
   Selected Measure = SELECTEDVALUE(DisplayMeasure[Measure ID])
   ```

   I call this a harvester measure, and it uses the same technique used with what-if earlier in the chapter: It checks to see if there is a single value selected for `DisplayMeasure[Measure ID]`, and if so, it returns that value; otherwise, it returns BLANK. It "harvests" the selection from the user when it is used with a slicer.

5. Go back to the Report view and create a new page. Place a card on the report (see #1 below) and add the `DisplayMeasure[Measure]` column to the card Fields list (#2). Then place a slicer on the report (#3) and place `DisplayMeasure[Measure]` on the slicer (#4).

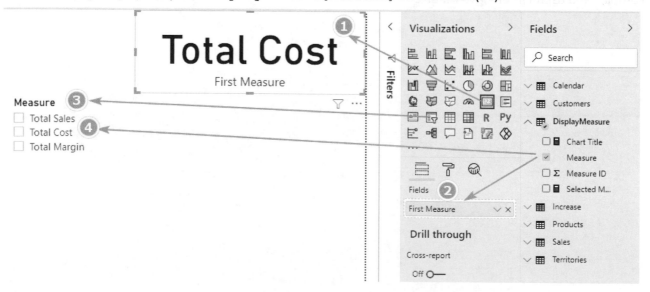

Now when you click on the slicer, the card updates to show which measure you have selected. This card will be the title for the chart that will be added next.

6. Click on the card, go to the Format pane, and turn off Category Label.

7. Right-click on the `Sales` table in the Fields pane, select New Measure, and write the following measure:

```
Measure to Display =
    SWITCH([Selected Measure],
        1,[Total Sales],
        2,[Total Cost],
        3,[Total Margin $]
    )
```

8. Add a new column chart to the report. (Either a clustered or stacked column chart will work.) Place `CalendarYear` on Axis and the new `[Measure to Display]` measure on Values, as shown below.

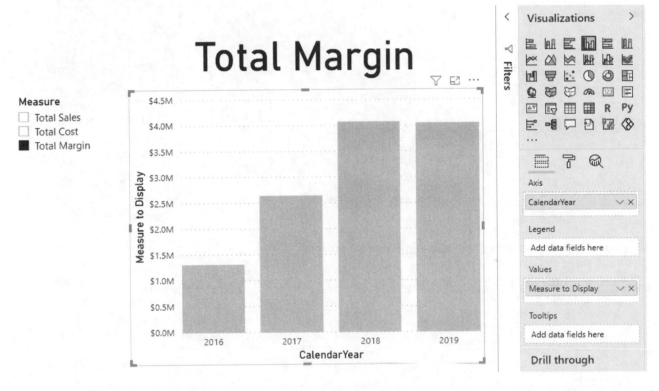

9. Go to the Format pane for the chart and turn off the default title. Also expand the X-axis section and set Type to Categorical.

You should now have an interactive chart that displays the measure that a user selects in the slicer.

Expression-Based Formatting

The example above uses a card as the report title. This works, but there is a better way: You can use expression-based formatting. Expression-based formatting exists in many areas throughout Power BI, and you can use it in more ways with each new release. If you navigate back to the Format pane and turn on the title of the chart, you see an Fx button like the one highlighted in the image below. The Fx button allows you to apply expression-based formatting. Any time a formatting option has an Fx button, you know that you can write a DAX formula to control the formatting item (the chart title in this instance).

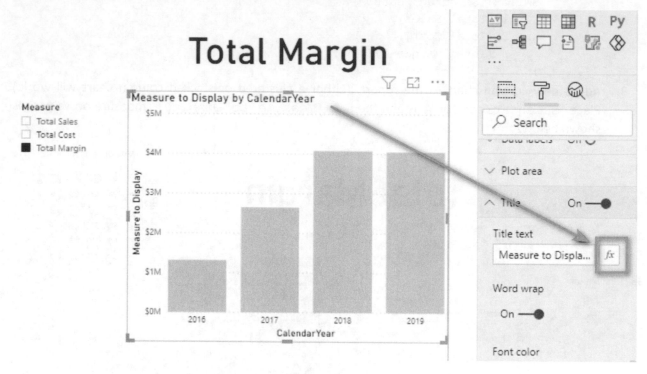

To create this chart, I created the following new measure:

```
Chart Title = SELECTEDVALUE(DisplayMeasure[Measure])
```

I then clicked on the Fx button next to the chart title and set the title text as shown below.

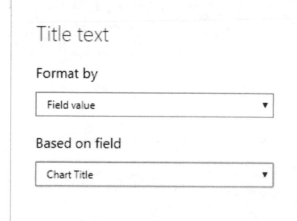

Thanks to this change, the card at the top is no longer needed, and the title in the chart automatically updates with the selection in the slicer, as shown below.

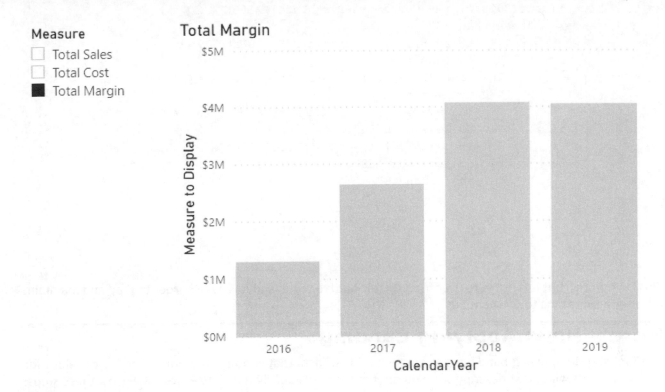

Using Banding

Banding is a disconnected table technique I learnt about from Marco Russo and Alberto Ferrari at http://sqlbi.com.

To understand banding, think about the earlier example in which you created a slicer based on the year the customer was born. A more common and practical need is to be able to analyse customers based on their age groups rather than their actual ages, like this:

- Under 20
- 20 but less than 30
- 30 to less than 40
- 40 to less than 50
- 50 to less than 60
- 60 and over

You could write a calculated column in the Customers table that creates these age group bands. But it would require a very complex formula that would be hard to edit.

> **Note:** For the sake of the exercise, I use January 1, 2018, as the "current date" from which to work out the age of each customer. Of course, in reality, each customer's age band will change over time, but I have ignored that fact for this example so that the results you see onscreen will be the same as my results shown below. If I used TODAY() in this exercise, my results would be different from yours; this is why I have not done so in this case.

A hard-coded calculated column formula for age group might look like this:

```
= IF(
    ((date(2018,1,1) - Customers[BirthDate])/365) < 20,
        "Less than 20",
        IF (((date(2018,1,1) - Customers[BirthDate])/365) < 30,
            "20 to less than 30",
            IF(((date(2018,1,1) - Customers[BirthDate])/365) < 40,
            "30 to less than 40",
            IF(((date(2018,1,1) - Customers[BirthDate])/365) < 50,
            "40 to less than 50",
            IF(((date(2018,1,1) - Customers[BirthDate])/365) < 60,
            "50 to less than 60",
            "Greater than 60"
                )
            )
        )
    )
)
```

This DAX works, but it is not very user friendly, it is hard to write, and it is even harder to read and maintain. A better approach is to use banding.

Here's How: Applying Banding

The first step in applying banding is to create a table of data that contains the upper and lower values for each band, as well as text descriptions. You can type these values directly into Power BI. Follow these steps:

1.   On the Home tab in Power BI, click Enter Data.

2.   Enter data into the form as shown below. Name the table AgeBands and then click Load.

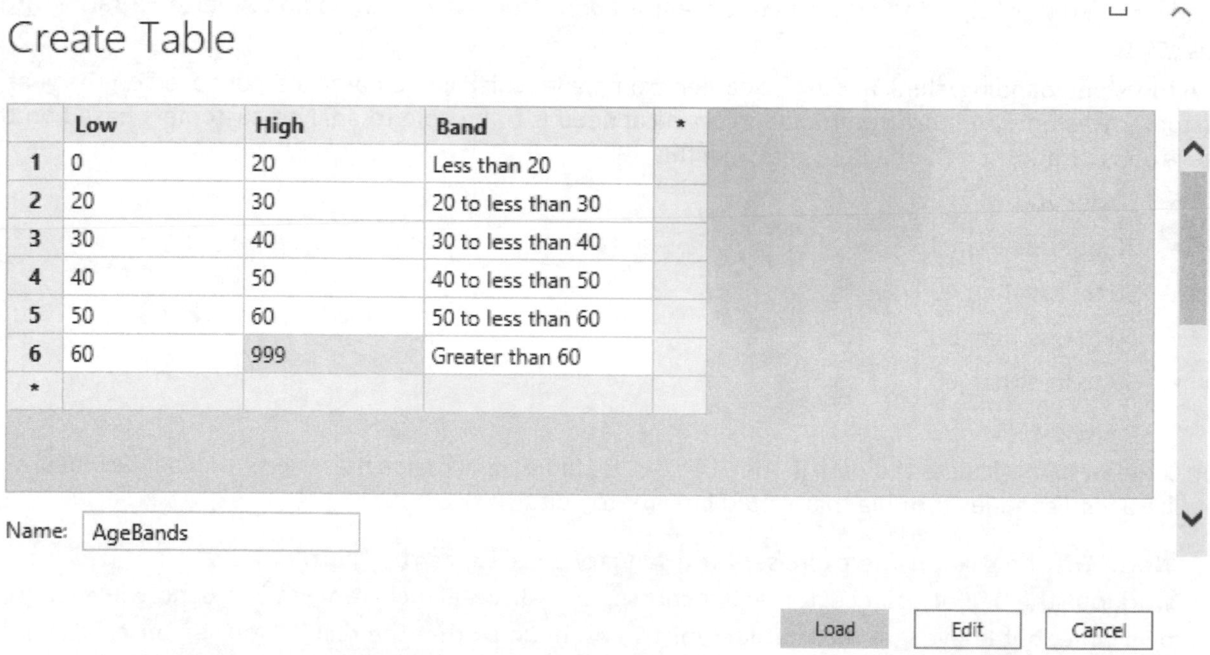

Create Table

	Low	High	Band	*
1	0	20	Less than 20	
2	20	30	20 to less than 30	
3	30	40	30 to less than 40	
4	40	50	40 to less than 50	
5	50	60	50 to less than 60	
6	60	999	Greater than 60	
*				

Name: AgeBands

Load   Edit   Cancel

Note: It is important to set up the banding table so there is no crossover of ages between the low and high ranges. The table above covers all possible ages between 0 and 999, without any duplication. Of course, the 999 value is an arbitrarily large value to catch everyone.

Note: There is no need to join this table to any other table in the data model. In fact, there is no workable way you can do that. Even if there were an age column in the Customers table, you still couldn't join this table to the age column. This banding table doesn't contain all the possible ages for customers; it just has the age bands. So if you first create a customer age column and then join the Low column to this new column, the data will only match for customers who are 20, 30, 40, etc. There will be no match for customers with ages that don't end in a zero (e.g., 21, 22, 23)—so that is not going to work. Because this table is not joined, it is called a disconnected table.

3. In the Data view, right-click the Customers table in the Fields pane, select New Column, and enter the following formula:

```
Age =(DATE(2018,1,1) - Customers[BirthDate])/365
```

Note: Although it is not required to make this banding technique work, you could enhance this formula with some rounding, as follows:

```
Age = ROUNDDOWN((DATE(2018,1,1) -
        Customers[BirthDate])/365, 0)
```

Now you have a new calculated column, as shown below, and you can write some DAX to create the banding column.

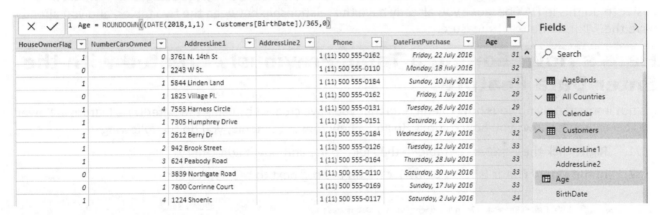

4. Right-click the Customers table in the Fields pane, select New Column, and enter the following formula:

```
Age Group =
    CALCULATE(VALUES(AgeBands[Band]),
        FILTER(AgeBands,
            Customers[Age] >= AgeBands[Low]
            && Customers[Age] < AgeBands[High]
        )
    )
```

The key to this formula is the FILTER() function. This function iterates over the AgeBands table and checks each customer's age against the low and high values for each band. There is only ever one single row in the AgeBands table that matches the age of the customer. The FILTER() function inside CALCULATE() first filters the AgeBands table so that only the one row that matches the age band is left visible. Then CALCULATE() evaluates the expression VALUES(AgeBands[Band]), and because there is only one row visible, VALUES() returns the name of the band as a text value into the column.

There are two main benefits of taking this approach to banding:

*   The DAX formula is easier to read and understand. Once you get used to the concept, it is easier to write, too.

*   It is easy to make changes in the future. For example, if you want to add another age band to your analysis (e.g., a new "Greater than 70" age band), all you need to do is add another row to your AgeBands table and then click Refresh.

Power Query or DAX?

Quite a few scenarios in this book could be handled by using Power Query rather than DAX. When should you use each of them? This is a DAX book, so I am teaching you how to solve these problems with DAX, but using Power Query may often be a better approach. The rules I use to decide which approach to use are as follows:

- Do the work as close to the source as possible: Change it in the source data if possible; otherwise, do it in Power Query.

- Use a DAX calculated column when:

  ◊ You need to use a measure from your model as part of the calculation.

  ◊ You need to leverage the relationships in the model as part of the calculation.

  ◊ You don't know how to do it in Power Query.

Say that you wanted to add the column Large Customers to your Customers table. How would you do this in Power Query? You would have to do a table merge between customers and sales in Power Query, you would need to aggregate all the sales in the Sales table per customer, and then you would need to create a new conditional column to group the customers into small, medium, and large categories. It would be a lot easier to do this in DAX because you already have the relationship between the two tables, and you already have the [Total Sales] measure.

Here's How: Editing a Table Previously Created with the Enter Data Feature

It's not immediately obvious how to edit data that you have created by using the Enter Data feature in Power BI. This example shows you how to do it. To add a new row to the table, you do the following:

1. Right-click the AgeBands table in the Fields pane and select Edit Query.

2. In the Query Editor (shown below), click on the cog next to the Source step.

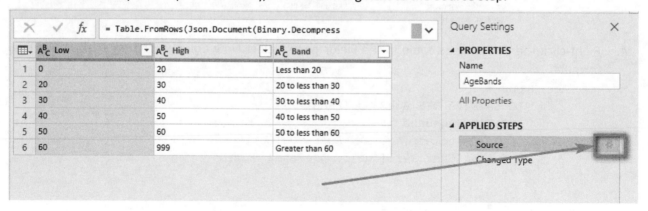

3. In the dialog box that appears, enter the data to add the new bands of data. Your table should look like the one shown below.

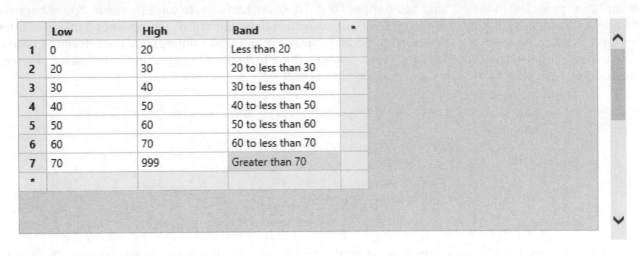

Create Table

	Low	High	Band	*
1	0	20	Less than 20	
2	20	30	20 to less than 30	
3	30	40	30 to less than 40	
4	40	50	40 to less than 50	
5	50	60	50 to less than 60	
6	60	70	60 to less than 70	
7	70	999	Greater than 70	
*				

OK   Cancel

4. Click OK.

5. Click Close & Apply on the Query Editor tab and then save the .pbix workbook.

Note: Maintaining a banding table like this is much easier than editing a complex nested IF() statement.

6. To use this new calculated column in a visual, create a new matrix on a new page, put Customers[Age Group] on Rows, and add the following measures, which you wrote in Practice Exercises 1 and 15:

    ```
    [Total Sales]
    [Total Customers That Have Purchased]
    ```

7. Add some conditional formatting so that the matrix is easier to read, as shown below.

Age Group	Customers That Have Purchased	Total Sales
20 to less than 30	5,428	$9,495,753
30 to less than 40	5,902	$9,559,614
40 to less than 50	3,808	$6,235,170
50 to less than 60	1,888	$2,416,427
60 to less than 70	438	$358,476
Greater than 70	54	$14,475
Less than 20	966	$1,278,762
Total	**18,484**	**$29,358,677**

It is easy to see the power of banding. You are unlikely to ever want to analyse a business based on sales to customers age 20 or 21 or 22. Grouping customers into age brackets is more practical, and this disconnected table banding technique makes such grouping easy.

Houston, We Have a Problem

Do you see the problem in the image above? The Age Group column is sorted alphanumerically, so "Less than 20" appears last in the list but should appear first. There are two ways to solve this issue. You either need to name the columns in such a way that they sort correctly (alphanumerically), or you need to add another column that can be used as a sort override. To add another column, you simply copy the calculated column from above and use the DAX to create a new column with a few minor changes. In the following measure, VALUES() now returns the low value in place of the band:

```
Age Group Sort =
    VAR Age = ROUNDDOWN((DATE(2018,1,1) - Customers[BirthDate])/365,0)
    RETURN
        CALCULATE(VALUES(AgeBands[Low]),
            FILTER(AgeBands,
                Age >= AgeBands[Low] &&
                Age < AgeBands[High]
            )
        )
```

You then sort the Age Group column based on the Age Group Sort column, as discussed in Chapter 13. After you make this change, the matrix looks as shown below.

Age Group	Customers That Have Purchased	Total Sales
Less than 20	966	$1,278,762
20 to less than 30	5,428	$9,495,753
30 to less than 40	5,902	$9,559,614
40 to less than 50	3,808	$6,235,170
50 to less than 60	1,888	$2,416,427
60 to less than 70	438	$358,476
Greater than 70	54	$14,475
Total	**18,484**	**$29,358,677**

Interim Calculated Columns

In the banding example, you first created an Age calculated column and then created an Age Group calculated column. Breaking the problem into parts like this makes the DAX easier to read, write, and debug. However, you should be aware that it is generally not considered good practice to leave interim calculated columns in a data model—unless you want to use these columns in your data model as well, of course—as they inefficiently take up extra space. What you really should do after you get your model working as expected is combine all the unwanted interim columns into a single final calculated column and then delete the interim columns. This saves space in your workbook, which improves reporting and refresh efficiency. However, making such a change could also make the formula harder to read (although it is almost always easier if you use variables). In this case, the Age column is useful, so you can keep it. But if the interim columns you create are not useful in your model, you are better off removing them and hard coding the needed information into the final calculated column.

Variables Syntax for the Final Calculated Column

The formula for the Age Group calculated column is shown below, using variables.

```
1   Age Group =
2   VAR Age =
3       ROUNDDOWN ( ( DATE ( 20118, 1, 1 ) - Customers[BirthDate] ) / 365, 0 )
4   RETURN
5       CALCULATE (
6           VALUES ( AgeBands[Band] ),
7           FILTER ( AgeBands, Age >= AgeBands[Low] && Age < AgeBands[High] )
8       )
```

Here's How: Deleting Interim Calculated Columns

Follow these steps to combine the interim column into the final banding calculated column and then delete the interim column:

1. Navigate to the Age interim calculated column in the table.

2. Highlight the formula, as shown below, and then press Ctrl+C to copy the entire formula from the interim column.

```
1   Age = ROUNDDOWN((DATE(2018,1,1) - Customers[BirthDate])/365,0)
```

3. Navigate to the final Age Group banding calculated column. You can enlarge the formula bar by clicking the drop-down arrow at the top right, if needed.

4. Create two new blank lines after the = in the formula by pressing Shift+Enter. The formula bar should now look as shown below.

```
1   Age Group =
2
3
4           CALCULATE(VALUES(AgeBands[Band]),
5               FILTER(AgeBands,
6                   Customers[Age] >= AgeBands[Low]
7                   && Customers[Age] < AgeBands[High]
8               )
9           )
```

5. Type the keyword VAR (see #1 below), paste in the Age column code (#2), and then type the RETURN keyword (#3).

```
1   Age Group = VAR Age = ROUNDDOWN((DATE(2018,1,1) - Customers[BirthDate])/365,0)
2           RETURN
3           CALCULATE(VALUES(AgeBands[Band]),
4               FILTER(AgeBands,
5                   Customers[Age] >= AgeBands[Low]
6                   && Customers[Age] < AgeBands[High]
7               )
8           )
```

6. Replace the two instances of the original column named Customers[Age] with the reference to the variable Age, as shown below.

```
1  Age Group = VAR Age = ROUNDDOWN((DATE(2018,1,1) - Customers[BirthDate])/365,0)
2           RETURN
3       CALCULATE(VALUES(AgeBands[Band]),
4           FILTER(AgeBands,
5               Age >= AgeBands[Low] &&
6               Age < AgeBands[High]
7           )
8       )
```

7. Delete the interim column Customers[Age].

Note: Of course, if you need the interim column in your table, you should keep it. But if you don't need it, you should remove it by using the process shown here. You can find deeper coverage of the use of variables at my blog: http://xbi.com.au/variables.

21: Concept: Multiple Data Tables

So far in this book, we have used only a single data table, the Sales table. It is quite likely that you will want or need to use multiple data tables in your data models. When bringing a second data table into Power BI, people sometimes think that they should join the new data table to the original data table, but this is incorrect. The correct way to join a second data table to a data model is to treat the new data table exactly the same as the first data table; data tables should be joined to lookup tables.

To better understand how to handle multiple data tables, let's look at a common business scenario in which a business wants to load a Budget table as well as a Sales table. One of the challenges in this scenario is that a budget and sales are often at different levels of granularity. For example, sales may be captured and reported every day for every individual product, but budgets may be set only for each month and for each product category.

Before we step through the process of modelling this data, let me explain a problem that needs to be solved.

Many-to-Many Relationships

The Budget table has data that looks as shown below. There is a Category column with repeating values and a Period column with repeating values. These are the columns that need to be used to join the new data table to the rest of the model.

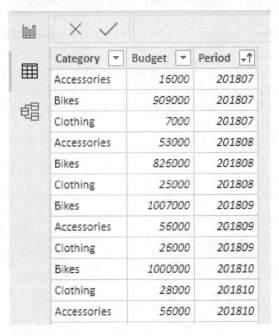

The Category column needs to be joined to the Products table, and the Period column needs to be joined to the Calendar table.

The image below shows a subset of the `Products` table (on the left) and a subset of the `Calendar` table (on the right). Take a close look. Do you see the problems?

Products **Table**

ProductKey ▼	ModelName ▼↑	Category ▼
522	ML Touring Seat/Saddle	Components
218	Mountain Bike Socks	Clothing
219	Mountain Bike Socks	Clothing
478	Mountain Bottle Cage	Accessories
449	Mountain Pump	Accessories
528	Mountain Tire Tube	Accessories
351	Mountain-100	Bikes
344	Mountain-100	Bikes
345	Mountain-100	Bikes

Calendar **Table**

Date ▼	MonthName ▼	Period ▼
Sunday, 1 July 2018	July	201807
Monday, 2 July 2018	July	201807
Tuesday, 3 July 2018	July	201807
Wednesday, 4 July 2018	July	201807
Thursday, 5 July 2018	July	201807
Friday, 6 July 2018	July	201807
Saturday, 7 July 2018	July	201807
Sunday, 8 July 2018	July	201807
Monday, 9 July 2018	July	201807

There are two main problems:

- The `Budget[Category]` column needs to be joined to the `Product[Category]` column, but both columns contain duplicate values.

- The `Budget[Period]` column needs to be joined to the `'Calendar'[Period]` column, but both columns contain duplicate values.

Power BI is optimised for one-to-many relationships. The "one" side (the lookup table) should have a column of unique values (a primary key), and the "many" side (the data table) can have duplicate values (a foreign key). Power BI is built and optimised to work this way. If you try to join two tables that have duplicate values in both columns, you get a warning message like the one shown below.

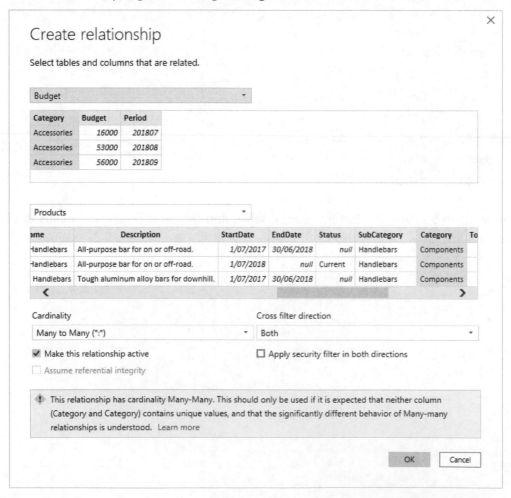

There is a very good reason that there is a warning message at the bottom of this dialog. Creating many-to-many relationships is very dangerous in Power BI, particularly if you don't know what you are doing. It can be done successfully under certain conditions in Power BI (although you cannot do this in Power Pivot for Excel). This is a big topic that is mostly beyond the scope of this book, but there is a way to model the data without the need for many-to-many relationships: by using bridging tables.

Here's How: Bridging a Budget Table

The following steps walk you through the process of importing a budget table, loading the required bridging tables, and writing measures for the budget:

1. In Power BI, click Get Data, Excel and navigate to the Excel file you used in Chapter 2.

2. Select the `Budget` and `BudgetPeriod` tables from the Navigator list, as shown below. In this case, the `Budget` table is the data table, and the `BudgetPeriod` table is a bridging table.

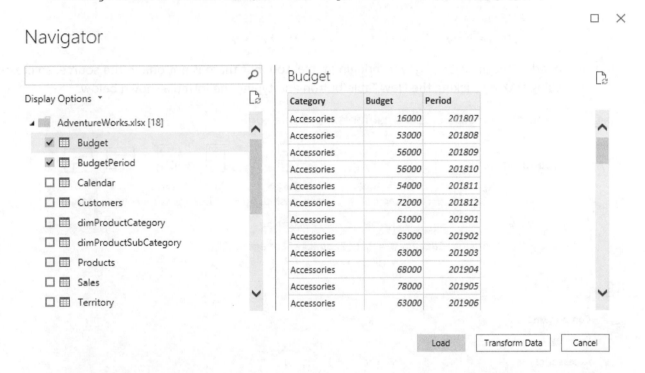

3. Click Load. As shown below, the `Budget` table has a monthly sales budget for each category, and the `Period` column is in the format YYYYMM for year and month.

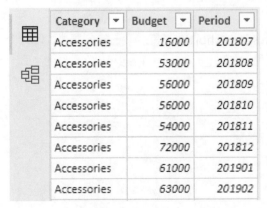

The `BudgetPeriod` table is both a bridging table and a type of calendar table, but it is a different type of calendar table from what you have used so far. Technically, it is still a calendar table, but it is a monthly calendar table instead of a daily calendar table. Like the `Budget` table, it contains a `Period` column in the format YYYYMM, as shown below.

CalendarYear	MonthName	Month Number	Period
2018	July	7	201807
2018	August	8	201808
2018	September	9	201809
2018	October	10	201810
2018	November	11	201811
2018	December	12	201812
2019	January	1	201901
2019	February	2	201902

4.   You need a `ProductCategory` bridging table, too, but there is not one in the source, so create one using DAX by clicking the New Table button and typing the formula shown below.

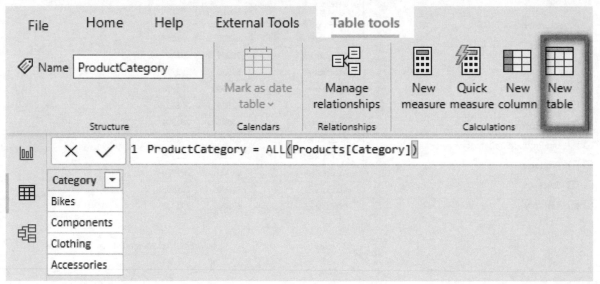

As you can see above, the new `ProductCategory` table has a list of the four possible product categories.

Note: How all these bridging tables will be used will make sense shortly.

5.   Switch to the Model view.

6. Rearrange the tables as shown below: Place the `BudgetPeriod` table (see #1 below) above the `Calendar` table and place the `Budget` table (#2) next to the `Sales` table. Put the `ProductCategory` table (#3) above the `Products` table, as shown.

Note: The relationship between `BudgetPeriod` and `Budget` is a physical relationship that Power BI automatically created when the new `BudgetPeriod` table was created.

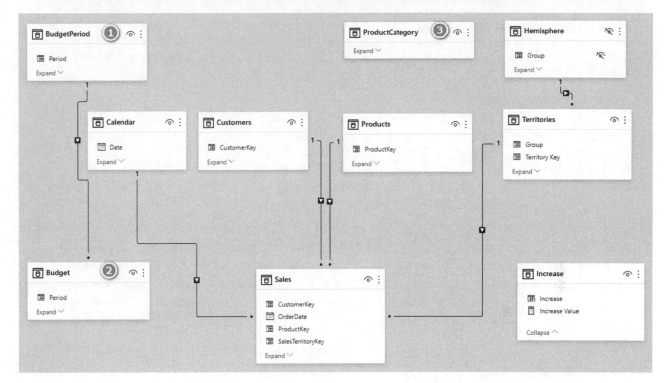

7.   To see why you need the bridging tables, try to join the `Budget` table to the `Calendar` table. When you try to create a new relationship between the `Budget[Period]` column and the `'Calendar'[Period]` column, you get the warning message shown earlier and repeated below.

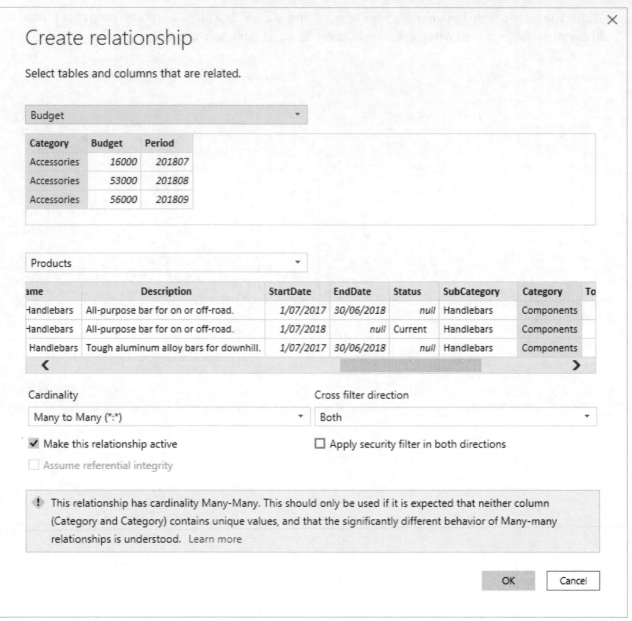

8.   Click Cancel to close the Create Relationship window.

The `Calendar` table is a daily calendar, but the `Budget` table is a monthly budget (a very common business scenario). The `'Calendar'[Period]` column has between 28 and 31 entries for each month, and the `Budget[Period]` column has repeating values, too. Technically, you can create a many-to-many relationship in Power BI, but as mentioned earlier, such a relationship can be inefficient and also dangerous, and I don't teach that method in this book.

To solve this data modelling problem, you can use bridging tables in order to join the tables using only one-to-many relationships. The `BudgetPeriod` table is a bridging table, and it has a `Period` column that contains unique values (a primary key). You can therefore join the `Budget` table to the `BudgetPeriod` table by using a one-to-many relationship. In fact, this relationship (see #1 below) was auto-created when the data was loaded.

9. Join the `Calendar` table to the `BudgetPeriod` table by dragging the `'Calendar'[Period]` column to the `BudgetPeriod[Period]` column (see #2 below).

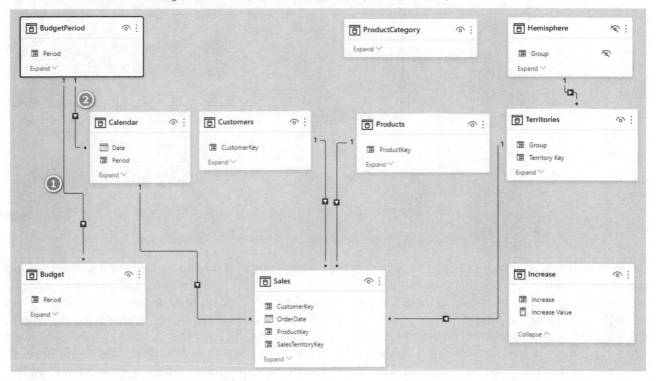

Now you need to join the `ProductCategory` table (which is also a bridging table) to the `Budget` table. If you try to join the `Budget[Category]` column to the `Products[Category]` column, you get the same warning as before.

10. To join the `Budget` table to the `ProductCategory` bridging table, click and drag the column `Budget[Category]` to `ProductCategory[Category]`.

11. To join the `Products` table to the `ProductCategory` table, click and drag the column `Products[Category]` to the `ProductCategory[Category]` column.

When you are finished, you should have something like the layout shown below. Notice that it becomes difficult to keep track of all the relationships when you have lots of tables in a data model. This is one reason I recommend arranging the tables using the Collie layout methodology, as shown below.

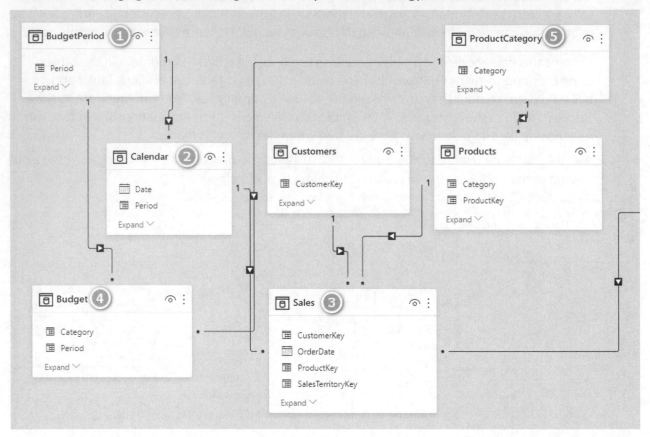

As you can see in the image above, the tables on the "many" side of the relationships are down below, and the tables on the "one" side of the relationships are up high. The filters flow downhill, and this layout makes it much easier to understand how the tables interact with each other. If you place a filter on the BudgetPeriod table (see #1 above), this table directly filters the Budget table (#4) via the direct relationship. In addition, the BudgetPeriod table (#1) directly filters the Calendar table (#2), and the Calendar table (#2) filters the Sales table (#3). The net result is that any filter you apply to the BudgetPeriod table (#1) filters both the Sales table (#3) and the Budget table (#4). The same concept applies with the ProductCategory table (#5).

When working with data tables of different granularities, as in this case, it is important to use the correct tables and columns in your matrix filters. So when working with both the Sales table and the Budget table in a model like this, you should use the columns from the BudgetPeriod table and ProductCategory table in your visuals; columns from the Calendar table and Products table will not correctly filter both the Sales and Budget tables.

Using One Table for Each Object

One of the general rules I introduced in Chapter 2 is that you should aim to use one table (e.g., `Calendar`, `Product`) for each object. One reason for this is that it makes it easier for people using your data model to find what they are looking for. As mentioned earlier, when you have the bridging tables loaded as shown above, you must use the bridging table columns in your visuals instead of the columns in the lookup tables. Only the bridging table columns can filter both the `Budget` table (directly) and the `Sales` table (indirectly, via the lookup tables). This can be confusing to people building new visuals in your reports. Take a look at the tables that now appear in the Fields pane.

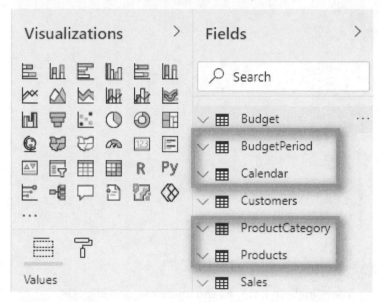

There are two calendar tables (`Calendar` and `BudgetPeriod`) and two product tables (`Products` and `ProductCategory`). If the report writer uses the wrong table, the results will be wrong. In the image below, the `Category` column comes from the `Products` table, not the `ProductCategory` table, so the `Budget` table is not filtered.

Category	Total Sales	Total Budget
Accessories	$700,760	$29,841,000
Bikes	$28,318,145	$29,841,000
Clothing	$339,773	$29,841,000
Components		$29,841,000
Total	**$29,358,677**	**$29,841,000**

In addition, there are columns (e.g., `Year`) in the `Calendar` table that you might want to use in the reports that don't exist in the bridging table. This is one of the few situations in which I recommend using bidirectional cross-filtering in a data model.

Enter Bidirectional Cross-Filtering

Generally speaking, you should aim for single-directional cross-filtering; that is, the lookup tables should filter the data tables—and not the other way around. But in this case, I highly recommend using bidirectional cross-filtering, where each table filters the other, because it solves both problems mentioned above:

- It removes confusion about which columns to use for reports. (It restores the concept of using one table for each object—at least as presented to the end users.)

- It opens up use of the other columns in the lookup tables to roll up your data to a higher level of aggregation.

Here's How: Enabling Bidirectional Cross-Filtering

To enable bidirectional cross-filtering, follow these steps:

1. Switch to the Model view.

2. Double-click the relationship between the `Calendar` table and the `BudgetPeriod` table (shown below).

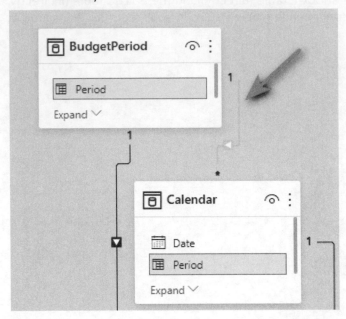

3. Change the Cross Filter Direction setting from Single to Both, as shown below, and click OK.

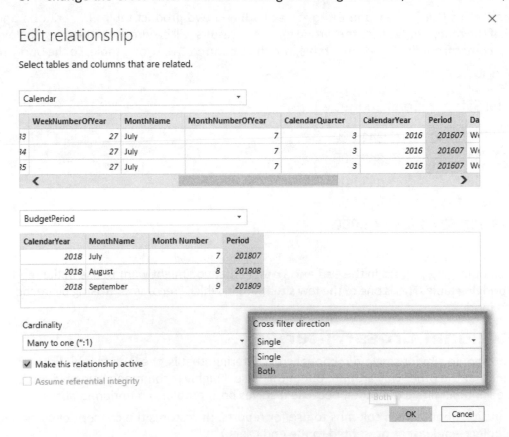

Edit relationship

Select tables and columns that are related.

Calendar

WeekNumberOfYear	MonthName	MonthNumberOfYear	CalendarQuarter	CalendarYear	Period	Da
33	27	July	7	3	2016	201607	W
34	27	July	7	3	2016	201607	W
35	27	July	7	3	2016	201607	W

BudgetPeriod

CalendarYear	MonthName	Month Number	Period
2018	July	7	201807
2018	August	8	201808
2018	September	9	201809

Cardinality

Many to one (*:1)

☑ Make this relationship active

☐ Assume referential integrity

Cross filter direction

Single

Single

Both

OK   Cancel

4. Repeat this process for the relationship between the `ProductCategory` table and the `Products` table. The image below shows the Model view after these changes are made.

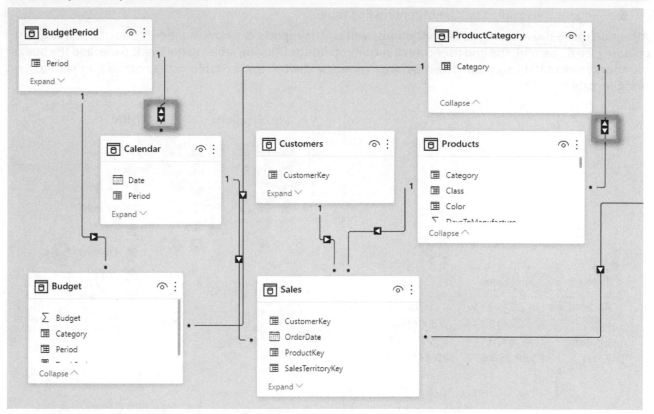

Note: The relationships now indicate that filters flow in both directions. The implications are that if you use a column in the `Calendar` table, it will directly filter the `Sales` table (the same as before you changed the cross-filter direction), but the `Calendar` table will also now filter the `BudgetPeriod` bridging table. The `BudgetPeriod` table directly filters the `Budget` table, so now the `Calendar` table will filter both the `Sales` and the `Budget` tables. The same is true for the `Products` table.

5. Hide the `BudgetPeriod` bridging table from the end user by clicking the eyeball icon, as shown below.

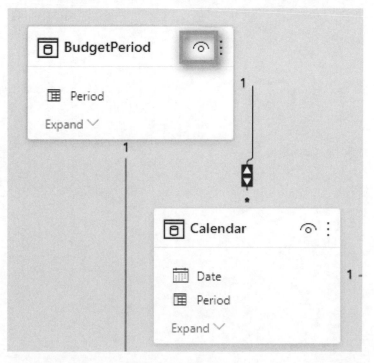

6. Repeat these steps for the other bridging table.

After you make these changes, everything just works. The reports can now use the `Products[Category]` column (see #1 below), the end user cannot see any confusing bridging tables in the Fields pane, and the budget numbers work (#2). In addition, the reports can now use the `Calendar` table instead of the `BudgetPeriod` bridging table.

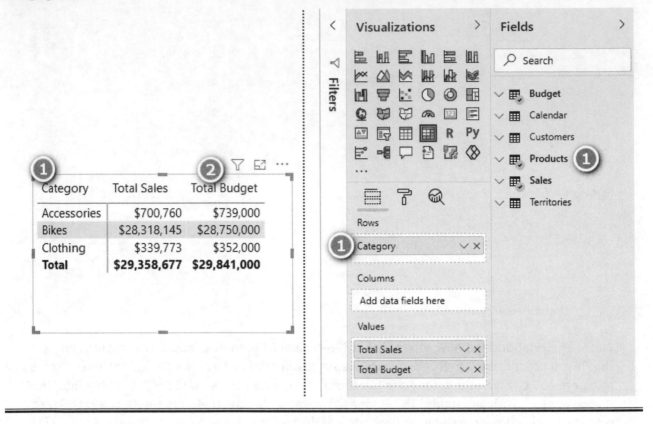

Aggregating Rolls Up, Not Down

One thing you should note at this point is that the budget data is at the month and product category level; this is the lowest level of granularity contained in the budget data. The lowest level of data can be easily aggregated up (e.g., months can be aggregated up to create yearly data), but the data cannot automatically disaggregate to create a lower level of granularity (e.g., categories do not automatically disaggregate into subcategories). To illustrate this point, the image below shows `'Calendar'[Year]` and `Products[SubCategory]` in a matrix.

CalendarYear SubCategory	2018 Total Sales	Total Budget	2019 Total Sales	Total Budget	Total Total Sales	Total Budget
Bike Racks	$16,440	$307,000	$22,920	$432,000	$39,360	$739,000
Bike Stands	$18,921	$307,000	$20,670	$432,000	$39,591	$739,000
Bottles and Cages	$23,280	$307,000	$33,518	$432,000	$56,798	$739,000
Cleaners	$3,045	$307,000	$4,174	$432,000	$7,219	$739,000
Fenders	$19,408	$307,000	$27,211	$432,000	$46,620	$739,000
Helmets	$92,584	$307,000	$132,752	$432,000	$225,336	$739,000
Hydration Packs	$16,772	$307,000	$23,536	$432,000	$40,308	$739,000
Lights		$307,000		$432,000		$739,000
Locks		$307,000		$432,000		$739,000
Mountain Bikes	$3,989,638	$9,730,000	$3,814,691	$9,027,000	$7,804,330	$18,757,000
Panniers		$307,000		$432,000		$739,000
Pumps		$307,000		$432,000		$739,000
Road Bikes	$3,952,029	$9,730,000	$2,920,268	$9,027,000	$6,872,297	$18,757,000
Tires and Tubes	$103,260	$307,000	$142,270	$432,000	$245,529	$739,000
Touring Bikes	$1,417,435	$9,730,000	$2,427,366	$9,027,000	$3,844,801	$18,757,000
Total	$9,652,812	$10,037,000	$9,569,375	$9,459,000	$19,222,187	$19,496,000

The years (columns in the matrix) are correctly adding up the budget from months to years (i.e., the budget numbers add up correctly horizontally across the matrix). However, the subcategories (rows on the matrix) are all showing the same budget total (vertically down the matrix). It is technically possible to write a budget measure that will apportion the category budget down to the subcategory level by using sales history (for example). You could have a go at writing the formula yourself if you are feeling brave. I do not provide a solution in this book, but I do suggest the following process steps:

1. Create a plan for how to solve the problem. Do it in Excel first, if that helps.

2. Use what you have learnt about using the `ALL()` function in calculating the percentage of a column (see Chapter 14) to work out the historical sales percentage for each subcategory.

3. Break the problem into pieces, using variables, and solve each part of the problem before moving on. Check each variable component in a visual before moving on.

Good luck. Feel free to contact me via my website (http://xbi.com.au/contact-matt) and tell me how you did with this challenge.

Practice Exercises: Multiple Data Tables

It's time to get some practice writing new DAX formulas across the two data tables Budget and Sales. First, create a new matrix. Then put Products[Category] on Rows, put 'Calendar'[Period] on Rows, and put [Total Sales] on Values.

When your matrix is set up, click on the Expand All Down One Level in the Hierarchy icon, as shown below, to expand all levels in the matrix.

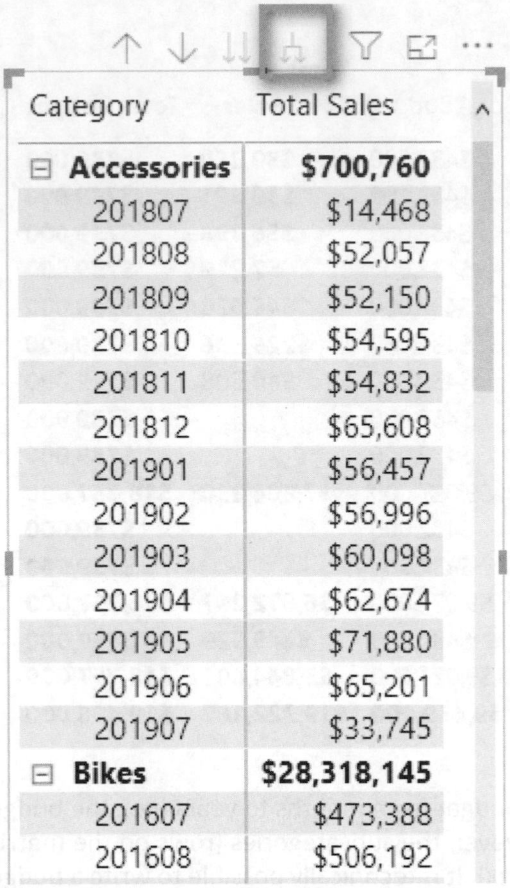

Category	Total Sales	
⊟ **Accessories**	**$700,760**	
201807	$14,468	
201808	$52,057	
201809	$52,150	
201810	$54,595	
201811	$54,832	
201812	$65,608	
201901	$56,457	
201902	$56,996	
201903	$60,098	
201904	$62,674	
201905	$71,880	
201906	$65,201	
201907	$33,745	
⊟ **Bikes**	**$28,318,145**	
201607	$473,388	
201608	$506,192	

To create the following measures, right-click the Budget table in the Fields pane, select New Measure, and then write each measure. Find the solutions to these practice exercises in "Appendix A: Answers to Practice Exercises" on page 252.

71. [Total Budget]

72. [Change in Sales vs. Budget]

73. [% Change in Sales vs. Budget]

How Did It Go?

Did you end up with a matrix like the one below (which has conditional formatting added)?

Category	Total Sales	Total Budget	Change in Sales vs. Budget	% Change in Sales vs. Budget
⊟ **Accessories**	**$700,760**	**$739,000**	**-$38,240**	**-5.2%**
201807	$14,468	$16,000	-$1,532	-9.6%
201808	$52,057	$53,000	-$943	-1.8%
201809	$52,150	$56,000	-$3,850	-6.9%
201810	$54,595	$56,000	-$1,405	-2.5%
201811	$54,832	$54,000	$832	1.5%
201812	$65,608	$72,000	-$6,392	-8.9%
201901	$56,457	$61,000	-$4,543	-7.4%
201902	$56,996	$63,000	-$6,004	-9.5%
201903	$60,098	$63,000	-$2,902	-4.6%
201904	$62,674	$68,000	-$5,326	-7.8%
201905	$71,880	$78,000	-$6,120	-7.8%
201906	$65,201	$63,000	$2,201	3.5%
201907	$33,745	$36,000	-$2,255	-6.3%
⊟ **Bikes**	**$28,318,145**	**$28,750,000**	**-$431,855**	**-1.5%**
201607	$473,388	$483,000	-$9,612	-2.0%
201608	$506,192	$516,000	-$9,808	-1.9%
201609	$473,943	$502,000	-$28,057	-5.6%
201610	$513,329	$488,000	$25,329	5.2%
201611	$543,993	$560,000	-$16,007	-2.9%
201612	$755,528	$718,000	$37,528	5.2%
201701	$596,747	$615,000	-$18,253	-3.0%

22: Concept: Using Analyze in Excel and Cube Formulas

So far in this book, you have consumed and visualised the information from data models in reports directly inside Power BI Desktop. But even after you have invested so much time and effort building Power BI data models, you may want to get to the data by using good old traditional Excel. Fortunately, there is an easy way to do this from PowerBI.com. As long as you have a Power BI Pro licence, you can use Analyze in Excel to directly connect to the data model. Before you can use Analyze in Excel, however, you must first publish your Power BI Desktop file to PowerBI.com.

> **Note:** If for some reason you are not able to use Analyze in Excel from PowerBI.com, you can still complete the cube formulas exercises later in this chapter. Simply go to my website, http://xbi.com.au/local-host, and follow the instructions on how to connect Excel to a local instance of Power BI Desktop running on your PC.

Here's How: Publishing a Report to PowerBI.com

Follow these steps to publish a report to PowerBI.com:

1. Save the Power BI workbook.

2. On the Home tab (see #1 below), click the Publish button (#2).

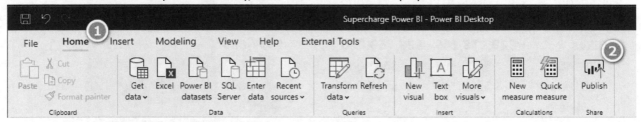

3. If this is the first time you are using PowerBI.com, you are prompted to create an account. Simply follow the instructions to create a new account for yourself. If you already have an account, just sign in using your credentials. You get a success message when the file has been loaded to PowerBI.com. If you are creating an account for the first time, you need to activate the 60-day Pro trial in order to use Analyze in Excel.

> **Note:** Your access to PowerBI.com may be controlled by your IT department. If you cannot create an account as described here, you may need to contact your IT department for support. Also, as of this writing, it is not possible to sign up to PowerBI.com by using a generic email address such as @gmail.com or @hotmail.com. You need to use a business or school email address.

4.   In a browser, navigate to http://powerbi.com and click the sign-in link in the top-right corner of the website, using the same credentials you specified in step 3.

5.   Once you are logged in, expand the menu on the left-hand side (see #1 below) and open the work-space where you uploaded your workbook, such as My Workspace (#2).

6.   Locate your data model under Datasets (see #3 below) and all your reports in the Reports section (#4).

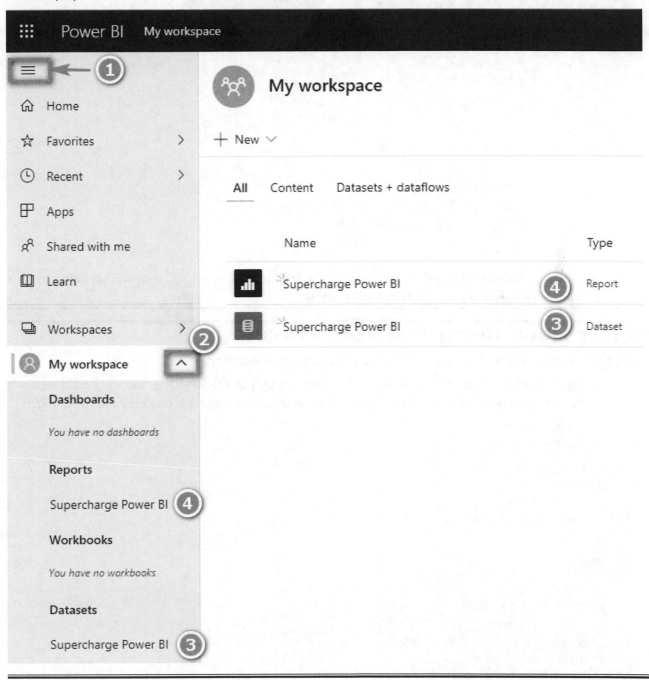

Here's How: Installing Analyze in Excel

Before you can use Analyze in Excel the first time, you need to install the Analyze in Excel updates. Follow these steps:

1. Click on the download arrow in the top-right corner of the browser (see #1 below) and select Analyze in Excel Updates (#2).

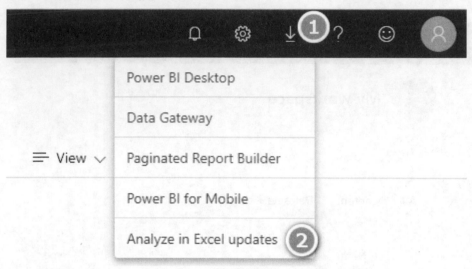

2. After the update is downloaded, run the downloaded file on your PC. You need admin rights on your computer to be able to complete the installation.

Here's How: Using Analyze in Excel

Using Analyze in Excel could not be easier. Simply follow these instructions:

1. Navigate to either Reports (see #1 below) or Datasets (#2) on the left-hand side, click on the ellipsis to open the menu, and then select Analyze in Excel (#3). An Excel file is downloaded to your PC.

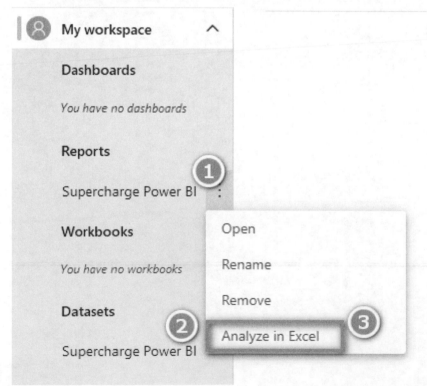

2. Find the Excel file that was downloaded (probably in your Downloads folder, depending on your browser settings) and double-click to open it.

3. When the Excel file opens, and you are prompted to log in to Power BI, use your Power BI login credentials to log in.

> **Note:** The first time you do this, you may be prompted to log in with your credentials and enable editing view, enable external data connections, etc. You should check for messages and follow the instructions to enable this process. When you sign in, make sure you sign in using the same approach and credentials you use for PowerBI.com.

If everything has gone well, you should now have a new pivot table in a new Excel workbook that looks like the one shown below.

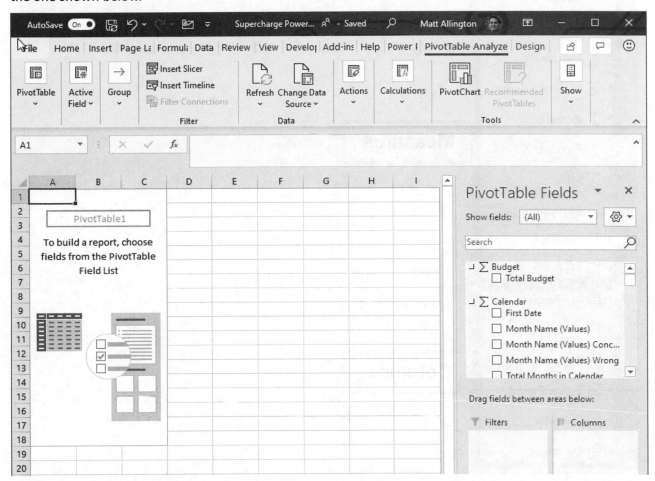

The really cool thing about this Excel workbook/pivot table is that it has a direct, live connection to PowerBI.com. The data model remains at PowerBI.com, and only the data needed to display the pivot table is stored in the Excel workbook. The data model could be 10 GB or larger on PowerBI.com, but the Excel workbook could be as small as 20 KB. These workbooks are commonly referred to as "thin workbooks."

The PivotTable Fields list on the right-hand side of Excel looks slightly different from this list for a regular pivot table. There are measure tables and also column tables, sometimes with the same names and differentiated only by the two different icons shown below.

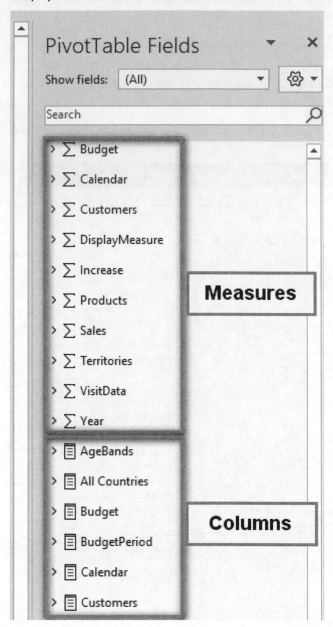

One important difference between Analyze in Excel pivot tables and Power BI visuals is that Analyze in Excel does not support implicit measures. You cannot drag a column from one of the column tables into the Values section of a pivot table. If you want to aggregate data in an Analyze in Excel pivot table, you must first write an explicit measure in the data model.

When you have a connection, you should be able to build pivot tables similar to the matrixes you have already built in Power BI Desktop. (See the example below.)

Occupation		Total Sales	Column Labels			
		Row Labels	Accessories	Bikes	Clothing	Grand Total
Clerical		2016		$3,266,374		$3,266,374
Management		2017		$6,530,344		$6,530,344
Manual		2018	$293,710	$9,359,103	$138,248	$9,791,060
Professional		2019	$407,050	$9,162,325	$201,525	$9,770,900
Skilled Manual		Grand Total	$700,760	$28,318,145	$339,773	$29,358,677

Using Cube Formulas

The final concept topic in this book is one of my favourites: cube formulas. Cube formulas have been around for many years. But before Power BI was launched, the main way you could use cube formulas was to connect to a SQL Server Analysis Services (SSAS) multidimensional cube. Some large companies have SSAS multidimensional set up. Some of those companies may connect directly to SSAS from Excel, and some of the ones that do may have discovered cube formulas. But given how rare this scenario is, most people have not come across cube formulas prior to discovering Power BI.

Pivot tables in Excel are great, and I use them all the time, but they do have some limitations. The biggest limitation is that a pivot table locks you into a particular format (or shape/structure). What if you want to put a single value in a single cell in a workbook? In that case, you could create a pivot table and set it to show just the number you want, but that involves a lot of overhead. In addition, if the pivot table changes shape at any time (e.g., on refresh), it is likely that the cell positions will change, which could mean that other parts of your workbook might break. The best-case scenario is that you realise there is a problem. The worst-case scenario is that your formula points to another similar cell in the pivot table, and you don't even notice that it is wrong!

"What about GETPIVOTDATA()?" you might ask. Well, yes, you can use GETPIVOTDATA(), but you still have the overhead of the pivot table, and the bottom line is that using cube formulas is often a much better solution. The easiest way to get started with cube formulas is to convert an existing pivot table to cube formulas. The following section walks you through how to do this.

Here's How: Converting a Pivot Table to Cube Formulas

Follow these steps to convert a pivot table in a thin workbook to cube formulas:

1. Create a new blank sheet in an Excel workbook and insert a pivot table like the one shown below, which is the same one you created earlier in this chapter.

Occupation		Total Sales	Column Labels			
		Row Labels	Accessories	Bikes	Clothing	Grand Total
Clerical		2016		$539,623		$539,623
Management		2017		$1,217,500		$1,217,500
Manual		2018	$52,969	$1,761,493	$25,269	$1,839,731
Professional		2019	$76,212	$1,761,077	$33,718	$1,871,007
Skilled Manual		Grand Total	$129,182	$5,279,693	$58,987	$5,467,862

2. Put `'Calendar'[CalendarYear]` on Rows, `Products[Category]` on Columns, and `[Total Sales]` on Values. Also add a slicer for `Customers[Occupation]`. Click on the slicer and make sure it works before proceeding.

3. Click inside the pivot table and then select the PivotTable Analyze tab (see #1 below), click OLAP Tools (#2), and select Convert to Formulas (#3).

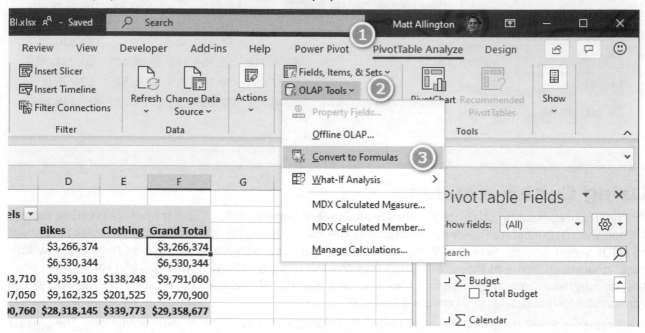

Bam! As shown below, your pivot table is converted to a stack of standalone formulas that you can move around as you want on the spreadsheet.

Occupation	Total Sales	Column Labels		
	Row Labels	Accessories	Bikes	Clothing	Grand Total
Clerical	2016		$3,266,374		$3,266,374
Management	2017		$6,530,344		$6,530,344
Manual	2018	$293,710	$9,359,103	$138,248	$9,791,060
Professional	2019	$407,050	$9,162,325	$201,525	$9,770,900
Skilled Manual	Grand Total	$700,760	$28,318,145	$339,773	$29,358,677

What's more, the slicer still works! Go ahead and drag the formulas around to new locations in your spreadsheet and then click on the slicer to verify that it works.

Occupation	Total Sales	Column Labels		
	Row Labels	Accessories	Bikes	Clothing	Grand Total
Clerical	2016				$539,623
Management	2017		$1,217,500		$1,217,500
Manual	2018	$52,969	$1,761,493	$25,269	$1,839,731
Professional	2019	$76,212	$1,761,077	$33,718	$1,871,007
Skilled Manual	Grand Total	$129,182	$5,279,693	$58,987	$5,467,862

$539,623

Writing Your Own Cube Formulas

Converting a pivot table to cube formulas is dead easy, but there is a better way: You can easily write your own cube formulas from scratch once you know how. There are seven cube formulas in total, and they all start with the word CUBE. You can see the list by typing =CUBE into any cell of a workbook, as shown below.

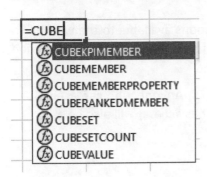

This book covers the two most commonly used cube formulas, CUBEVALUE() and CUBEMEMBER(). Once you have mastered these two formulas, you can do some research to learn about the other five.

CUBEVALUE() vs. CUBEMEMBER()

To get an idea of the difference between CUBEVALUE() and CUBEMEMBER(), go back to the pivot table that you just converted and double-click inside the grand total cell (see #1 below) so that Excel is in Edit mode. Notice in the formula bar that this grand total cell is a CUBEVALUE() formula (#2), and it points to a number of other cells (#3). The formulas inside each of these other cells (#3) are CUBEMEMBER() formulas.

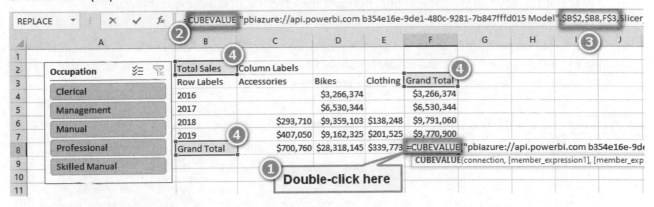

CUBEVALUE() is used to extract the value of a measure from the data model, and CUBEMEMBER() is used to extract a value from a column/lookup table. When they are used together, CUBEMEMBER() filters the data model and then calculates the CUBEVALUE() expression.

Now that you know about cube formulas, you can build a pivot table that contains the cube formulas you want in your spreadsheet and then simply select PivotTable Analyze, OLAP Tools, Convert to Formulas. Once you have done this, you can copy and paste the resulting formulas wherever you want. But it actually isn't very hard to write cube formulas from scratch, and the following section shows how.

Here's How: Writing CUBEVALUE() from Scratch

The important keyboard keys when writing cube formulas are the double quote, the square brackets, and the full stop (or period). This information will make sense as you work through these steps. Be sure to follow these steps exactly:

1. Click in an empty cell in a workbook and type =CUBEVALUE(. Notice the tooltip that pops up, asking for a connection and one or more member expressions. The member expressions can be either measures or table columns from your data model.

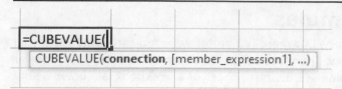

2. Type " (a double quote). You are presented with a list of connections available to the workbook. Given that this is a thin workbook created using Analyze in Excel, you should have a connection string that looks something like the one shown below.

Note: The long number (GUID) is unique to your instance of Power BI. Anyone who can access your Power BI data set (e.g., someone else in your organisation who has access) will also be able to interact with this thin workbook when it is done.

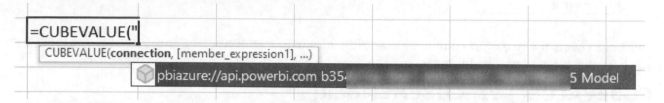

Note: If you are writing a cube formula using my localhost workbook http://xbi.com.au/local-host, you will get a different connection string experience than shown above.

3. Press the Tab key to select the connection and then type " (a double quote) again.
4. Type , (a comma).
5. Type " (a double quote) again to start the next parameter. This time notice that the tooltip shows a list of all the tables in the data model (as shown below). There is also one additional item in the list, [Measures]. All your DAX formulas are stored in [Measures].

6. Type [and then M and press Tab to select [Measures].
7. Type . (a full stop/period), and you see a list of all the measures that exist in the data model. From here you can either keep typing [followed by the name of the measure or use the up and down arrow keys on the keyboard to navigate to the measure you want to select.

=CUBEVALUE("pbiazure://api.powerbi.com b35   5 Model","[Measures].|

CUBEVALUE(connection, **[member_expression1]**, [member_expression2], ...)

- [Measures].[% Change in Sales vs. Budget]
- [Measures].[% of All Customer Sales]
- [Measures].[% of Global Sales]
- [Measures].[% of Selected Territories ONE STEP]
- [Measures].[% of Selected Territories]
- [Measures].[% Sales for All Days Selected Dates]
- [Measures].[% Sales to Selected Customers]
- [Measures].[Average Price Paid for a Product]
- [Measures].[Average Safety Stock]
- [Measures].[Average Sell Price per Item]
- [Measures].[Average Tax Paid]
- [Measures].[Avg Spent per visit Correct]

8. Type [and then type `Total S`. This brings the [Total Sales] measure to the top.
9. Press Tab, type `")`, and press Enter.

If you follow these instructions exactly, you end up with a value in a cell, as shown below. This is your first handwritten cube formula:

```
= CUBEVALUE(<your connection string>,"[Measures].[Total Sales]")
```

Note: In the formula above, I have used *<your connection string>* in place of the actual connection string because what you have on your screen will be different.

fx | =CUBEVALUE("pbiazure://api.powerbi.com b35   5 Model","[Measures].[Total Sales]")

B	C	D	E	F	G	H	I	J
$29,358,677								

You have probably noticed that the value you end up with after writing this cube formula is the grand total for all the data in the data model. It should therefore be clear that the data model is completely unfiltered. It is possible to filter this formula just as in a pivot table by adding some column parameters to the formula (sort of like adding a column to Rows in a pivot table).

Note: Before moving on, you should rewrite the formula above a couple of times for practice. Remember that the most important keys on your keyboard in this process are double quotes, square brackets, and the full stop/period, along with Tab to select the highlighted selection. Practice the rhythm of writing these formulas using these keys on the keyboard. Do it four or five times with a few different measures until you get the hang of it. Trust me, you will better understand the process if you do this.

Here's How: Applying Filters to Cube Formulas

To filter an existing formula, follow these steps:

1. Select one of the formulas you have already written.
2. Start editing the formula by deleting the last) and then typing , (a comma). The tooltip asks for *member_expression2*.
3. Type `"[`.
4. Use the down arrow key to select [Calendar] and then press Tab.
5. Type . (full stop/period) and use the down arrow key to select [CalendarYear]. Then press Tab.
6. Type . (full stop/period) and notice that the tooltip offers only a single choice, [All]. Select [All] and then press Tab.
7. Type . (full stop/period) again and notice that you now have a list of the possible years to select from. Select [2018].
8. Finish the formula by typing `")` and pressing Enter.

This is the final formula:

```
= CUBEVALUE(<your connection string>, "[Measures].[Total Sales]",
  "[Calendar].[CalendarYear].[All].[2018]")
```

9. Go back into this formula again and delete the closing bracket,), add another , (a comma), and then follow the same process as above to add another cube member, this time for Products[Category] = "Clothing". This is the formula you need:

```
= CUBEVALUE(<your connection string>, "[Measures].[Total Sales]",
    "[Calendar].[CalendarYear].[All].[2018]",
    "[Products].[Category].[All].[Clothing]")
```

You can add to your spreadsheet any measure from your data model by writing a cube formula like this. You can further filter the measure in your cube formula by adding additional column parameters inside the cube formula you are writing.

Here's How: Adding a Slicer Without a Pivot Table

Connecting your cube formulas to slicers is surprisingly easy. You should have a slicer for Customers[Occupation] on the sheet already. If you don't have this slicer, then go ahead and add it now. Here are the steps to add a slicer when there is no pivot table:

1. Select Insert, Slicer.

> **Note:** In this case, you can't right-click on a column in the PivotTable Fields list because there is no pivot table.

2. In the Existing Connections dialog that appears, select the Connections tab (see #1 below), and under Connections in This Workbook (#2), select <your connection string> (#3). Then click Open.

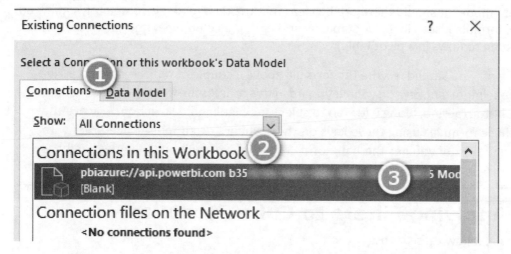

3. Find the Products[color] column in the list, select the correct check box, and click OK. You now have a slicer on your sheet. (However, it is not connected to your formula.)

Here's How: Connecting a Slicer to a Cube Formula

Follow these steps to connect a slicer to a cube formula:

1. Check the unique name for the slicer you want to connect by right-clicking on the slicer and selecting Slicer Settings.

2. In the Slicer Settings dialog that appears, note and memorise the value that appears next to Name to Use in Formulas. You will need this name in the next step. In the example shown here, the name is Slicer_Products. In your case, the name may be different. Once you've noted the slicer name, click Cancel.

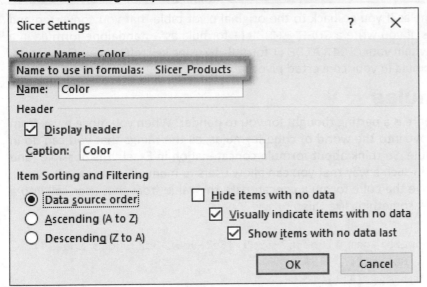

3. Write a new version of the `Total Sales` cube formula, this time adding the slicer to the formula. Simply add a comma after `[Total Sales]`, followed by the slicer name from step 2, and then type `)`. Your formula should now look something like this (though your slicer may have a slightly different name):

```
= CUBEVALUE(<your connection string>,
    "[Measures].[Total Sales]", Slicer_Products)
```

When you add a slicer name as a parameter inside a cube formula like this, the slicer is acting as a filter back to the data model.

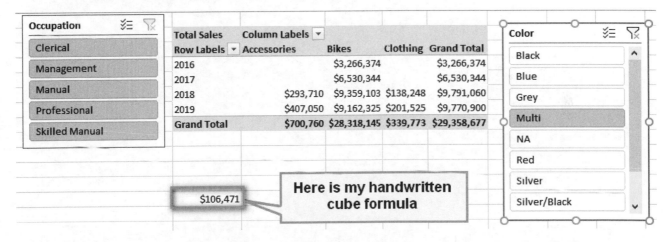

Note: You do not use double quotes around slicer names. This is an unfortunate inconsistency, but this is just how it works.

4. Now test it: Click on your slicer and watch your cube formula update.

Take a deep breath and be amazed. How cool are cube formulas?!

Writing CUBEMEMBER() Formulas

In addition to referencing a column name inside a `CUBEVALUE()` formula, it is possible to write a `CUBEMEMBER()` formula directly in a cell in a workbook. This formula can be used to extract column values from your data model.

Here is an example of a `CUBEMEMBER()` formula:

```
= CUBEMEMBER(<Your Connection String>,
    "[Customers].[Occupation].[All].[Manual]")
```

You can see a lot more of these formulas if you go back to the original pivot table that you converted and click in the column and row headings. If you write a CUBEMEMBER() formula as a standalone formula in a cell, you can reference that cell from within your CUBEVALUE() formula by using cell references. Once again, you can see this by examining the formula in your converted pivot table.

Concatenating Formulas

If you are not amazed already, then here is a parting thought for you to ponder: When you move away from the structure of a pivot table and move into the world of cube formulas, all the things that you can do in regular Excel formulas become possible. So think about formula concatenation in Excel. It is possible (and not too hard) to build cube formulas in such a way that you can allow users to manually enter a value (e.g., a product code) in a cell and then have the cube formula concatenate the value from that user cell into a master formula. The formula may look something like this:

```
=CUBEVALUE(
    "pbiazure://api.powerbi.com 175b2867-59d9-46e7-9c9f-3d23d0d83 Model",
    "[Measures].[Total Sales]",
    "[Products].[ProductKey].[All].["
    & D2 & "]"
)
```

This cube formula concatenates the value in cell D2 to extract the sales for the product number entered. This is a very powerful capability indeed!

23: Concept: Transferring DAX Skills to Excel

Power BI is a relatively new product from Microsoft, certainly compared to Excel. Power BI first became generally available in July 2015, and the pace of change over the years since its release has been phenomenal. The fact that you have purchased this book and have now arrived at this point probably means that you already know this. But the truth is that the main data technologies inside Power BI were first released as Power Pivot and Power Query for Microsoft Excel. Microsoft didn't (and still doesn't) do a really great job at marketing the existence of these products as part of Excel, and as a result, many (most?) people who could benefit from the technologies inside Excel don't know they exist. The good news, however, is that the skills you have learnt in this book are completely transferable to Power Pivot for Microsoft Excel. This chapter is here to help you with the transfer.

Differences Between Power BI and Power Pivot for Excel

There are a couple differences between Power BI and the various versions of Power Pivot for Excel that you should be aware of, as explained here.

> **Note:** I use the following terminology in this section:
> - Power Pivot is a data modelling engine that is an add-in for Excel. Power BI Desktop also has this data modelling engine, but it is not called Power Pivot inside Power BI.
> - Power Query is the data acquisition tool that exists in both Excel and Power BI Desktop.

All Versions of Excel

Different versions of Excel may have different versions of Power Pivot, and not all DAX functions are available in all versions. Power BI contains the latest and most up-to-date version of the data modelling engine. I keep an up-to-date quick guide to all the DAX functions that you can download from http://xbi.com.au/dax-functions.

There is also a DAX function quick reference list at the back of this book. See "Appendix B - DAX Quick Reference List" on page 260.

All Excel versions of Power Pivot support one-to-many relationships; they do not support the one-to-one or many-to-many relationships that are supported in Power BI. This is not a major issue, however, as one-to-one and many-to-many are not common relationship types.

There is no bidirectional cross-filtering available in any of the Excel versions of Power Pivot.

You can convert the data models produced in Excel 2010 to Excel 2013 or 2016 data models, but you can't go back the other way. That is, you can upgrade but not downgrade.

Excel 2013/2016 data models can be opened in both Excel 2013 and Excel 2016.

Excel 2010 and 2013 have a different user experience in the Diagram view compared to Excel 2016 and Power BI Desktop. You can see the differences between the different UIs in the image below. The earlier versions of Excel (see #1 below) have an arrow pointing to the "one" side of the relationship (#3) and a black dot on the "many" side (#5). Excel 2016 and Power BI have a new, improved UI (#2) with a 1 on the "one" side of the relationship (#4) and an asterisk (*) on the "many" side (#6).

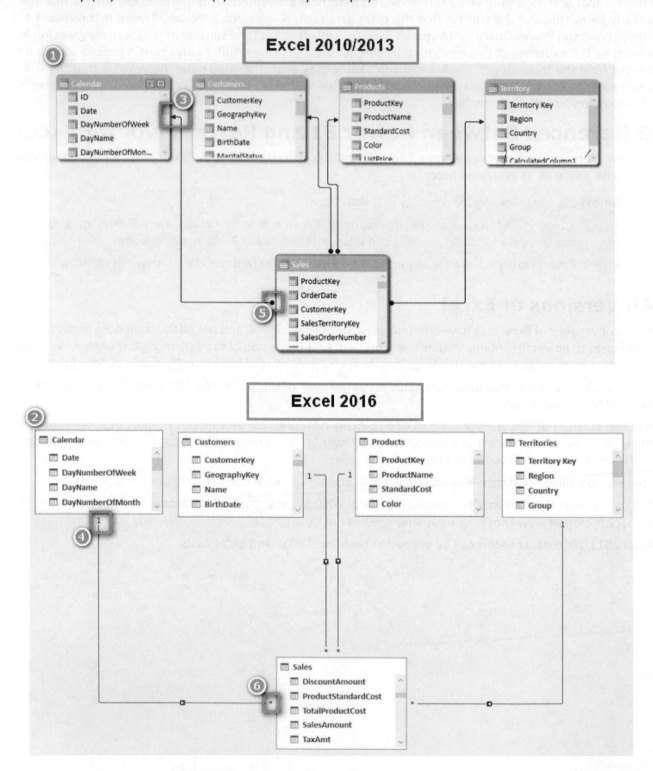

Excel 2013

In Excel 2013, the term calculated field is used instead of measure. This was an unfortunate change made in Excel 2013 that—thankfully—lasted for this one version of Excel only.

Excel 2010

The ribbon in Excel 2010 is unique in that it has a PowerPivot Window option (as shown below) instead of Manage, which appears in later versions of Excel. The Power Pivot icon is the same in all Excel versions.

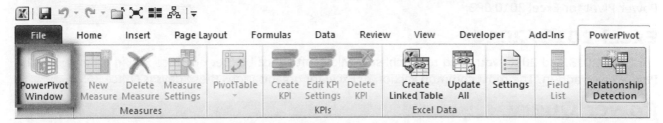

Excel 2010 is the only version that uses a completely separate add-in to deploy Power Pivot, and this means there are two completely different field lists for pivot tables. The first time you stumble on the traditional PivotTable Field List pane, you might be confused about what is happening; being forewarned allows you to be forearmed. In the image below, note the different titles in the two different field list panes. The one on the left (see #1 below) is the newer PowerPivot Field List pane; this is the one you should be using when working with Power Pivot. The one on the right (#2) is the original PivotTable Field List pane, and you don't use it with Power Pivot pivot tables. However, it is possible to have both of these panes open at the same time, and, confusingly, you can accidently open the wrong one without realising it. The key visual clues about which one you have open are easy to spot: The titles are different, the PivotTable Field List pane has special icons (#3), and the PowerPivot Field List pane has a slicer drop zone (#4).

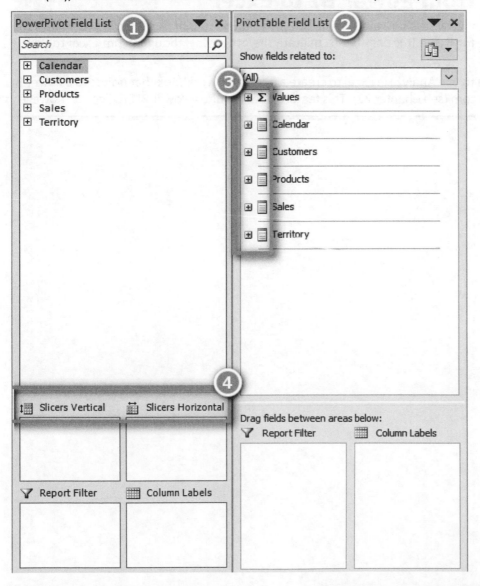

Excel 2010

For Excel 2010 you can download the free Power Pivot add-in from the Microsoft website. You can use a browser to search for the add-in. Just make sure you find and install Service Pack 2. You should search for Power Pivot for Excel 2010 SP2.

Excel 2013/2016

For Excel 2013 and 2016, you need to purchase a Microsoft Office box set or Office 365 in order to get the Power Pivot add-in. The most common version of Excel for organisations these days is Office 365 E3.

Power Query

Excel 2010/2013

Power Query is a free add-in that you can download from Microsoft. If you use Excel 2010 or 2013, just search for Power Query in a web browser. After you install it, you see a new tab called Power Query.

Excel 2016

Power Query comes bundled with Excel 2016. There are many different versions of Excel 2016, and the way it integrates Power Query does vary. You will find it on the Data tab either as Get and Transform or Get External Data.

Migrating Data from Power BI to Excel

If you read this heading and got excited, then I am sorry to tell you that you cannot migrate a Power BI Desktop data model into Power Pivot for Excel. It is possible to migrate the other way, though (from Excel to Power BI), as described below.

Don't forget that it is possible to use Analyze in Excel to create a new Excel workbook that points to a Power BI workbook loaded to PowerBI.com (see Chapter 22). This feature does require a Power BI Pro licence, however.

Here's How: Importing Excel Power Pivot Workbooks to Power BI Desktop

It is possible to import a Power Pivot data model from an Excel workbook into Power BI Desktop, along with all the data connections, relationships, and measures. Unfortunately, any reports you have created in Excel are not migrated and need to be re-created in Power BI.

Follow these steps to import a Power Pivot workbook from Excel into Power BI Desktop:

1. In Power BI Desktop, select File, New. A new blank Power BI Desktop file opens.

2. Select File, Import (see #1 below), Power Query, Power Pivot, Power View (#2).

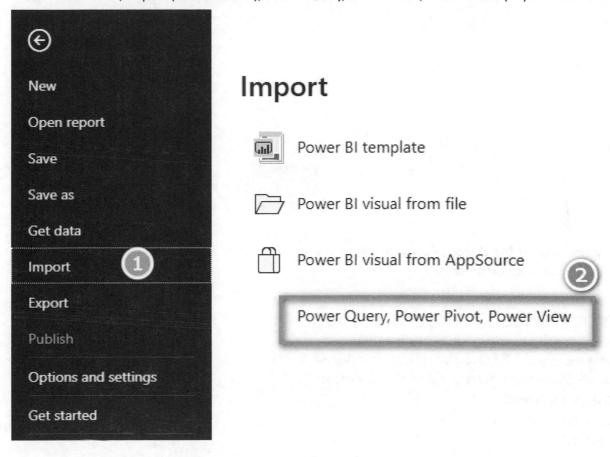

3. Navigate to the Excel workbook you want to migrate, select it, and click OK.

4.   When you get the message shown below, click Start.

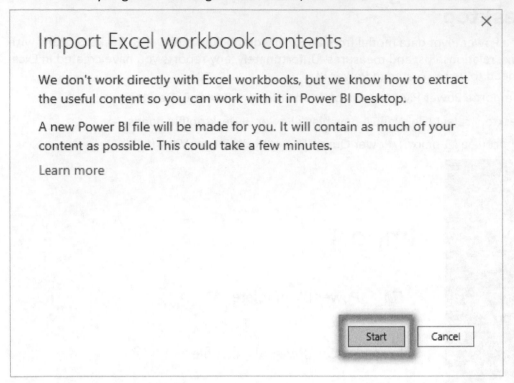

Import Excel workbook contents

We don't work directly with Excel workbooks, but we know how to extract the useful content so you can work with it in Power BI Desktop.

A new Power BI file will be made for you. It will contain as much of your content as possible. This could take a few minutes.

Learn more

Start   Cancel

5.   When you get the choice to copy the data from your queries or keep the connection (as shown below), click Keep Connection.

Import Excel workbook contents

There are queries and data model tables that depend on the following worksheet tables in the original workbook:
- DatesSamePeriodLY
- TempTableFromFilter
- YearTable
- AgeBands
- Hemisphere

Do you want to copy the data from those tables to your Power BI Desktop file or keep a connection to the original Excel workbook for this data?

Copy data   Keep connection   Cancel

Note: Power BI Desktop doesn't include the concept of linked tables. When you import an Excel workbook that contains linked tables into Power BI Desktop, you can either bring the data in as a one-off migration or retain the link to the original linked table in the original Excel workbook.

The Excel workbook data model is imported into Power BI Desktop, and you can proceed to use Power BI Desktop instead of Excel and build your own visualisations on top of the Power Pivot data model.

Writing DAX Measures in Excel

If you have learnt how to use Power BI from this book and want to try out Power Pivot for Excel, you need to be aware of a few differences (mainly related to the user interfaces).

There are three places you can write DAX measures in Power Pivot for Excel:

- You can write a measure in the formula bar in the Power Pivot window, as shown below. If you use this method, you must specify the measure name followed by a colon and then the formula.

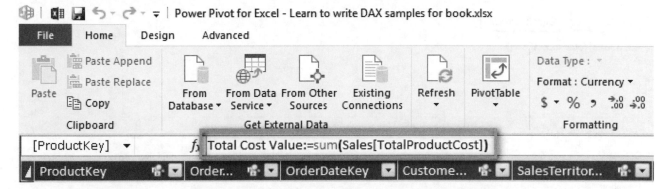

- You can write and edit measures in any empty cell in the calculation area at the bottom of the Power Pivot window, as shown below. You also need to add a colon when writing a measure here.

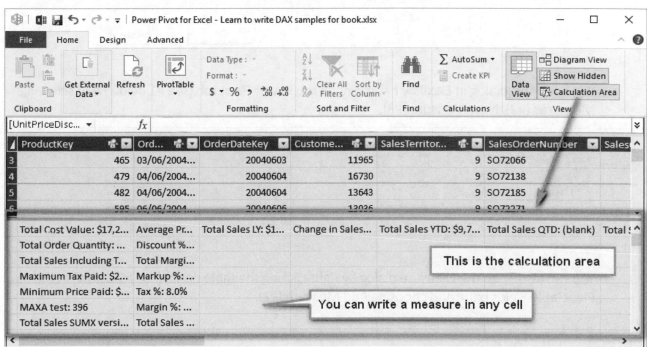

- You can write measures in the Measure dialog in Excel, as shown below.

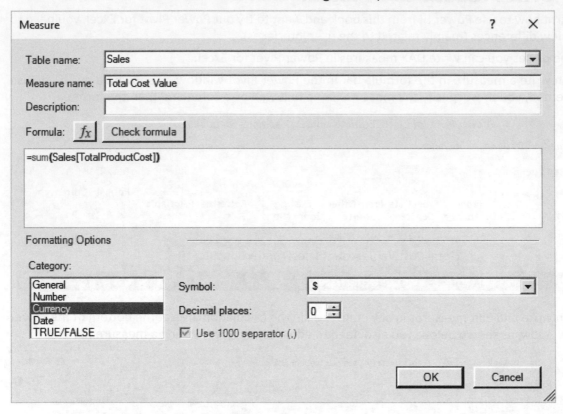

You open this dialog in Excel by navigating to the Power Pivot tab (see #1 below) and selecting Measures (#2), New Measure (#3).

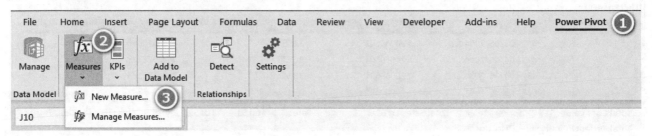

You can also open the Measure dialog by right-clicking the table name (see #1 below) in the PivotTable Fields pane and choosing Add Measure (#2).

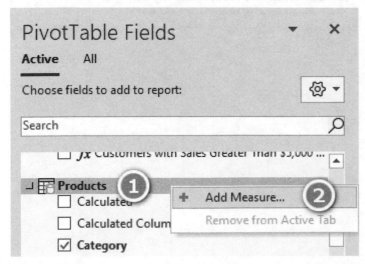

However, at this writing, adding a measure by right-clicking and selecting Add Measure is problematic, and I do not recommend that you do it this way. The UI looks the same as when you select Measure, New Measure, but the Measure dialog box is actually a completely different piece of code. The behaviour of the Tab key when editing the measure is completely different (frustratingly so), and there is no colour coding of the formula language. For these reasons, I recommend that you not use the right-clicking and selecting Add Measure approach. I have to say, however, that it is very difficult to avoid doing it this way as it comes naturally after you learn to write measures in Power BI Desktop.

Tip: In general, I recommend that Excel users write DAX in the Measure dialog box in Excel. I also recommend first creating a pivot table that provides some context for the measure you are about to write. If you do it this way, you will immediately see the measure appear in the pivot table when you click OK, and this helps you quickly see whether the formula looks correct.

Here's How: Writing Measures

To create a new measure in Power Pivot for Excel, follow these steps:

1. Create a new blank pivot table connected to your data model (or use an existing one if you already have something appropriate).

2. Add some relevant data to the rows in your pivot table (see #1 below).

3. Click inside the pivot table, navigate to the Power Pivot tab, click the Measures drop-down arrow (#2), and then select New Measure (#3). The Measure dialog appears.

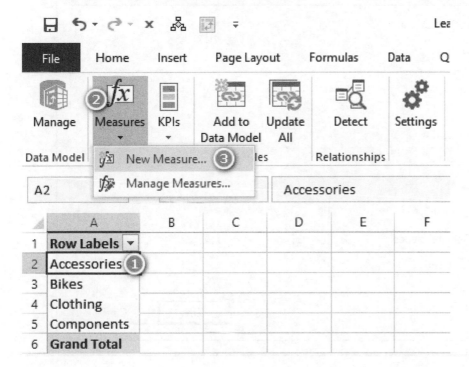

Tip: You should use the Measure dialog shown below as a process flow/guide. If you don't do this, you risk missing one or more of the steps. Missing a step will end up costing you time and causing rework. Get in the good habit of following the process steps I describe here, using the dialog as a reminder of all the steps. Always follow the order outlined here.

4. In the Table Name drop-down (see #1 below), select the table where your measure will be stored.

5. In the Measure Name text box (#2), give the new measure a name.

6. In the Formula box (#3) write the DAX formula.

7. Click Check Formula (#4) to check whether the formula you wrote is syntactically correct. Fix any errors that occur.

8. Select an appropriate formatting option from the Category list (#5), including a suitable symbol and decimal places in the area to the right of the Category list.

9. Click OK (#6) to save the measure.

Note: I generally don't enter anything in the Description box, but it is there for you to use if you like. It's for reference only and doesn't impact the behaviour of the formulas.

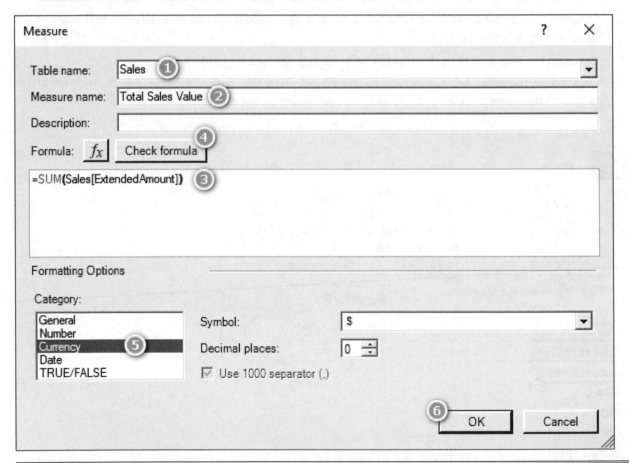

24: Concept: Next Steps on Your DAX Journey

You have almost finished reading all the chapters of this book. Now what? First of all, let me assure you that this is just the start, not the end, of your journey to learning how to supercharge Power BI (and Excel) by learning to write DAX. As I have been saying all through the book, the most important thing is to practice, practice, practice. Start using your new skills at work and at play so that you build your depth of skill and knowledge. It will take you a few months of using your new skills to become competent (if you practice regularly), but you are well on your way already. Now that you have a basic understanding of Power BI and DAX, you can incrementally learn and improve over time. But there are some things that will help you learn more and faster.

Guided Online Learning

You might have found certain DAX concepts—such as filter propagation, evaluation contexts, context transition, and custom time intelligence—difficult to master, and you may not yet have the solid understanding you need to apply them to your real-life business problems. If this is the case, you might want to enrol in my Supercharge Power BI online training (http://xbi.com.au/scpbi-online-training), which includes the following:

- Guided study of DAX with this book

- Online videos to cement your learning

- Weekly online live Q&A sessions with me, where you can bring your questions/problems and get answers/solutions from me

- A video recording of each live Q&A session you attend that you can download and keep for future reference

What's more, when you enrol in the training, you get access to the online videos for one year and can attend any of the Q&A sessions throughout the year.

Video Training

I offer video training for learning DAX. You can find more details at http://xbi.com.au/dax-online-training.

Live Instructor-Led Classroom and Online Training

Some people learn best in a classroom environment. If you're one of them, you might want to attend a live instructor-led training.

If you are in Australia, you can attend live classroom training courses delivered personally by me or my accredited trainers. For details about upcoming events, see http://xbi.com.au/live-training.

If you are outside Australia, you can attend online live training courses delivered personally by me or my accredited trainers. For details about upcoming training sessions, see http://xbi.com.au/live-online-training. I am also considering licensing some training providers outside Australia. If I do that in the future, you will be able to find the announcement at http://xbi.com.au/global-training.

I also deliver customised in-house training for companies that have larger groups of users and are looking for a more personalised experience. Once again, this can be at the company premises if in Australia (see http://xbi.com.au/inhouse-training) or can be live online training for those outside Australia (see http://xbi.com.au/live-online-inhouse-training). Contact me on my website for details.

There are many great things about these training courses, but one super benefit is that my accredited trainers and I teach DAX using the same techniques I have used in this book. By attending one of our live training courses, you will continue to learn using the same methodology used in this book.

Reports and Dashboards

In this book I have used only a few basic visuals to teach you how to write DAX. But Power BI supports literally hundreds of other visuals and has many interactivity concepts that can set your reports apart from the pack. To learn more about what Power BI has to offer, you might want to consider my video training course "Foundations of Power BI—Data to Dashboard" (http://xbi.com.au/d2d-online-training).

Power Query

Power Query is a desktop ETL (extract, transform, and load) tool for Power BI and Excel users. It is the same technology that comes bundled with Power BI and Excel. Power Query allows you to connect to data from anywhere, change the shape of that data, and then load it into your workbooks. Once the data is loaded with Power Query, you can easily refresh data at any time with a single click or, better still, with an automated refresh. Power Query has its own language, called M, but it also has a simple-to-use interface that allows you to do most common tasks without the need to learn M.

I offer a Power Query video course (http://xbi.com.au/pq-training) created in collaboration with Ken Puls and Miguel Escobar. You can start with the free course Power Query Fundamentals and proceed from there.

Advanced DAX

When you are making progress with DAX and have been using it regularly for 6 to 18 months, you may be ready to take your learning to the next level. I have an excellent follow-up training course called Demystifying DAX (http://xbi.com.au/adv-dax-training) that will help you move to the next level.

Enhancing Your Skills

Once you learn Power BI, you need to keep yourself up to date with the latest developments in the product. (Remember that Power BI is evolving continuously at a rapid phase.) You also need to be aware of a number of tips and tricks. There are many ways of accomplishing this, as described in the following sections.

Third-Person Teaching/Learning

I am a big believer in "third-person teaching/learning." I first heard of this concept from Stephen Covey, at one of his seminars. The basic idea is that you learn more when you learn with the intent to teach others, and you learn more from the process of teaching others. For this reason, I really believe in the benefits of participating in user forums. As I mentioned at the start of the book, I have set up a forum at http://xbi.com.au/scpbi-forum, and it is free for anyone and everyone to ask questions and also to help others. If you want to really cement your new skills and knowledge, then sign up and ask for help. Even better, answer questions and teach others on the forum. When you teach others, you cement your knowledge and become better and stronger with your DAX. There is also an excellent Power BI community and forum at http://community.powerbi.com. You can participate in the forums and maybe also join a local Power BI user group in your region. The Sydney Power BI user group is at http://xbi.com.au/syd-pug. You can use http://xbi.com.au/all-pug to search for a group in your area.

Blogs

There are a number of Power BI blogs that I recommend you subscribe to. Reading blogs is a great way to keep in touch with the latest thinking from people who spend their life working with Power BI. Here are some that I think are especially useful:

- My blog: http://xbi.com.au/matt-blog
- Marco Russo and Alberto Ferrari's blog: http://sqlbi.com
- Reza Rad's blog: http://radacad.com/blog
- Gilbert Quevauvilliers' blog: https://www.fourmoo.com/
- Ken Puls' blog: http://www.excelguru.ca/blog/
- Chris Webb's blog: http://blog.crossjoin.co.uk/
- Gil Raviv's blog: https://datachant.com

Books

There are a few really good DAX books that I recommend (and have mentioned previously). I keep a list of books I recommend on my website and update it over time. You can always find an updated list at http://xbi.com.au/power-books.

That's All, Folks

I hope you have enjoyed this book and that it has successfully started you on your journey to becoming a DAX superstar. If you like this book, please tell your Power BI and Excel friends and colleagues so they, too, can become DAX superstars. I have had feedback from many hundreds of people that my book has helped them immensely. If I have helped you, the best way you can say thanks is to write a positive review of the book at Amazon.com.

Appendix A: Answers to Practice Exercises

This appendix provides answers to the practice exercises scattered throughout the book. The answers appear in the same order as the exercises in the book and are numbered so you can easily match up the exercises and the answers.

SUM()

These practice exercises appear in Chapter 4. As you compare your answers to the ones shown here, consider the following questions: Did you remember to put your measures in the correct table? Did you put the measure in the table the data comes from? Did you format with an appropriate number format? Have you used a matrix visual with relevant fields to check the values of the measure?

1. Total Sales = SUM(Sales[ExtendedAmount])

    or:

    Total Sales = SUM(Sales[SalesAmount])

2. Total Cost = SUM(Sales[TotalProductCost])

    or:

    Total Cost = SUM(Sales[ProductStandardCost])

3. Total Margin $ = [Total Sales] - [Total Cost]
4. Total Margin % = [Total Margin $] / [Total Sales]

    or:

    Total Margin % = DIVIDE([Total Margin $], [Total Sales]

    Note: I haven't covered DIVIDE() yet, but that is coming later in Chapter 4.

5. Total Sales Tax Paid = SUM(Sales[TaxAmt])
6. Total Sales Including Tax = [Total Sales] + [Total Sales Tax Paid]
7. Total Order Quantity = SUM(Sales[OrderQuantity])

COUNT()

These practice exercises appear in Chapter 4.

8. Total Number of Products = COUNT(Products[ProductKey])
9. Total Number of Customers = COUNT(Customers[CustomerKey])

    Note: Counting the "key" columns is generally pretty safe because, by definition, each one must have a value. Technically, you can count any column that has a value in each cell, and you will get the same answer. Just be careful if you are counting a column that may have blank values because COUNT() does not count blanks. Try it out with the Products[Status] column. You can verify your results in the Data view by manually placing a filter on the Products[Status] column at the top of the table.

COUNTROWS()

These practice exercises appear in Chapter 4.

    Note: Remember that COUNTROWS() takes a table, not a column, as input.

10. Total Number of Products COUNTROWS Version = COUNTROWS(Products)
11. Total Number of Customers COUNTROWS Version = COUNTROWS(Customers)

DISTINCTCOUNT()

These practice exercises appear in Chapter 4.

12. `Total Customers in Database DISTINCTCOUNT Version = DISTINCTCOUNT(Customers[CustomerKey])`

13. `Count of Occupation = DISTINCTCOUNT(Customers[Occupation])`

14. `Count of Country = DISTINCTCOUNT(Territories[Country])`

15. `Total Customers That Have Purchased = DISTINCTCOUNT(Sales[CustomerKey])`

MAX(), MIN(), and AVERAGE()

These practice exercises appear in Chapter 4.

16. `Maximum Tax Paid on a Product = MAX(Sales[TaxAmt])`

17. `Minimum Price Paid for a Product = MIN(Sales[ExtendedAmount])`

18. `Average Price Paid for a Product = AVERAGE(Sales[ExtendedAmount])`

COUNTBLANK()

These practice exercises appear in Chapter 4.

19. `Customers Without Address Line 2 = COUNTBLANK(Customers[AddressLine2])`

20. `Products Without Weight Values = COUNTBLANK(Products[Weight])`

DIVIDE()

These practice exercises appear in Chapter 4.

21. `Margin % = DIVIDE([Total Margin $], [Total Sales])`

22. `Markup % = DIVIDE([Total Margin $], [Total Cost])`

23. `Tax % = DIVIDE([Total Sales Tax Paid], [Total Sales])`

Calculated Columns

This practice exercise appears in Chapter 7.

24.
```
= IF(
    OR('Calendar'[CalendarQuarter]=1, 'Calendar'[CalendarQuarter]=2),
    "H1","H2"
)
```

or you could write:

```
= IF(
    'Calendar'[CalendarQuarter] in {1,2},
    "H1","H2"
)
```

Note: There are a number of ways to write this calculated column. If yours is different from this but works, then all is well and good.

SUMX()

These practice exercises appear in Chapter 8.

25. Total Sales SUMX Version =

    SUMX(Sales, Sales[OrderQuantity] * Sales[UnitPrice])

Note: In this sample database, the order quantity is always 1.

26. Total Sales Including Tax SUMX Version =

    SUMX(Sales,Sales[ExtendedAmount] + Sales[TaxAmt])

27. Total Sales Including Freight =

    SUMX(Sales,Sales[ExtendedAmount] + Sales[Freight])

28. Dealer Margin =

    SUMX (Products,Products[ListPrice] - Products[DealerPrice])

AVERAGEX()

These practice exercises appear in Chapter 8.

29. Average Selling Price Including Tax per Item =

    AVERAGEX(Sales, Sales[ExtendedAmount] + Sales[TaxAmt])

Note: There are a few columns in the Sales table that have the same value. If you used one of the others and got the same answer, then that is fine.

30. Average Profit Per Item Sold =

    AVERAGEX(Sales, Sales[ExtendedAmount] - Sales[ProductStandardCost])

31. Average Value of Safety Stock Per Product =

    AVERAGEX(Products, Products[SafetyStockLevel]
    * Products[ListPrice])

CALCULATE() with a Single Table

These practice exercises appear in Chapter 9.

32. Total Male Customers =

    CALCULATE([Total Number of Customers], Customers[Gender] = "M")

33. Total Customers Born Before 1970 =

    CALCULATE([Total Number of Customers],

        Customers[BirthDate] < DATE(1970,1,1)

)

34. Total Customers Born in January =

    CALCULATE([Total Number of Customers],

        MONTH(Customers[BirthDate]) = 1

)

35. Customers Earning at Least $100,000 per Year =

      CALCULATE([Total Number of Customers],

          Customers[YearlyIncome] >=100000

)

CALCULATE() with Multiple Tables

These practice exercises appear in Chapter 9.

36. Total Sales of Clothing =

      CALCULATE([Total Sales],

          Products[Category]="Clothing"

)

37. Sales to Female Customers =

      CALCULATE([Total Sales], Customers[Gender]="F")

38. Sales of Bikes to Married Men =

      CALCULATE([Total Sales],

          Customers[MaritalStatus]="M",

          Customers[Gender]="M",

          Products[Category]="Bikes"

)

VALUES()

These practice exercises appear in Chapter 13.

39. Number of Color Variants = COUNTROWS(VALUES(Products[Color]))

40. Number of SubCategories = COUNTROWS(VALUES(Products[SubCategory]))

41. Number of Size Ranges = COUNTROWS(VALUES(Products[SizeRange]))

42. Product Category (Values) =

      IF(HASONEVALUE(Products[Category]), VALUES(Products[Category]))

   or:

  SELECTEDVALUE(Products[Category])

43. Product Subcategory (Values) =

      IF(HASONEVALUE(Products[SubCategory]),

          VALUES(Products[SubCategory])

)

   or:

  SELECTEDVALUE(Products[SubCategory])

44. Product Color (Values) =

    IF(HASONEVALUE(Products[color]),

        VALUES(Products[color])

)

    or:

    SELECTEDVALUE(Products[color])

45. Product SubCategory (Values) edited =

    IF(HASONEVALUE(Products[SubCategory]),

        VALUES(Products[SubCategory]),

        "More than 1 SubCategory"

)

    or:

  = SELECTEDVALUE(Products[SubCategory],"More than 1 SubCategory")

46. Product Color (Values) edited =

    IF(HASONEVALUE(Products[color]),

        VALUES(Products[color]),

        "More than 1 Color"

)

    or:

  = SELECTEDVALUE((Products[color],"More than 1 Color")

ALL(), ALLEXCEPT(), and ALLSELECTED()

These practice exercises appear in Chapter 14.

47. Total Sales to All Customers = CALCULATE([Total Sales], All(Customers))

> **Note:** This measure belongs in the Sales table, not the Customers table.

48. % of All Customer Sales =

        DIVIDE([Total Sales], [Total Sales to All Customers])

49. Total Sales to Selected Customers =

        CALCULATE([Total Sales], ALLSELECTED(Customers))

50. % of Sales to Selected Customers =

        DIVIDE([Total Sales], [Total Sales to Selected Customers])

51. Total Sales for All Days Selected Dates =

        CALCULATE([Total Sales], ALLSELECTED('Calendar'))

> **Note:** Did you know to use ALLSELECTED() and not ALLEXCEPT()?

52. % Sales for All Days Selected Dates =

        DIVIDE([Total Sales],[Total Sales for All Days Selected Dates])

53. Total Orders All Customers =

```
CALCULATE([Total Order Quantity], ALL(Customers))
```

54. Baseline Orders for All Customers with This Occupation =

```
CALCULATE([Total Order Quantity],

    ALLEXCEPT(Customers, Customers[Occupation])

)
```

55. Baseline % This Occupation of All Customer Orders =

```
DIVIDE(

    [Baseline Orders for All customers with this Occupation],

    [Total Orders All Customers]

)
```

56. Total Orders Selected Customers =

```
CALCULATE([Total Order Quantity], ALLSELECTED(Customers])
```

57. Occupation % of Selected Customers =

```
DIVIDE([Total Order Quantity], [Total Orders Selected Customers])
```

58. Percentage Point Variation to Baseline =

```
[Occupation % of Selected Customers] -

[Baseline % this Occupation is of All Customer Orders]
```

FILTER()

These practice exercises appear in Chapter 15.

59. Total Sales of Products That Have Some Sales but Less Than $10,000 =

```
CALCULATE([Total Sales],

    FILTER(Products,

        [Total Sales] < 10000 && [Total Sales] >0

    )

)
```

or:

```
= CALCULATE([Total Sales],

    FILTER(Products, [Total Sales] <10000),

    FILTER(Products, [Total Sales] >0)

)
```

60. Count of Products That Have Some Sales but Less Than $10,000 =

```
CALCULATE(COUNTROWS(Products),

    FILTER(Products, [Total Sales]<10000 && [Total Sales] >0)

)
```

or:

```
= CALCULATE(COUNTROWS(Products),

    FILTER(Products, [Total Sales] <10000),

    FILTER(Products, [Total Sales] >0)

)
```

Time Intelligence

These practice exercises appear in Chapter 16.

61. Total Sales Month to Date = TOTALMTD([Total Sales], 'Calendar'[Date])

62. Total Sales Quarter to Date = TOTALQTD([Total Sales], 'Calendar'[Date])

63. Total Sales FYTD 30 June =

```
TOTALYTD([Total Sales],'Calendar'[Date],"30/6")
```

64. Total Sales FYTD 31 March =

```
TOTALYTD([Total Sales],'Calendar'[Date],"31/3")
```

65. Total Sales Previous Month =

```
CALCULATE([Total Sales], PREVIOUSMONTH('Calendar'[Date]))
```

66. Total Sales Previous Day =

```
CALCULATE([Total Sales], PREVIOUSDAY('Calendar'[Date]))
```

67. Total Sales Previous Quarter =

```
CALCULATE([Total Sales], PREVIOUSQUARTER('Calendar'[Date]))
```

68. Total Sales Moving Annual Total =

```
CALCULATE([Total Sales],

    FILTER(ALL('Calendar'),

        'Calendar'[Date] > MAX('Calendar'[Date]) - 365

        && 'Calendar'[Date] <= MAX('Calendar'[Date])

    )

)
```

69. Total Sales Rolling 90 Days =

```
IF(MAX('Calendar'[ID])>=90,
    CALCULATE([Total Sales],
        FILTER(ALL('Calendar'),
            'Calendar'[Date] > MAX('Calendar'[Date]) - 90
            && 'Calendar'[Date] <= MAX('Calendar'[Date])
        )
    )
)
```

Harvester Measures

This practice exercise appears in Chapter 20.

70. Total Customers Born Before Selected Year =

```
CALCULATE([Total Number of Customers],
    FILTER(Customers,
        Customers[BirthDate] < DATE([Selected Year],1,1)
    )
)
```

Multiple Data Tables

These practice exercises appear in Chapter 21.

71. Total Budget = SUM(Budget[Budget])

> **Note:** This measure should be placed in the Budget table.

72. Change in Sales vs. Budget = [Total Sales] – [Total Budget]

> **Note:** This measure could be placed in either the Sales table or the Budget table. I normally place it in the Sales table because the name of the measure is [Change in Sales vs. Budget].

73. % Change in Sales vs. Budget =

```
DIVIDE([Change in Sales vs. Budget], [Total Budget])
```

> **Note:** Also place this measure in the Sales table.

Appendix B - DAX Quick Reference List

This DAX function quick reference list contains all the current DAX functions in an easy-to-use categorised list. Due to limited space in this book, this is simply a list of the function names. I have prepared a more comprehensive quick reference guide that contains details about how each function works and can be used. You can download a free PDF copy of the full quick reference guide at http://xbi.com.au/online-shop.

DAX Aggregation Functions (Aggregators)

DAX Aggregation Functions (called aggregators for short) take a column or a table as the argument and aggregate the values.

AVERAGE(column)

AVERAGEA(column)

COUNT(column)

COUNTA(column)

COUNTBLANK(column)

COUNTROWS(table)

DISTINCTCOUNT(column)

DISTINCTCOUNTNOBLANK(column)

MAX(column)

MAX(expression1, expression2)

MAXA(column)

MIN(column)

MIN(expression1, expression2)

MINA(column)

PRODUCT(column)

SUM(column)

TOPN(n_value, tablename, orderByexpression1, [Order],
    [orderByexpression2, [Order]], …)

DAX Date and Time Functions

You can use DAX Date and Time Functions in the calculations based on dates and time. DAX Date and Time Functions are like the Excel date and time functions but use a datetime data type and can take values from a column as an argument.

CALENDAR(startdate, enddate)

CALENDARAUTO([endmonthoffiscalyear])

DATE(year, month, day)

DATEDIFF(startdate, enddate, interval)

DATEVALUE(datetext)

DAY(date)

EDATE(startdate, months)

EOMONTH(startdate, months)

HOUR(datetimevalue)

MINUTE(datetimevalue)

MONTH(datetimevalue)

NOW()

QUARTER(datetimevalue)

SECOND(datetimevalue)

TIME(hour, minute, second)

TIMEVALUE(timetext)

TODAY()

UTCNOW()

UTCTODAY()

WEEKDAY(date, returntype)

WEEKNUM(date, returntype)

YEAR(datetimevalue)

YEARFRAC(start_date, end_date, [basis])

DAX Filter Functions

DAX Filter Functions are very different to Excel functions. They are used to (typically) return filtered tables that can be used in your data model. These new "virtual" tables retain lineage with the physical data model and hence they can "filter" the physical data model on the fly. Lookup functions work by using tables and relationships between them. Filtering functions let you manipulate data context to create dynamic calculations.

DAX FILTER and VALUES functions are the most complex and powerful functions.

```
ADDMISSINGITEMS(showAllColumn[, showAllColumn] …, table,
    groupingColumn[, groupingColumn]…[, filterTable] …)
```

```
ADDMISSINGITEMS(showAllColumn[, showAllColumn]…, table,
    [ROLLUPISSUBTOTAL()groupingColumn[, isSubtotal_columnName]
    [, groupingColumn][, isSubtotal_columnName] … )],
    [, filterTable] …)
```

```
ALL([TableOrColumn][, TableOrColumn] …)
```

```
ALLCROSSFILTERED(table)
```

```
ALLEXCEPT(table, column[, column] …)
```

```
ALLNOBLANKROW(table|column)
```

```
ALLSELECTED([tableName|columnName])
```

```
CALCULATE(expression[, filter1][, filter2]…)
```

```
CALCULATETABLE(expression, filter1, filter2, …)
```

```
CROSSFILTER(columnName1, columnName2, direction)
```

```
DISTINCT(column)
```

```
DISTINCT(table)
```

```
EARLIER(column[, number])
```

```
EARLIEST(column)
```

```
FILTER(table, filter)
```

```
FILTERS(columnName)
```

```
HASONEFILTER(columnName)
```

```
HASONEVALUE(columnName)
```

```
ISCROSSFILTERED(columnName)
```

```
ISFILTERED(columnName)
```

```
KEEPFILTERS(expression)
```

```
RELATED(column)
```

```
RELATEDTABLE(tableName)
```

```
REMOVEFILTERS([table|column[, column[, column[, …]]]])
```

```
SELECTEDVALUE(columnName[, alternateResult])
```

```
SUBSTITUTEWITHINDEX(table, indexColumnName, indexColumnsTable,
    orderBy_expression[, order][, orderBy_expression[, order]] …)
```

```
TREATAS(table_expression, column1[, column2][, column3] …)
```

```
USERELATIONSHIP(columnName1, columnName2)
```

```
VALUES(TableNameOrColumnName)
```

DAX Financial Functions

DAX Financial Functions are used in formulas that perform financial calculations. These functions are similar to Excel financial functions.

```
ACCRINT(issue, first_interest, settlement, rate, par, frequency
    [, basis[, calc_method]])

ACCRINTM(issue, maturity, rate, par[, basis])

AMORDEGRC(cost, date_purchased, first_period, salvage, period, rate
    [, basis])

AMORLINC(cost, date_purchased, first_period, salvage, period, rate
    [, basis])

COUPDAYBS(settlement, maturity, frequency[, basis])

COUPDAYS(settlement, maturity, frequency[, basis])

COUPDAYSNC(settlement, maturity, frequency[, basis])

COUPNCD(settlement, maturity, frequency[, basis])

COUPNUM(settlement, maturity, frequency[, basis])

COUPPCD(settlement, maturity, frequency[, basis])

CUMIPMT(rate, nper, pv, start_period, end_period, type)

CUMPRINC(rate, nper, pv, start_period, end_period, type)

DB(cost, salvage, life, period[, month])

DDB(cost, salvage, life, period[, factor])

DISC(settlement, maturity, pr, redemption[, basis])

DOLLARDE(fractional_dollar, fraction)

DOLLARFR(decimal_dollar, fraction)

DURATION(settlement, maturity, coupon, yld, frequency[, basis])

EFFECT(nominal_rate, npery)

FV(rate, nper, pmt[, pv[, type]])

INTRATE(settlement, maturity, investment, redemption[, basis])

IPMT(rate, per, nper, pv[, fv[, type]])

ISPMT(rate, per, nper, pv)

MDURATION(settlement, maturity, coupon, yld, frequency[, basis])

NOMINAL(effect_rate, npery)

NPER(rate, pmt, pv[, fv[, type]])

ODDFPRICE(settlement, maturity, issue, first_coupon, rate, yld,
    redemption, frequency[, basis])

ODDFYIELD(settlement, maturity, issue, first_coupon, rate, pr,
    redemption, frequency[, basis])

ODDLPRICE(settlement, maturity, last_interest, rate, yld,
```

```
    redemption, frequency[, basis])

ODDLYIELD(settlement, maturity, last_interest, rate, pr,
    redemption, frequency[, basis])

PDURATION(rate, pv, fv)

PMT(rate, nper, pv[, fv[, type]])

PPMT(rate, per, nper, pv[, fv[, type]])

PRICE(settlement, maturity, rate, yld, redemption, frequency[, basis])

PRICEDISC(settlement, maturity, discount, redemption[, basis])

PRICEMAT(settlement, maturity, issue, rate, yld[, basis])

PV(rate, nper, pmt[, fv[, type]])

RATE(nper, pmt, pv[, fv[, type[, guess]]])

RECEIVED(settlement, maturity, investment, discount[, basis])

RRI(nper, pv, fv)

SLN(cost, salvage, life)

SYD(cost, salvage, life, per)

TBILLEQ(settlement, maturity, discount)

TBILLPRICE(settlement, maturity, discount)

TBILLYIELD(settlement, maturity, pr)

VDB(cost, salvage, life, start_period, end_period[, factor
    [, no_switch]])

XIRR(table, values, dates[, guess])

XNPV(table, values, dates, rate)

YIELD(settlement, maturity, rate, pr, redemption, frequency[, basis])

YIELDDISC(settlement, maturity, pr, redemption[, basis])

YIELDMAT(settlement, maturity, issue, rate, pr[, basis])
```

DAX Information Functions

DAX Information Functions provide required information based on the given argument.

CONTAINS(table, columnName, value[, columnName, value]…)

CONTAINSROW(table, scalarexpression1[, scalarexpression2, …])

CUSTOMDATA()

Scalarexpression IN table
    OR
    (scalarexpression1, scalarexpression2, …) IN table

ISBLANK(value)

ISEMPTY(table_expression)

ISERROR(value)

ISEVEN(number)

ISINSCOPE(column)

ISLOGICAL(value)

ISNONTEXT(value)

ISNUMBER(value)

ISODD(number)

ISONORAFTER(scalarexpression, scalarexpression[, sortorder]
    [, scalarexpression, scalarexpression[, sortorder]], …)

ISTEXT(value)

LOOKUPVALUE(result_columnName, search_columnName, search_value[,
    search_columnName, search_value], … [, <alternateResult>])

USERNAME()

DAX Logical Functions

DAX Logical Functions return values based on the conditional results.

```
AND(logical_value, logical_value)
```

```
COALESCE(expression, expression[, expression] …)
```

```
FALSE()
```

```
IF(logicaltest, value_if_true[, value_if_false])
```

```
IFERROR(value, value_if_error)
```

```
NOT(logical_value)
```

```
OR(logical_value, logical_value)
```

```
SWITCH(Expression, value1, expression1[, value2, expression2] … [, else,
expression])
```

```
TRUE()
```

DAX Math and Trig Functions

DAX Math and Trig Functions are similar to Excel mathematical and trigonometric functions.

ABS(number)

ACOS(number)

ACOSH(number)

ASIN(number)

ASINH(number)

ATAN(number)

ATANH(number)

CEILING(number, significance)

COMBIN(number, number_chosen)

COMBINA(number, number_chosen)

COS(number)

COSH(number)

CURRENCY(value)

DEGREES(angle)

DIVIDE(numerator, denominator[, alternate-result])

EVEN(number)

EXP(number)

FACT(number)

FLOOR(number, significance)

GCD(number1[, number2] …)

INT(number)

ISO.CEILING(number[, significance])

LCM(number1[, number2] …)

LN(number)

LOG(number, [base])

LOG10(number)

MOD(number, divisor)

MROUND(number, multiple)

ODD(number)

PERMUT(number, number_chosen)

PI()

POWER(number, power)

QUOTIENT(numerator, denominator)

```
RADIANS(angle)

RAND()

RANDBETWEEN(bottom, top)

ROUND(number, num_digits)

ROUNDDOWN(number, num_digits)

ROUNDUP(number, num_digits)

SIGN(number)

SIN(number)

SINH(number)

SQRT(number)

SQRTPI(number)

TAN(number)

TANH(number)

TRUNC(number, num_digits)
```

DAX Other Functions

These functions perform unique actions that cannot be defined by any of the categories.

```
CONVERT(Expression, Datatype)
```

```
ERROR(text)
```

```
VAR VarName = Expression
```

DAX Other Special Functions (X-Functions / Iterators)

These functions perform specific actions that complement the other DAX functions.

DAX Iterator Functions, called iterators for short, take a column or a table as the argument and aggregate the values just as aggregation functions—but using a different approach. These functions aggregate the values in a row context.

These are "X-functions" (i.e., any function that has an X on the end of the name). The iterators given below also include statistical iterator functions.

DAX also has two financial functions that got added in Excel 2016.

AVERAGEX(table, expression)

CONCATENATEX(table, expression[, delimiter])

COUNTAX(table, expression)

COUNTX(table, expression)

GEOMEANX(table, expression)

MAXX(table, expression)

MEDIANX(table, expression)

MINX(table, expression)

PERCENTILEX.EXC(table, expression, k)

PERCENTILEX.INC(table, expression, k)

PRODUCTX(table, expression)

RANKX(table, expression, [value], [order], [ties])

STDEVX.P(table, expression)

SUMX(table, expression)

VARX.P(table, expression)

VARX.S(table, expression)

DAX Other Special Functions (Argument Functions)

In DAX, there are also some special functions that have a very specific purpose of usability in other DAX functions only. i.e., they can be used only as arguments to certain DAX functions. These functions cannot be used as standalone functions.

CURRENTGROUP()

IGNORE(expression)

NONVISUAL(expression)

ROLLUPADDISSUBTOTAL(groupBy_columnName, isSubtotal_columnName, [groupBy_columnName, isSubtotal_columnName], …)

ROLLUPGROUP(groupBy_columnName, groupBy_columnName)

ROLLUPISSUBTOTAL(groupingColumn, isSubtotal_columnName, [groupingColumn, isSubtotal_columnName], …)

DAX Parent and Child Functions

DAX Parent and Child functions help to manage data that is presented as a parent/child hierarchy in the data model.

For more information read Understanding Functions for Parent-Child Hierarchies in DAX (https://msdn.microsoft.com/en-us/library/gg492192.aspx).

PATH(ID_columnName, parent_columnName)

PATHCONTAINS(path, item)

PATHITEM(path, position, [type])

PATHITEMREVERSE(path, position, [type])

PATHLENGTH(path)

DAX Query Functions

These DAX functions are helpful in writing queries in DAX. These functions return tables that can be used in other DAX functions as input. The resulting tables are virtual and are not materialised.

DAX Studio is a great way to learn about table functions because you can "see" the tables materialised on the screen. Read about DAX Studio as a tool to query your data model here http://xbi.com.au/dax-studio.

```
ADDCOLUMNS(table, name, expression[, name, expression] …)

CROSSJOIN(table, table[, table] …)

DATATABLE(ColumnName1, DataType1, ColumnName2, DataType2, …,
    {{Value1, Value2 …}, {Value1, Value2…}, …})

EXCEPT(table_expression1, table_expression2)

GENERATE(table1, table2)

GENERATEALL(table1, table2)

GROUPBY(table, [<groupBy_columnName1>], [<name, expression>] …)

GENERATESERIES(StartValue, EndValue[, IncrementValue])

INTERSECT(table, table)

NATURALINNERJOIN(leftJoinTable, rightJoinTable)

NATURALLEFTOUTERJOIN(leftJoinTable, rightJoinTable)

ROW(name, expression[, name, expression] …)

SELECTCOLUMNS(table, name, scalar_expression
    [, name, scalar_expression] …)

SUMMARIZE(table, groupBy_columnName[, groupBy_columnName] …,
    name, expression, [name, expression] …)

SUMMARIZECOLUMNS(groupBy_columnName[, groupBy_columnName] …,
    [filterTable] … [, name, expression] …)

TableConstructor {scalar_expression1, scalar_expression2, …}
    {(scalar_expression11, scalar_expression12, …, scalar_expression1N),
    (scalar_expression21), scalar_expression22, …, scalar_expression2N),
    …}

UNION(table_expression1, table_expression2)
```

DAX Statistical Functions

Following are the DAX Statistical Functions:

BETA.DIST(x, alpha, beta, cumulative[, A][, B])

BETA.INV(probability, alpha, beta[, A][, B])

CHISQ.INV(probability, deg_freedom)

CHISQ.INV.RT(probability, deg_freedom)

CONFIDENCE.NORM(alpha, standard_dev, size)

CONFIDENCE.T(alpha, standard_dev, size)

EXPON.DIST(x, lambda, cumulative)

GEOMEAN(column)

MEDIAN(column)

NORM.DIST(X, Mean, Standard_dev, Cumulative)

NORM.INV(Probability, Mean, Standard_dev)

NORM.S.DIST(Z, Cumulative)

NORM.S.INV(Probability)

PERCENTILE.EXC(column, k)

PERCENTILE.INC(column, k)

POISSON.DIST(x, mean, cumulative)

RANK.EQ(value, columnName, [order])

SAMPLE(n_value, table, orderBy_expression, [order][, orderBy_expression, [order], …])

STDEV.P(ColumnName)

STDEV.S(ColumnName)

T.DIST(X, Deg_freedom, Cumulative)

T.DIST.2T(X, Deg_freedom)

T.DIST.RT(X, Deg_freedom)

T.INV(Probability, Deg_freedom)

T.INV.2T(Probability, Deg_freedom)

VAR.P(ColumnName)

VAR.S(ColumnName)

DAX Text Functions

DAX Text Functions are based on the Excel string functions but have been modified to work with tables and columns.

BLANK()

CODE(text)

COMBINEVALUES(delimiter, expression, expression[, expression] …)

CONCATENATE(text1, text2)

CONTAINSSTRING(within_text, find_text)

CONTAINSSTRINGEXACT(within_text, find_text)

FIND(find_text, within_text[, start_num][, NotFoundValue])

FIXED(number, decimals[, no_commas])

FORMAT(value, format_string)

LEFT(text[, num_chars])

LEN(text)

LOWER(text)

MID(text, start_num, num_chars)

REPLACE(old_text, start_num, num_chars, new_text)

REPT(text, num_times)

RIGHT(text, [num_chars])

SEARCH(find_text, within_text[, start_num], [, NotFoundValue])

SUBSTITUTE(text, old_text, new_text, instance_num)

TRIM(text)

UNICHAR(number)

UPPER(text)

VALUE(text)

DAX Time Intelligence Functions

DAX Time Intelligence Functions enable you to manipulate data using time periods, including days, months, quarters and years, and then build and compare calculations over those periods.

There are 3 classes of DAX Time Intelligence functions based on their return value.

- Those that return scalar values (e.g. TOTALYTD). They are stand-alone functions and so can be used as a stand-alone measure/function.
- Those that return a table containing a single column and single row with a date value (e.g. FIRSTNONBLANK). They can be used either as stand-alone functions to define a measure (as a scalar value) or as an argument to any function that requires a table in its arguments. These types of functions therefore behave as both a scalar value and a table, depending on the use case.
- Those that return a table of dates (e.g. DATESYTD) and are designed to be used inside a CALCULATE function.

DAX Time Intelligence Functions that return Scalar Values

CLOSINGBALANCEMONTH(expression, dates, [filter])

CLOSINGBALANCEQUARTER(expression, dates, [filter])

CLOSINGBALANCEYEAR(expression, dates, [filter], [year_end_date])

OPENINGBALANCEMONTH(expression, dates[, filter])

OPENINGBALANCEQUARTER(expression, dates[, filter])

OPENINGBALANCEYEAR(expression, dates[, filter])

TOTALMTD(expression, dates[, filter])

TOTALQTD(expression, dates[, filter])

TOTALYTD(expression, dates[, filter][, year_end_date])

DAX Time Intelligence Functions that return both a Table and a Scalar

These functions return a table containing a single column and single row with a date value (can be used as a scalar value or a table input to another function).

ENDOFMONTH(dates)

ENDOFQUARTER(dates)

ENDOFYEAR(dates[, year_end_date])

FIRSTDATE(dates)

FIRSTNONBLANK(column, expression)

FIRSTNONBLANKVALUE(column, expression)

LASTDATE(dates)

LASTNONBLANK(column, expression)

LASTNONBLANKVALUE(column, expression)

STARTOFMONTH(dates)

STARTOFQUARTER(dates)

STARTOFYEAR(Dates, [yearenddate])

DAX Time Intelligence Functions that return a Table of Dates

DATEADD(dates, number_of_intervals, interval)

DATESBETWEEN(dates, start_date, end_date)

DATESINPERIOD(dates, start_date, number_of_intervals, interval)

DATESMTD(dates)

DATESQTD(dates)

DATESYTD(dates[, year_end_date])

NEXTDAY(dates)

NEXTMONTH(dates)

NEXTQUARTER(dates)

NEXTYEAR(dates[, year_end_date])

PARALLELPERIOD(dates, number_of_intervals, interval)

PREVIOUSDAY(dates)

PREVIOUSMONTH(dates)

PREVIOUSQUARTER(dates)

PREVIOUSYEAR(dates[, year_end_date])

SAMEPERIODLASTYEAR(dates)

Table of Here's How Sections

Index

Symbols

Ready to Learn More?

PQ

Power Query Online Training

- Over 7 hours of video lessons
- Free sample videos
- Lessons taught using real world examples
- Sample files available for you to practice

"

Now that you know how to write DAX, it's time to learn how to cleanse and load data using Power Query.

Developed by
Microsoft® MVP
Matt Allington

Find Out More at
http://xbi.com.au/pqtb

Need More Help?

Visit Matt's website to continue your learning journey

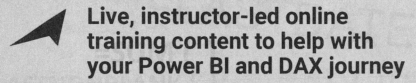 Live, instructor-led online training content to help with your Power BI and DAX journey

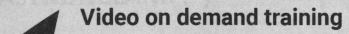 Video on demand training

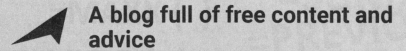 A blog full of free content and advice

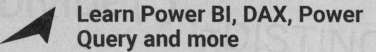 Learn Power BI, DAX, Power Query and more

Find Out More at
http://xbi.com.au/learn-more